JUDGMENT AND PLANNING
IN CHESS

JUDGMENT
AND
PLANNING
IN CHESS

BY

DR. MAX EUWE

Translated and edited by

J. DU MONT

LONDON

G. BELL AND SONS LTD

1973

THIS BOOK IS DEDICATED IN FRIENDSHIP TO
MR. AND MRS. I. NAPIER
OF LELANT, CORNWALL

First published 1953
Reprinted 1954, 1955, 1957, 1962, 1967, 1970, 1973

ISBN 0 7135 0429 3

Printed in Great Britain by
William Clowes & Sons, Limited, London, Beccles and Colchester

AUTHOR'S PREFACE

DURING the Plymouth Congress in August 1948 I met Mr. J. du Mont, then editor of the *British Chess Magazine*, who suggested that I should write a book on the lines of the present volume.

His idea was to give the practical player some guidance as to how to proceed in a game from the point where the books on opening theory leave off. The result is the present volume, and I am grateful to Mr. du Mont for giving me the opportunity of carrying out his idea and suggestions.

M. E.

March 1953

TRANSLATOR'S NOTE

I WISH to express my thanks to Leonard Barden, Daniel Castello and Eric Leyns who read the proofs.

J. d. M.

CONTENTS

INTRODUCTION

OFTEN when a player has a fair understanding of the principles of chess and can make quite pretty combinations, two or three moves deep and occasionally, in simple positions, even four, he suddenly notices, as he meets stronger players, that his development seems to have come to a standstill. He loses games without being able to assess the cause. He works out a series of moves as far ahead as he possibly can and then notices that his opponent has planned and thought in an entirely different direction; in short, he loses the grip on the game which he had possessed at a previous stage. He learns opening variations by heart without accurately knowing why just these moves are played, with the result that he finds himself in totally unfamiliar positions —positions which may well be favourable though he has neither any idea why they are so nor knowledge as to how to turn them to his advantage.

A new element enters the chess battle at this stage—namely, 'positional understanding.' It does not grow of itself but must be developed by the process of drawing conclusions in practical play. It represents the increasing ability to form a judgment on any position whatever without going into the details of exact calculation.

Just like the doctor, who first has to gain a clear picture of the diseased condition in order afterwards to plan the process of the cure —diagnosis, treatment—the chess player must make a plan on the basis of such characteristics as he has found in the examination of a given position. Steinitz' axiom that the plan to be made must be in keeping with the characteristics of the position appears self-evident to us, for it is the logical outcome of our present method of taking effective action, though sixty years ago Steinitz' stipulation created a very revolution in chess thought.

Judging and planning. Coming back to our remarks on opening variations, we find that the theoretical work judges for us, generally by means of such symbols as $+ - =$, etc. But this judgment in itself is not enough: we have to know not only which of the two players stands better, but also why. And with this the first step is taken, on the basis of Steinitz' axiom, towards the making of a plan. The forming of a judgment, and the making of a plan, are the topics to be dealt with in this book. They form for the beginner, the bridge, that takes him across to those higher regions where not impulse but reason determines the choice of a move without, however, minimising the significance of what we call 'intuition.'

CHAPTER I

FIRST STEPS IN JUDGING AND PLANNING

THE task is so vast and varied, that we must deal with it step by step, starting with the most elementary examples before approaching more difficult and complicated problems.

We shall first examine positions which require nothing more than a knowledge of the relative value of the pieces and no other ability than that of checking the accuracy of a series of forced moves. The positions we shall now proceed to illustrate are the outcome of fairly well-known opening variations in which one side has a forced mate or a winning advantage in material.

1. P—K4, P—K4; 2. Kt—KB3, Kt—QB3; 3. B—B4, B—B4; 4. P—B3, Kt—B3; 5. P—Q4, P×P; 6. P×P, B—Kt5 ch; 7. Kt—B3, Kt×KP; 8. Castles, B×Kt; 9. P—Q5, Kt—K4; 10. P×B, Kt×B; 11. Q—Q4, Kt (B5)—Q3; 12. Q×KtP, Q—B3; 13. Q×Q, Kt×Q; 14. R—K1 ch,

1	*2*

K—B1; 15. B—R6 ch, K—Kt1; 16. R—K5, Kt (Q3)—K5; 17. Kt—Q2 (*No. 1*).

White has an easily won game, for neither Knight can move because of mate by the Rook either at K8 or Kt5. But if 17. ..... P—Q3; 18. Kt×Kt, P×R; 19. Kt×Kt mate.

There are no variations, no problems.

More simple still is the situation after:

1. P—K4, P—K4; 2. Kt—KB3, Kt—QB3; 3. B—B4, B—B4; 4. P—QKt4, B×P; 5. P—B3, B—R4; 6. P—Q4, P×P; 7. Castles, Kt—B3; 8. B—R3, P—Q3; 9. P—K5, P×P; 10. Q—Kt3, Q—Q2; 11. R—K1, P—K5; 12. QKt—Q2, B×P; 13. Kt×KP, B×KR; 14. R×B, K—Q1; 15. QKt—Kt5, Kt—QR4; 16. Kt—K5, Kt×Q (*No. 2*).

White mates in four:

17. Kt (K5)×P ch	Q×Kt		19. B—Kt5 ch	P—B3
18. Kt×Q ch	K—Q2		20. R—K7 mate	

The next will not cause the reader any headache:

1. P—K4, P—K4; 2. P—KB4, P×P; 3. Kt—KB3, P—KKt4; 4. B—B4, P—Kt5; 5. Castles, P×Kt; 6. Q×P, Q—B3; 7. P—Q3, Kt—B3; 8. B×P, B—Kt2; 9. Kt—B3, Kt—Q5; 10. Q—B2, P—Q3; 11. Kt—Q5, Q—Q1; 12, P—K5, P—QB3; 13. B—KKt5, Q—Q2; 14. Kt—B7 ch, Q×Kt; 15. B×P ch, K—Q2 (*No. 3*).

White mates in two by—

16. Q—B5 ch	Kt×Q		17. P—K6 mate

More complicated is the next example:

1. P—K4, P—K4; 2. Kt—KB3, Kt—QB3; 3. B—B4, B—B4; 4. P—QKt4, B×P; 5. P—B3, B—R4; 6. P—Q4, P×P; 7. Castles, Kt—B3; 8. B—R3, Kt×P; 9. Q—Kt3, P—Q4; 10. B×P, Kt—Q3; 11. B×P

3	*4*

ch, K—B1; 12. R—K1, B—Q2; 13. QKt—Q2, B×P; 14. Kt—B4, Kt—R4; 15. Kt×Kt, B×Kt; 16. Kt—K5, B×R; 17. R×B, B—B3; 18. B—R5, Q—B3; 19. Kt×B, P—KKt3; 20. R—K6, Q—B4; 21. Kt× QP, Q×B (*No. 4*).

White now mates in 14!

22. B×Kt ch   P×B

It is instructive to note how far the mate can be accelerated by deviating from the main variation, e.g. 22. .... K—Kt2; 23. R—K7 ch, K—R3; 24. B—B4 ch, P—Kt4; 25. Kt—B5 ch, K—Kt3; 26. Q—B7 mate. It is not of paramount importance, whether the loser runs into a mate or suffers decisive material loss, but, for our purposes and for the cultivation of combinative powers, it is of real importance to make a sharp distinction between the two forms of decisive advantage—the opportunity to mate or great material superiority

23. R—B6 ch   K—Kt2

It would lead too far to give a complete analysis of the position, and we shall therefore confine ourselves to the main variation, but we would urge our readers thoroughly to examine all the possible ramifications. 24. R—B7 ch, K—R3; 25. Q—K3 ch, Q—Kt4; 26. Kt—B5 ch, P×Kt; 27. R—B6 ch, K—R4; 28. Q—R3 ch, Q—R5; 29. Q×P ch, Q—Kt4; 30. Q—R3 ch, Q—R5; 31. P—Kt4 ch, K—Kt4; 32. R—B5 ch, K—Kt3; 33. Q×Q, P—KR3; 34. Q—R5 ch, K—R2; 35. Q—B7 mate.

The illustrations given so far have one thing in common: the position in every case led to a forced mate, so that our theme may here be described briefly thus:

Assessment: White (or Black) wins. *Plan:* the appropriate mating continuation.

We shall now give a few examples in which the main variation likewise leads to a mate, but where the losing side has one or two opportunities to escape with some substantial material loss which deprives the illustration of its forced character.

An important variation of the so-called Vienna Variation is as follows:

1. P—Q4, P—Q4; 2. P—QB4, P—K3; 3. Kt—KB3, Kt—KB3; 4. B—Kt5, B— Kt5 ch; 5. Kt—B3, P×P; 6. P—K4, P— B4; 7. B×P, P×P; 8. Kt×P, Q—R4; 9. B×Kt, B×Kt ch; 10. P×B, Q×P ch; 11. K—B1, Q×B ch; 12. K—Kt1, Castles; 13. Q—Kt4 (*No. 5*).

5

It is now of the greatest importance, in assessing the value of the Vienna Variation as a whole, to ascertain whether this variation does indeed lead to a decisive advantage. Here it would not do to dismiss the position with a remark that 'White has attacking chances' when he can indeed force mate or loss of Queen. There follows:

13. ....   P—KKt3

Forced.

14. Q—B4   Kt—Q2   15. P—K5   Kt×B
16. P×Kt

Mate is still threatened by 17. Q—R6, etc.

16. ....   K—R1   17. R—QB1

An important intermediary manœuvre, intended in the first place to safeguard the Rook from attack by the Queen.

17. ....   Q—Q4

Other moves are worse.

18. Q—R6   R—KKt1   19. Kt—B3

Threatens 20. Kt—Kt5, and mate; to be sure, Black could at any time exchange his Queen for the Knight, but he would remain at a great, we may say a decisive, disadvantage in material. e.g.:

1. 19. .... P—KKt4; 20. P—KR4, R—Kt3 (he has nothing better); 21. Q—B8 ch, R—Kt1; 22. Q×P (now 23. Kt×P, or 23. P×P, are threatened), 22. .... Q—Q2; 23. Kt—K5 (Black cannot exchange Queens because 24. Kt×Q would be mate, and other moves by the Queen lead to a similar result) 23. .... Q—Q7; 24. Q×P ch, K×Q; 25. P×P mate, or

1. (*a*) 20. .... P—K4 (preparing B—B4, protecting the Pawn on KR2); 21. R×B!, QR×R; 22. Kt×KtP, R—B8 ch (Black cannot protect KR2 without abandoning KB2); 23. K—R2, R×R ch; 24. K×R, R×Kt (he has nothing better); 25. P×R, and there is no defence against the mate on Kt2.

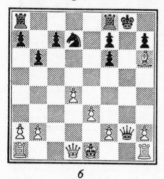

6

2. 19. .... Q—KR4; 20. Kt—Kt5, again a surprise sacrifice. Black can parry the mate only by giving up his Queen for the Knight.

1. P—Q4, P—Q4; 2. P—QB4, P—K3; 3. Kt—QB3, Kt—KB3; 4. B—Kt5, QKt—Q2; 5. P—K3, B—K2; 6. Kt—B3, P—QKt3?; 7. P×P, P×P; 8. B—Kt5, B—Kt2; 9. Kt—K5, Castles; 10. B—B6, B×B; 11. Kt×B, Q—K1; 12. Kt×B ch, Q×Kt; 13. Kt×P, Q—K5; 14. Kt×Kt ch, P×Kt; 15. B—R6, Q×KtP (the Pittsburgh Variation) (*No. 6*).

White now obtains a decisive advantage with the surprising move—

16. Q—B3

for if 16. .... Q×Q; there is a mate after 17. R—Kt1 ch, K—R1:

18. B—Kt7 ch, K—Kt1; 19. B×P dis. ch, etc., while after 16. ....
Q—Kt3; 17. B×R, R×B; 18. Castles, White has won the exchange
and has a strong attack (*No. 7*).

From a consideration of this position there arises perhaps the question: what should be my plan, how can I convert my material advantage into a win? It would be a colossal as well as a thankless task to write a book dealing with the various methods of bringing material advantage to fruition. There nearly always are so many ways to win that in general no real problem arises. I fancy too that few beginners would have the patience to wade through such a huge work; in the course of their studies they would make such progress that they would no longer be interested in problems which would, by then, have become obvious.

Nevertheless, it will be useful to make a few remarks on this subject.

1. If you have an advantage in material, the guiding line is to simplify the position by exchanges with certain reservations as follows:

  (*a*) do not exchange automatically, for there are positions in which exchanges cause your material superiority to lose its effect;

  (*b*) in end games R and B *v*. R, R and Kt *v*. R, and R *v*. B or R *v*. Kt are mostly drawn, though there are some few exceptions. The simplification in such cases must therefore not be allowed to go too far.

But as long as a single Pawn is left on the board, it is nearly always sufficient to ensure a win.

7

2. Do not think that the win will come by itself, either here or at any time. If you wish to derive the full benefit of your advantage in material, you must make it work for you. A Rook is more valuable than a Bishop only as long as proper use is made of its powers. Don't go out of the way of complications as a matter of course unless they are risky. It happens frequently enough that the player who has an advantage in material is inclined to play passively, awaiting events. This is the worst possible attitude and has been fatal to many.

3. Only attack can exploit material advantage. Therefore play aggressively, though, of course, not recklessly. Once you have the initiative the potentialities of voluntary exchanges become greater (see *No. 1*).

In this connection we shall now revert in greater detail to the variation we have just examined. (See Diag. 7.)

After 18 Castles, we continue:

18. ....   K—R1

More or less forced because of the threat 19. R—Kt1.

Now White must play a Rook to KKt1, but which one? The King's Rook because, after 19. QR—Kt1, the black Queen can move to Q6? The wrong argument. Don't take things for granted, for after the black Queen's *sortie*, 20. Q—Kt4, wins the Knight because of the mating threat. And thus, as it makes little difference which Rook moves, White plays

19. QR—Kt1   Q—R3

And what does White do now? He has several lines of play to choose from:

1. 20. Q—B6, winning a Pawn.

2. 20. R—Kt3, followed by 21. KR—Kt1, continuing the King's side attack, the best, but not—

3. 20. Q—B4, exchanging Queens. The pawn formation on White's King side would be ruined and the win made much more difficult (an example of 'exchange at all cost').

4. 20. R—Kt4, followed by 21. Q—B4, so that now the exchange of Queens does not imply a deterioration of White's pawn formation.

8   9

This being said, White's best continuation is: 20. R—Kt3, with, as a likely sequel, 20. .... P—QB4; 21. KR—Kt1, with the threat 22. R—R3, and the black Queen is cornered. But even now Black has a resource with 21. .... P×P; 22. R—R3, R—B1 ch; 23. K—Kt1, Q—B1; but White forces the win with 24. Q—B5. An alternative after 21. KR—Kt1, would be 21. .... R—B1; but White wins by 22. Q—B6.

Even in positions in which one side has achieved material superiority, combinations are possible, one might even say, particularly so.

We now give a number of positions in which there is no question of mate but only of a preponderance in material. By this we mean an advantage of two pawns or the exchange or perhaps a piece with a minority of one or two pawns.

When the excess material is represented by a Rook or Queen, the position may be abnormal:

1. P—Q4, P—Q4; 2. P—QB4, P—K3; 3. Kt—QB3, Kt—KB3; 4. Kt—B3, P—B4; 5. B—Kt5, P×QP; 6. KKt×P, P—K4; 7. Kt (Q4)—Kt5, P—QR3; 8. Kt×P, P×Kt; 9. Kt×Kt ch (*No. 8*).

A well-known trap by which White appears to win the exchange after 9. .... P×Kt; 10. Q×Q ch, K×Q; 11. B×P ch.

But Black had a stronger line in—

| 9. .... | Q×Kt | 11. Q—Q2 | B×Q ch |
| 10. B×Q | B—Kt5 ch | 12. K×B | P×B |

and Black remains a piece up.

1. P—Q4, P—Q4; 2. P—QB4, P—K3; 3. Kt—QB3, P—QB4; 4. P×QP, KP×P; 5. Kt—B3, Kt—QB3; 6. P—KKt3, Kt—B3; 7. B—Kt2, B—K2; 8. Castles, Castles; 9. B—Kt5, P—B5; 10. Kt—K5, Q—Kt3; 11. B×Kt, B×B; 12. Kt×QP, Q×QP? (*No. 9*).

White wins a piece:

| 13. Kt×B ch | P×Kt | 15. Kt—K7 ch K—R1 |
| 14. Kt×Kt | Q×Q | 16. QR×Q |

A well-known manœuvre which occurs in various other positions as, for instance, in the following:

1. P—Q4, P—Q4; 2. P—QB4, P—K3; 3. Kt—QB3, P—QB4; 4. P×QP, KP×P; 5. Kt—B3, Kt—QB3; 6. P—KKt3, P—B5; 7. B—Kt2, B—QKt5; 8. Castles, KKt—K2; 9. P—K4, Castles; 10. Kt×P, Kt×Kt; 11. P×Kt, Q×P; 12. P—QR3 (to free K7 for the white Knight), B—R4; 13. Kt—K5, Q×P; 14. Kt×Kt, Q×Q; 15. Kt—K7 ch, K—R1; 16. R×Q, and again White has won a piece.

10

1. P—QB4, Kt—KB3; 2. Kt—QB3, P—K3; 3. P—K4, P—B4; 4. P—KKt3, P—Q4; 5. P—K5, P—Q5; 6. P×Kt, P×Kt; 7. KtP×P, Q×P; 8. P—Q4, P×P; 9. P×P, B—Kt5 ch; 10. B—Q2, Q×P; 11. B×B, Q—K5 ch; 12. B—K2, Q×R; 13. Q—Q6, Kt—B3 (*No. 10*).

White wins with a combinative idea which required exact calculation:

14. B—KB3   Q×Kt ch   15. K—K2

and wins because 15. .... Q×R fails after 16. B×Kt ch, and mate next move.

1. P—Q4, P—Q4; 2. P—QB4, P—K3; 3. Kt—KB3, Kt—KB3; 4. Kt—B3, B—K2; 5. P—K3, Castles; 6. P—QKt3, P—B4; 7. B—Q3, P—QKt3; 8. Castles, B—Kt2; 9. B—Kt2, Kt—B3; 10. R—B1, R—B1;

11   *12*

11. Q—K2, BP×P; 12. KP×P, P×P; 13. P×P, Kt×P?; 14. Kt×Kt, Q×Kt (*No. 11*).

Black has been too greedy and has carelessly exposed his Queen to an indirect attack, a common fault in this type of opening, which here receives short shrift.

15. Kt—Q5   Q—B4   16. B×Kt

and now:

1. 16. .... B×B; 17. Q—K4, and wins.

2. 16. .... P×B; 17. Q—Kt4 ch, K—R1; 18. Q—R4, P—B4; 19. Kt×B, etc.

1. P—Q4, P—Q4; 2. P—QB4, P—QB3; 3. Kt—KB3, Kt—B3; 4. Kt—B3, P×P; 5. P—QR4, P—K3; 6. P—K4, B—Kt5; 7. P—K5, Kt—K5; 8. Q—B2, Q—Q4; 9. B—K2, P—QB4; 10. Castles, Kt×Kt; 11. P×Kt, P×P; 12. P×P, P—B6; 13. B—Q2, Q—R4; 14. B×P, B×B; 15. R—R3, B—Q2; 16. R×B, B×P (*No. 12*). Another example of greed punished.

White wins surprisingly with—

17. B—Kt5 ch

and now:

1. 17. .... Q×B; 18. R—B8 ch, K—K2; 19. Q—B7 ch, Kt—Q2; 20. Q—Q6 mate (if 19. .... Q—Q2; 20. Q—B5 ch, and mate next move).

2. 17. .... B×B; 18. R—B8 ch, K—Q2; 19. R×R, and wins, for if
19. .... B×R; 20. Q—B8 ch, and mate to follow.

1. P—K4, P—QB3; 2. P—Q4, P—Q4; 3. P×P, P×P; 4. P—QB4,
Kt—KB3; 5. Kt—QB3, Kt—B3; 6. B—Kt5, P×P; 7. P—Q5, Kt—
QR4; 8. P—QKt4, P×P *e.p.*; 9. P×P, P—K3; 10. B—Kt5 ch (*No. 13*).

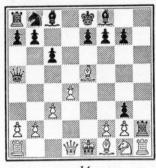

13   14

White obtains the advantage after 10. .... K—K2; 11. P—Q6 ch,
Q×P; 12. Q×Q ch, K×Q; 13. R×Kt.

If Black plays 10. .... B—Q2 (instead of K—K2) the sequel is:
11. B×Kt, with the following two alternative continuations: (*a*) 11.
.... Q×B; 12. B×B ch, K×B; 13. P×P db ch, or (*b*) 11. .... P×B;
12. B×B ch, Q×B; 13. KKt—K2, with a favourable game for White,
who threatens R×Kt,—not on move 13, because of 13. R×Kt (instead
of KKt—K2), B—Kt5—while the black King is in a precarious
situation.

1. P—K4, P—QB3; 2. P—Q4, P—Q4; 3. Kt—QB3, P×P; 4. Kt×P,
Kt—B3; 5. Kt—Kt3, P—KR4; 6. B—KKt5, P—R5; 7. B×Kt, P×Kt;
8. B—K5, Q—R4 ch; 9. P—B3, R×P (*No. 14*). White has allowed
the capture at KR2, because the Bishop is controlling that critical
square. He therefore plays 10. R×R, with full confidence. But his
confidence is rudely shattered by the surprise manœuvre: 10. .... Q×B
ch; 11. P×Q, P×R; and after queening his pawn Black remains a
piece ahead.

Let us finish this chapter with a more complicated example.
1. P—K4, P—QB3; 2. P—Q4, P—Q4; 3. Kt—QB3, P×P; 4. Kt×P,
Kt—B3; 5. Kt—Kt3, P—K4; 6. Kt—B3, P×P; 7. Kt×P, B—QB4; 8.
Q—K2 ch, B—K2; 9. B—K3, P—B4; 10. Kt (Q4)—B5, Castles; 11.
Q—B4, R—K1; 12. B—Q3, P—QKt3; 13. Castles QR, B—R3 (*No. 15*).
Black has left his Queen exposed to the Rook on the open Q

file, secure in the thought that White's Queen is *en prise*. He has overlooked the point, however, as the following variations will show:

14. Kt—R6 ch, P×Kt; 15. B×P ch, and now:

15

1. 15. .... K×B; 16. Q×P ch, K—R1; 17. R×Q, B×R; 18. Kt—R5.

2. 15. .... Kt×B; 16. Q—Kt4 ch, K—R1; 17. R×Q.
    (*a*) 17. .... R×R; 18. Q—K4.
    (*b*) 17. .... B×R; 18. Q—B3.

3. 15. .... K—R1 (the least evil); 16. R×Q, B×Q; 17. R×R ch, Kt×R; 18. B—K4, Kt—QB3; 19. B×Kt, and White will be two important pawns ahead, as Black's KR Pawn must fall.

In all the examples in this chapter, we have only touched the fringe of our main subject, *judging and planning in chess*. We had, however, to pay due attention to such positions in which possibilities of either mating or of extensive material gain were present. The problem in each case depended for its solution on some measure of tactical skill rather than positional judgment. Such possibilities are moreover easily overlooked by a player too intent on positional considerations.

The big problems have, however, still to be tackled.

CHAPTER II

PAWN MAJORITY ON THE QUEEN'S SIDE

BOTVINNIK—KMOCH, *Leningrad*, 1934

1. P—K4, P—QB3; 2. P—Q4, P—Q4; 3. P×P, P×P; 4. P—QB4, Kt—KB3; 5. Kt—QB3, Kt—B3; 6. B—Kt5, P—K3; 7. P—B5, B—K2; 8. B—Kt5, Castles; 9. Kt—B3, Kt—K5; 10. B×B, Kt×B; 11. R—QB1, Kt—Kt3; 12. Castles, B—Q2; 13. B—Q3, P—B4; 14. P—QKt4 (*No. 16*).

The comment of the 'theory' on this typical example is: 'White has the superior position.'

The average player may well ask, why is White's position superior?

The material is equal, each side has a Queen, two Rooks, two Knights, a Bishop and seven pawns. It cannot be said that White has progressed further than Black; on the contrary, Black's Knight, well established in White's half of the board, looks particularly threatening. The pieces on either side enjoy approximately equal mobility, one piece a little more, one piece a little less, but no considerable disparity can be noticed. Neither King has to fear a direct attack, and the reader will again ask, why is White's position

16

better, why can his advantage be called a winning one?

No doubt many chess players could give the correct answer straight away, but to not a few of these the answer would be a stereotyped phrase devoid of real meaning: *White stands better because he has a pawn majority on the Queen's side.*

Let us first examine this dictum in detail. Both White and Black have seven pawns but, and that is the crucial point, they are not evenly distributed over their respective fronts. If we divide the board into three sections by drawing two vertical lines between the QB and Q files and between the KB and K files respectively, as in *No. 17*, Section I represents the Q side, Section II the centre, and Section III the K side.

In positions such as that in *No. 16* which is under discussion, both sides have castled on the K side and we note that White has more pawns on the Q side than Black—three to two—while the position is reversed in the centre where Black has two pawns to one. On the K side White and Black have an equal number of pawns.

This is, of course, a particularly clear-cut case. The white pawn at QB5 has nothing more to do with the black pawns on the right, which would not be the case were it standing say at QB3. We can speak of a positive Q side majority for White, while all the remaining pawns can be summarised as K-side pawns. In other words, in *No. 16*, White has a majority of 3-2 on the Q side, and Black a majority of 5-4 on the K side. The front pawn on White's majority wing has passed the black K pawn, and thus the pawn chains on opposite wings are independent of each other. But the cardinal point is that White is able to force a passed pawn on his majority wing, while Black, with his majority of 5-4 on the K side, will normally be unable to do so.

It is, of course, not exclusively a question of arithmetic. Easy and

I   II   III

17

difficult positions must be taken into account, with or without doubled pawns, wherein it is not always a simple matter to obtain a passed pawn, and in which it may become necessary to sacrifice in order to achieve this end. For example, the white pawns may be at QR2, QKt3 and QB4 against black pawns at White's QKt4 and QB5, or White at QR2, QKt2 and QKt3 against Black at White's QR7 and QKt7.

This is not the case in the position under review. If there are no complications, White will always be able to force P—QKt5, with or without a preliminary P—QR4, so that he can at all times be sure of securing a passed pawn.

Let us, however, for the sake of argument, assume that White and Black have equal chances of securing a passed pawn, even then the pawn majority on the Q side must be looked upon as an advantage. And here are, in brief, some of the reasons why this is so:

1. The passed pawn on the Q side is at a great distance from the enemy King, who is thus unable to arrest its progress—something of the kind happens with distant passed pawns in pawn endings.

2. A passed pawn on the K side is more difficult to force through, and this often necessitates the advance of pawns, whose proper function is to guard their King.

While possessing this knowledge, however, it is wise not to make a fetish of it, for there is the danger of treating the whole subject by rote.

A pawn majority on the Q side, be it even of 1-0, is worth just so much as the player is able to make of it.

Let us now get a little closer to the substance of our task of judging and planning.

The first part is not difficult—White or Black has the advantage because of a pawn majority on the Queen's side. But we cannot be content with mere generalities. In deciding on our plan we must carefully ascertain whether the other side may not have compensating advantages, whether there are no factors in the enemy formation which counteract our positional advantage of a Q-side pawn majority.

We have now reached the next step in our disquisition, namely, how to exploit the advantage of a pawn majority on the Q side. To this end we shall again refer to *No. 16*.

14.	B—K1	15. P—Kt3

By preventing 9. .... Kt—B5 or R5, the text-move slows down a possible K-side attack by Black.

15.	R—B1	16. R—K1	Q—B3
	17. P—QR3		

White takes it calmly.

17.	Kt—K2

Not best, as it frees K5 for White's KKt. The better continuation is 17. .... Kt×Kt; 18. R×Kt, P—B5, with counter-chances on the KB file.

18. Kt—K5	Q—R3	19. P—B3	Kt—B7

Interesting. If White captures the Knight there is a perpetual check by 20. K×Kt, Q×P ch; 21. K—K3, P—B5 ch; 22. P×P, Q×P ch; 23. K—K2, Q—R7 ch, etc.

20. Q—K2	Kt—R6 ch	21. K—Kt2	P—KKt4
	22. Kt—Kt5	B×Kt	

He cannot allow the Knight to reach Q6 where it would occupy a commanding position.

23. B×B	R—KB3	24. B—Q7

The final preparation for the advance on the Q side (*No. 18*).

24.	R—Q1	25. P—Kt5	Q—R4

As Black can in no way prevent the execution of White's plan, he makes a last and desperate attempt to achieve some positive result on the K side.

26. P—B6   R—R3

With the threat 27. .... Kt—B5 ch, followed by .... Q×RP ch, which White, however, parries simply by protecting his R pawn.

27. K—R1

Black resigns, for he is powerless against the advance of White's passed pawn: 27. .... P×P; 28. P×P, Kt—B1; 29. P—B7, R—B1; 30. Kt—B6, with the double threat of 31. B×P ch or 31. B×Kt, followed by Kt—K7 ch.

It is quite clear that White owed his success to his pawn majority on the Q side, but, be it noted, he had to work for it. He had many oppor-

18

tunities of going wrong, and on several occasions he had to find just the right move to withstand Black's K-side attack (15. P—KKt3, 20. Q—K2, and 27. K—R1). He had to time with precision the moves preparatory to his Q-side advance (17. P—QR3, 18. Kt—K5, 22. Kt—QKt5, and 24. B—Q7), without which the advance of his Q-side pawns would have been premature. And that is the normal course of operations which can be summarised as follows:

1. Assess and analyse your opponent's counter-chances.

2. Thoroughly prepare your own action.

We could expatiate on this subject by reverting to the various types of complications which can influence the course of events. But these will become clear when we examine the illustrations given hereafter. One point, however, we wish to emphasise, which refers to the culmination of White's efforts to turn his pawn majority into a winning advantage.

In the position shown in *No. 16* zero hour will strike when White, after much manœuvring comprising defensive and offensive measures, thinks the time ripe to play the decisive P—B6.

Will this pawn, at that precise moment, have sufficient support from his own forces, to overcome any possible defensive measures, direct or indirect, which the opponent can then bring into operation?

However, a method in chess which solves all problems and eliminates all complications has (luckily) not yet been found, and we must be content with indicating guiding principles, ideas, and suggestions, to help the player's own judgment and imagination.

We shall now examine a number of examples illustrating various forms of the pawn majority on the Q side.

They will be shown in less detail and serve the double purpose of—

1. Elucidating still further the ideas already set out; and
2. Showing other forms of a pawn majority and their characteristics.

BOTVINNIK—KONSTANTINOPOLSKY, *Sverdlovsk*, 1943

1. P—K4, P—QB3; 2. P—Q4, P—Q4; 3. P×P, P×P; 4. P—QB4,
Kt—KB3; 5. Kt—QB3, Kt—B3; 6. B—Kt5, P—K3; 7. Kt—B3, B—
K2; 8. R—B1, Castles; 9. P—B5, Kt—K5;
10. B×B, Q×B; 11. B—K2, B—Q2; 12.
P—QR3 (*No. 19*).

19

The position shows great similarity
with the preceding one. Here, too, White
has a pawn majority on the Q side
against which Black's Knight at K5 is
not a sufficient compensation. Again
White's plan comprises: securing his pawn
formation on the Q side, obtaining command of the square QB6 and if possible
QB7 as well, and the advance P—QB6,
after P—QKt5.

During these operations White's K5 acquires a special significance,
for a Knight posted there adds to White's command of QB6.

After these remarks, the further course of the game is easy to understand.

12. ....   P—B4

Fine rightly criticises this move as weakening Black's K4 and thus
playing into his opponent's hand. Correct was: 12. .... P—B3; 13.
P—QKt4, Kt×Kt; 14. R×Kt, P—QR3; 15. Castles, QR—Q1; with
the object eventually to obtain a passed K pawn as a compensation
for White's Q-side pawn majority.

13. B—Kt5

It is often essential to act quickly. The text-move threatens 14.
B×Kt, followed by 15. Kt—K5, and a gradual exploitation of his
majority, as Black is practically powerless because of the solid position
of White's Knight at K5.

13. ....   Kt—Kt4

This cuts across White's intentions—occupying K5 with a Knight,
but at the cost of submitting to another drawback.

14. B×Kt   Kt×Kt ch   16. Q—B4   QR—K1
15. Q×Kt   P×B   17. Castles   P—K4

The only way in which Black can get rid of his backward pawn.

18. Q×KP   Q×Q   19. P×Q   R×P (*No. 20*)

20

21

The fight has assumed an entirely different character. To be sure, White's pawn majority is still in being, but Black's supported Q pawn is no less valuable an asset. However, White has secured a fresh advantage—he has a good Knight against Black's bad Bishop. The Bishop is bad because the black pawns stand on the same colour, and its mobility is thereby strictly limited. The Knight is strong because sooner or later it will be able to reach Q4, where it will be secure from both the adverse pawns and the Bishop.

The treatment of this type of position will be shown in Chapter IV, where we shall again refer to the position of *No. 20*.

1. P—K4, P—K4; 2. Kt—KB3, Kt—QB3; 3. B—Kt5, P—QR3; 4. B—R4, Kt—B3; 5. Castles, Kt×P; 6. P—Q4, P—QKt4; 7. B—Kt3, P—Q4; 8. P×P, B—K3; 9. P—B3, B—K2; 10. R—K1, Castles; 11. QKt—Q2, Kt—B4; 12. B—B2, P—Q5; 13. P×P, Kt×QP; 14. Kt×Kt, Q×Kt (*No. 21*).

The 'book' formerly found fault with Black's position on several counts. It was wrongly assumed that, with the Queens still on the board, White's position was entirely satisfactory with good chances of a K-side attack. Furthermore, after the exchange of Queens, White was still thought to have a satisfactory game because of his greater command of space and the favourable disposition of his forces.

In this last conclusion, the real meaning of the pawn majority on the Q side was completely left out of the reckoning.

As a double proof of this contention we give here two examples of the treatment of this position in actual play.

DR. LASKER—DR. TARRASCH, *St. Petersburg*, 1914

15. Kt—Kt3; the best in the circumstances. White is not afraid of getting a doubled pawn as his pieces will more rapidly get into play. Moreover, when it comes to stopping the advance of a pawn majority, a doubled pawn is an advantage rather than otherwise. 15. .... Kt × Kt; 16. P × Kt, Q × Q; 17. R × Q, P—QB4; 18. B—Q2, KR—Q1; 19. B—R5, R × R ch; 20. R × R, P—B3; 21. B—B3, P × P; 22. B × P, R—Q1; Black plays strongly. He forces the exchange of Rooks because, with only Bishops on the board, the doubled pawn becomes a weakness. The sequel demonstrates this fact.

23. R × R ch	B × R	30. B—Q6	B × KKtP
24. P—B4	K—B2	31. B × RP	K—K3
25. K—B2	B—B3	32. B—B8	K—Q4
26. B—Q6	B—Q5 ch	33. K—Kt5	B—B3 ch
27. K—B3	B—Q4 ch	34. K—Kt6	B—K5 ch
28. K—Kt4	K—K3	35. P—B5	K—K4
29. B—B8	K—B2	36. B × KtP	B × P ch
	37. K—B7 (*No. 22*)		

Black could now have obtained a decisive advantage by: 37. .... B—K3 ch; 38. K—B8, B × B ch; 39. K × B, B × P. He chose the inferior continuation—

22

37.	KB × B
38. B × B	K × B
39. K × B	P—R4
40. P—R4	K—Kt5

after which White secured the draw by the problem-like move 41. K—Kt6, as follows:

41. K—Kt6	K × P	44. K—Q5	K—K6
42. K—B5	K—Kt6	45. K × P	K—Q6
43. K—K4	K—B7	46. K × P	K—B7
	47. K × P	K × P (Kt6)	

One thing stands out clearly from this example: the pawn majority on the Q side can, in the later stages of the end-game, assume the same characteristics which obtain in the case of the 'distant passed pawn.'

H. JOHNER—DR. M. EUWE, *Zürich*, 1934

From *No. 21*—

15. Q—K2	KR—Q1	17. Q × Q	B × Q
16. Kt—B3	Q—QB5	18. B—K3	

(In a game Joss-Euwe from the same tournament, there followed 18. B—Kt5, B×B; 19. Kt×B, B—Q6; 20. B×B, R×B; 21. R—K2, R—Q4; equally to Black's advantage.)

18.	Kt—K3	20. B×B	R×B
19. B—K4	B—Q4	21. KR—Q1	QR—Q1
	22. R×R	R×R (*No. 23*)	

It is already clear that Black's pawn majority on the Q side represents a solid advantage, while there is no method at all by which White's

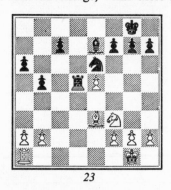

23

24

K-side majority can come into its own. Indeed, White's pawn at K5 can be looked upon as a definite weakness, as the necessity of defending it brings an additional strain on White's resources.

23. K—B1	K—B1	24. R—B1

A loss of a *tempo* which leaves White entirely without prospects.

24.	P—QB4	26. R—Q1	R×R
25. K—K2	K—K1	27. K×R	K—Q2
	28. Kt—Q2	P—Kt4	

Stopping White's P—B4, protecting the K pawn. The rest is no longer difficult. 29. P—B3, K—B3; 30. P—KKt3, K—Q4; 31. P—B4, P×P; 32. P×P, Kt—Q5; 33. Kt—B1, K—K5; 34. K—Q2, Kt—B4; 35. Kt—Kt3 ch, Kt×Kt; 36. P×Kt, K—B6; 37. K—Q3, K×P; 38. P—B5, P—KR4; 39. B—R6, P—R5; 40. P—B6, B—Q1; 41. P—K6, P×P; 42. P—B7, B—K2; 43. P—B8 (Q), B×Q; 44. B×B, P—R6; 45. B×P, P—K4; White resigns.

ELISKASES—FLOHR, *Semmering*, 1937

1. P—Q4, Kt—KB3; 2. P—QB4, P—KKt3; 3. Kt—QB3, P—Q4; 4. B—B4, B—Kt2; 5. P—K3, Castles; 6. Kt—B3, P—B4; 7. P×QP,

Kt×P; 8. B—K5, Kt×Kt; 9. P×Kt, P×P; 10. B×B, K×B; 11. BP×P, Q—R4 ch; 12. Q—Q2, Kt—B3; 13. B—K2, R—Q1 (*No. 24*).

The assessment of this position by the theory is: Black stands better.

By now the student will have progressed sufficiently to recognise the reason for this conclusion; Black has two pawns to one on the Q side.

But it requires considerable discernment to realise that this advantage, in spite of White's clear-cut majority in the centre, is in fact of importance. Special technical attainments are needed, not indeed to force a win, but even to extract some real winning chances from the situation.

An inexperienced player will make a blind rush, like the proverbial 'bull in a china shop.' He pushes forward and forces a pawn through, which becomes isolated and is promptly lost.

Let us examine the further course of the game:

14. Q×Q

More or less compulsory because 14. Castles KR, Q×Q; 15. Kt×Q, P—K4; loses a pawn;

14. ....   Kt×Q   15. Castles KR

On the whole it is unwise to castle the King away from the hostile pawn majority. He should be at hand when help is needed to stop a potential passed pawn. Instead of the move in the text, he should have played 15. K—Q2 and 16. KR—QB1.

15. ....   B—K3   16. P—K4

As is understandable, White tries to exploit his pawn majority in the centre, but to little effect, as will be seen.

16. ....   B—Kt5

An indirect attack on the Q pawn.

17. KR—Q1   P—K3

In order to isolate a prospective white passed pawn.

18. K—B1

The King, evidently sorry to have castled, gets on his way in the right direction.

18. ....   B×Kt   19. B×B   QR—B1

An important subsidiary part of Black's strategy in such cases: occupying the QB file. He threatens in the first place 20. .... R—B7.

20. R—Q2

Not 20. QR—B1, R×R; 21. R×R, R×P.

20. ....   P—K4   21. P—Q5

Not 21. QR—Q1, Kt—B5; 22. R—Q3, Kt—Kt7.

21.	Kt—B5	25. B—Kt2	R—B8 ch
22. R—K2	Kt—Q3	26. R × R	R × R ch
23. R—Kt1	R—B5	27. R—K1	R × R ch
24. P—Kt3	R (Q1)—QB1	28. K × R	(*No. 25*)

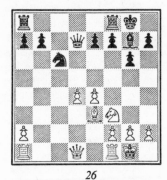

25   26

Black has made use of the QB file to force the exchange of Rooks in order to secure a favourable Knight *v*. Bishop ending (see *No. 20*, Botvinnik-Konstantinopolsky). The treatment of this ending will be elaborated later.

The rôle played here by Black's Q-side pawn majority was in the main a passive one. Black was in fact chiefly concerned with the question of making White's central majority harmless. But it must be conceded that Black had to thank his Q-side pawn majority for the ability to effect this object. In this type of position the QB file will always fall under Black's domination, at least when—as here—the white King fails to reach Q2 in good time (we note once more the damaging effect of White's castling on move 15).

It must be added that even before the general exchange which takes place in this example, Black is in a position to make use of the QB file for an attack on White's isolated QR pawn. This we shall see in the next example:

KOSTIC—GRÜNFELD, *Teplitz-Schönau*, 1922

1. P—Q4, Kt—KB3; 2. P—QB4, P—KKt3; 3. Kt—QB3, P—Q4; 4. P×P, Kt×P; 5. P—K4, Kt×Kt; 6. P×Kt, P—QB4; 7. Kt—B3, B—Kt2; 8. B—Kt5 ch, B—Q2; 9. B×B ch, Q×B; 10. Castles, P×P; 11. P×P, Kt—B3; 12. B—K3, Castles KR (*No. 26*).

This position is declared by the theory to be in favour of Black.

We give, without notes, the further course of the game which will throw more light on our subject.

13. R—Kt1	Kt—R4	32. P×P	R—R4
14. P—Q5	KR—B1	33. R—Q2	K—Kt2
15. B—Q4	B×B	34. P—B4	K—B3
16. Q×B	P—Kt3	35. R—K2	P—KKt4
17. Kt—K5	Q—Q3	36. P×P ch	K×P
18. Kt—Kt4	Q—B5	37. K—Kt2	K—B4
19. Kt—K3	R—B4	38. K—B3 (No. 27)
20. QR—B1	QR—QB1	
21. R×R	R×R	
22. P—B3	P—R4	
23. P—Kt3	Q—B2	
24. P—K5	Kt—B5	
25. Kt×Kt	R×Kt	
26. Q—K3	R—B6	
27. Q—Q4	R—B5	
28. Q—K3	R—B7	
29. P—K6	Q—B4	
30. Q×Q	R×Q	
31. R—Q1	P×P	

27

Here again Black made himself master of the QB file with his Knight at QR4, an effective post in connection with the jump to QB5. Black now again played for simplification in order to take advantage of the weaknesses which White has created for himself in the centre. In *No. 27* White has two pawns which require support and sooner or later White gets in *Zugzwang* and loses one of his pawns and the game.

38.	R—R6 ch	47. K—B3	P—Kt4
39. K—Kt2	R—R4	48. P—R4	K—B3
40. K—R3	R—R5	49. P—Kt4	R—Kt6 ch
41. R—QKt2	K×P	50. K—K4	P—R6
42. R—Kt5	R×P	51. R—R6 ch	K—Kt2
43. R×P	R—QKt7	52. K—B5	P—Kt5
44. R—R8	P—R4	53. R—R7	R—B6 ch
45. K—Kt4	P—R5	54. K—K4	R—B7
46. R—R8	R—Kt5 ch	55. K—K3	R—QKt7

White resigns.

We have shown that in trying to turn a Q-side pawn majority to advantage, the timing of the advance of the Q-side pawns requires great care. This actual advance has frequently to be held over while the necessary preparations are being made, and these, together with the exploitation of incidental advantages (*e.g.* open lines), take priority.

CHAPTER III

THE QUEEN'S SIDE ATTACK

THERE is a close affinity between the subject of our last article and the 'attack on the Queen's side,' although, in itself, the exploiting of a Queen's side majority does not, properly speaking, constitute an attack.

For the attack which we are about to examine aims at definite objects, pieces or pawns, whereas in the other case the purpose is to effect a break-through of at least a pawn, while frequently the real struggle rages on other fronts.

The Queen's side attack is local and in the nature of things far more violent. A practical example will illustrate the idea better than words.

BOGOLJUBOW—CAPABLANCA, *New York*, 1924

1. P—Q4, Kt—KB3; 2. Kt—KB3, P—Q4; 3. P—K3, P—K3; 4. B—Q3, P—B4; 5. P—QKt3, Kt—B3; 6. Castles, B—Q3; 7. B—Kt2,

28

Castles; 8. QKt—Q2, Q—K2; 9. Kt—K5, P×P; 10. P×P, B—R6; 11. B×B, Q×B; 12. QKt—B3, B—Q2; 13. Kt×Kt, B×Kt.

Here the 'book' says: Black stands better (*No. 28*).

Equal pawns, equal pieces, and approximately equal mobility. True, the black Queen is posted on white territory, but, if necessary, she can be driven off or exchanged by Q—B1.

Why, then, is Black's game preferable? Answer: *because he has attacking chances on the Queen's side.*

On White's Queen's wing the three pawns at QR2, QKt3, and QB2 are solid and well protected; where then are the chances of attack?

Let it be said that Black's attack cannot depend on single, unrelated moves, but rather on a broad, accurately-designed plan. White's QB pawn is weak, or, to be more accurate, can become weak. At present it is adequately guarded by the Bishop, but this piece might be exchanged—in fact, the black Bishop can force its exchange, after which this pawn will have to be protected by other, perhaps less reliable, means. The pawn will then be attacked on the open file by a Rook or two Rooks, by the Queen, and possibly still further by the black Knight.

It is then an open question whether White can, at the right moment, find adequate defensive measures.

This does not appear to be so difficult when White has equal forces at his disposal, but the problem is not as simple as it appears. While White's pieces are tied to the defence of the QB pawn, Black will in all probability, and without relaxing his grip, threaten other parts of the front and present White with additional problems which he may be unable to solve.

Let us examine the real reason of White's difficulties and the basis of Black's attacking chances. The open QB file is not the main factor, but the fact that White has played P—QKt3. If this pawn were still on its original square at QKt2, White could play P—QB3, and he would have little to fear.

Was, therefore, White's fifth move, P—QKt3, already faulty? No, for if we could come to such a drastic conclusion, we could hardly dare to make any move at all. The real mistake occurred when, at a later stage, White exchanged his Q Bishop on the eleventh move, for this exchange created 'holes' in White's Queen's side position (QKt2, and more particularly QB3), and these 'holes' gave Black the opportunity to exploit the open QB file.

It is therefore usual to play 8. P—QR3 (instead of 8. QKt—Q2), thus definitely preventing Black's manœuvre . . . . B—QR6.

Note well that White could not defer P—QR3, even for one move, without risking further damage: e.g. if in the game under review he had played 9. P—QR3 (instead of 9. Kt—K5), Black, with 9. . . . . P—K4, would have obtained a majority in the centre as well as the freer game.

The assessment of the position in *No. 28* therefore reads:

Black stands a little better, because he can initiate an attack on White's Q side along the open QB file, which attack will be helped by the fact that there are 'holes' at White's QKt2 and QB3.

The plan: before enlarging on this, let us first study the course of the game:

14. Q—Q2

Here are some alternative ideas:

1. 14. P—B4, in order to free the weak brother without delay. He threatens 15. P—B5, establishing a Q-side pawn majority, and so Black has no option but to exchange pawns: 14. . . . . P×P; 15. P×P. Now how do matters stand with regard to White's pawn formation; has it improved or deteriorated? It is definitely worse, for after 15. . . . . KR—Q1, White's Q pawn has clearly become weak. After, e.g. 16. Kt—K5, B—R5 (not 16. . . . . R×P; 17. B×P ch); 17. Q—Q2, Q—Q3; 18. Kt—B3, B—B3, it is clear that White will not get off scot-free.

Conclusion: with P—QB4, now or later, White transfers the weakness on the QB file to the Q file without otherwise strengthening his position.

2. 14. Kt—K5, QR—B1; 15. Kt×B, R×Kt. White has eliminated Black's Bishop, so that now the remaining white Bishop can well be expected to provide reliable protection for the QB pawn. But this does not cover the whole question; there is not only a weak pawn at QB2, but also a weak square at QB3. Sooner or later a Rook will settle down on that square and keep the whole of White's Q side under restraint. This again will afford the Knight full freedom of action and, once the Bishop is exchanged, Black will conquer White's QB2, which in turn will lead to further successes. It would lead too far to go into greater detail, but one fact stands out: Black can overcome difficulties, Black has the initiative.

3. 14. Q—B1. This would seem to be the best continuation, for if the attacker decides to accept the offer and exchanges Queens, he is deprived of his best attacking piece, which is another way of saying his attack has become far less dangerous. In addition, the white King, once the Queens are off the board, can play an important part in the defence of his Q side. At the same time White, with 14. Q—B1, abandons any idea of assuming the initiative and confesses that, as first player, he has failed to maintain his birthright, a confession not easy to make at any time.

14. ....   QR—B1   15. P—B3   P—QR3

Preparing for the next move:

16. Kt—K5   B—Kt4

An important intermediary part of Black's strategy. In order to increase the pressure on White's QB3, Black submits to his QKt pawn being doubled. This he does the more readily as his pawn at QKt4 will help the attack by preventing White's P—QB4.

17. P—B3

Let us examine 17. B×B, P×B (17. .... Kt—K5; 18. Q—B1, Q×Q; 19. KR×Q, P×B; 20. P—QB4 only leads to similar turns); and now—

1. 18. KR—B1, Kt—K5; 19. Q—K3 (not 19. Q—Q3, Q—Kt7, or even 19. .... Kt×QBP), 19. .... R—B2, with the following continuations:

(*a*) 20. P—QB4, KtP×P; 21. P×P, Q×Q; 22. P×Q, P—B3, winning a pawn; or

(*b*) 20. P—B3, Kt—Q3; 21. R—B2, KR—B1; 22. QR—QB1, P—Kt5, again winning a pawn because 23. P—QB4 fails after 23. .... P×P, because the white Queen is unguarded.

2. 18. P—B3, R—B2; 19. KR—B1, KR—B1; 20. R—B2, Kt—K1; 21. QR—QB1, Kt—Q3, and Black has prevented the advance of the QB pawn and exercises strong pressure on White's position.

17.	B×B	19. QR—B1	KR—B1
18. Kt×B	R—B2	20. R—QB2	Kt—K1
	21. KR—B1	Kt—Q3 (*No. 29*)	

The forces on either side have occupied the appropriate squares: Black's Rooks threaten the QB pawn, the black Knight commands White's QB4, while the white Rooks guard their Q side, and White's Knight has an option on K5 and QB5.

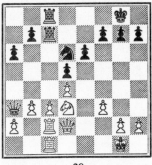

29

22. Kt—K5

An unlucky throw. He should play 22. Kt—B5, so as to be able to bring the Knight to QR4, should it become necessary to reinforce the defence of the weak QB pawn.

After 22. Kt—B5, Black can play 22. .... P—K4; but in that case, too, White plays 23. Kt—R4, and Black's advance has only weakened his position and given the white Queen chances of attack.

The correct development of Black's attack after 22. Kt—B5 is: 22. .... P—QKt3; 23. Kt—R4, R—B3 (not on any account 23. .... P—QKt4; 24. Kt—B5, Kt—Kt2; 25. P—QKt4, when Black would achieve nothing, a typical situation: White's weakness at QB3 is sealed off); 24. Q—Q3, R—R1, protecting the QR pawn and intending 25. .... Kt—Kt2 (controlling White's QB5), with the further threats of 26. .... P—QKt4 and 27. .... QR—QB1; and Black resumes his attack. In the meantime White will have played R—R1, to guard the R pawn, which is compulsory as the Knight will be forced back to QKt2. All this leaves White no chance of achieving anything.

We perceive that once this type of attack is well and truly launched, it is very tenacious and sets the defender a difficult, at times almost hopeless, task. Take care not to leave yourself open to such an attack. Caution is needed when playing 8. Kt—Q2, lest it allow 10. .... B—QR6.

22. ...... Q—R4

The time has come to let the Queen take a direct part in the attack, and now 23. .... Kt—Kt4 is threatened, after which four pieces would bear on White's vulnerable QB3.

23. P—QR4

With the twofold object of preventing 23. .... Kt—Kt4, and of carrying out the following manœuvre: the white Knight is to reach QB5 *via* Q3. Then P—QKt4 and P—QR5 would 'seal' White's weakness, very much as shown in a preceding note.

Black need not permit this to happen, and he can forestall White's intentions with some decisive blows.

Instead of 23. P—QR4, White should have played 23. Kt—Q3, e.g. 23. .... Kt—Kt4, and now White plays—

Not (*1*) 24. Kt—Kt4, because of 24. .... Kt—R6; 25. R—Kt2, Q×Kt; 26. P×Q, R×R ch; 27. K—B2, R (B8)—B7, etc.;

But (*2*) 24. Kt—B5, P—QKt3; 25. Kt—R4, and White can risk 26. P—QB4, even after 25. .... Kt—Q3.

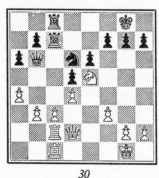

30   31

23. ....   Q—Kt3 (*No. 30*)

Now White cannot avoid the loss of a pawn as can be demonstrated by the following variations:

1. 24. P—QKt4, P—QR4;

(*a*) 25. P×P, Q×P, and White cannot defend the QR pawn without leaving the QB pawn in the lurch;

(*b*) 25. R—Kt2, P—B3; 26. P×P, Q×P; 27. Kt—Q3, Kt—B5;

(*c*) 25. R—Kt1, P×P; 26. R×P, Q×R; 27. P×Q, R×R; 28. Q—B4 (he was threatened with the loss of the Queen); 28. .... R—B8 ch; 29. K—B2, Kt—B4, etc.

(*d*) 25. P—Kt5, Kt—B5; 26. Kt×Kt (26. Q—K2 leads pretty much to the same result); 26. .... R×Kt; 27. R—R2, P—K4, etc.

2. 24. R—Kt2, Kt—B4 (threatening 25. .... Kt×P); 25. R (Kt2)—Kt1, P—B3;

(*a*) 26. Kt—Q3, R×P; 27. R×R, Q×P ch, etc.

(*b*) 26. Kt—Kt4, P—K4, and White's Q4 falls.

3. 24. R—Kt1, Kt—B4, with a similar continuation.

Note particularly how Black was able to make use of accessory circumstances (such as the pinning of White's Q pawn by the black Queen) in order to reach his objective. But these minor issues invariably come into the picture in some way or other when a player is tied up by the necessity of defending a weak point (as in this case White and his QB3), and he is in consequence unable to develop his game freely.

24. Kt—Q3

White gives up the pawn in order to try some counter-action; but all it does is to delay the execution. We give the rest without comment.
24. .... Q×P; 25. Kt—B5, Q—Kt3; 26. R—Kt2, Q—R2; 27. Q—K1, P—QKt3; 28. Kt—Q3, R—B5; 29. P—R5, P×P; 30. Kt—B5, Kt—Kt4; 31. R—K2, Kt×QP; 32. P×Kt, R (B1)×Kt. White resigns.

To recapitulate, Black's *plan* from *No. 28* was to engineer an attack on the Q side directed particularly against the QB pawn. Its *execution* comprised:
(*1*) Doubling Rooks on the QB file.
(*2*) Elimination of the principal defensive piece (Bishop at Q3) by an exchange (.... P—QR3 and .... B—QKt4).
(*3*) Preventing White from getting rid of his weakness by gaining control of his QB4.
(*4*) Suitable disposition of his remaining forces (here the Queen, the Knight, and the neighbouring pawns) which must occupy the right squares until the time is ripe for the final combination.

In the preceding example, we have seen that the creation of a second weakness (pawn at QKt3 after P—QR4) was followed by a swift débâcle, as nearly always happens in such circumstances. Here one can well generalise: the defence of one weakness is a difficult task, that of several is an impossible one.

In this respect the following game (again one of Capablanca's) is particularly characteristic. Black offers (or loses) a pawn on the Q side, but he thereby obtains lines of attack along which the white Q side pawns are subjected to threats so manifold and varied that at length the defence can no longer hold out.

NIMZOWITSCH—CAPABLANCA, *St. Petersburg*, 1914

1. P—K4, P—K4; 2. Kt—KB3, Kt—QB3; 3. Kt—B3, Kt—B3; 4. B—Kt5, P—Q3; 5. P—Q4, B—Q2; 6. B×Kt, B×B; 7. Q—Q3, P×P; 8. Kt×P, P—KKt3; 9. Kt×B, P×Kt; 10. Q—R6, Q—Q2; 11. Q—Kt7, R—B1; 12. Q×RP, B—Kt2.
The theory says (*No. 31*): 'Black has a strong attack for his pawn,' by which of course is meant our Q side attack.

In the present instance there are no weaknesses in White's position, but Black has lines of attack in the open QR and QKt files and, above all, the long black diagonal, which will enable him to develop great pressure on White's Q side.

But I am convinced that no critic would have ventured to characterise a position such as this as favourable to Black had it not been for the grand and convincing tale which this particular example unfolds. He would presumably have had to be content with the dictum: 'Black has little compensation for his pawn.'

Let us see how Black makes use of his opportunities.

13. Castles   Castles   14. Q—R6

White decides on defensive measures and wishes to play the Queen to Q3. It is remarkable how the gain of a pawn is apt to make a player over-cautious, almost as possessions frequently do in real life.

It does not affect our investigation, whether or no a more enterprising method would have had better results for White, though it might well be so. Indeed, he could hardly have fared worse than in the actual game.

14. ....   KR—K1   15. Q—Q3   Q—K3

Attacking the K pawn once more and preparing the important manœuvre Kt—Q2—K4—B5.

16. P—B3   Kt—Q2   17. B—Q2   Kt—K4
        18. Q—K2   Kt—B5 (*No. 32*)

32   33

Quite suddenly Black's attack has broken out in full force. Its first objective is White's QKt pawn, and the special significance of Black's Bishop at KKt2 becomes manifest in the following *petite combinaison*! 19. P—QKt3, B—Q5 ch; 20. K—R1, Kt×B; 21. Q×Kt, Q—K4; and wins (22. P—B4, B×Kt). One perceives why Black, a few moves back, provoked 16. P—B3. A check at Q5 can be handy at times.

19. QR—Kt1   R—R1 *(No. 33)*

Now White's second weak point is under fire, and he can no longer
avoid the loss of a pawn. To be sure, this is not so serious for, after all,
he is a pawn up and need not feel the loss. In fact he can, by giving
back the pawn, hope to improve his position, as, for instance, after
20. P—QKt3, Kt—R6; 21. QR—B1, B×Kt; 22. B×B, Kt—Kt4; 23.
B—Kt2, R×P; 24. R—Kt1, and White has a very good game, and his
Bishop has a most effective range.

In fact, 20. P—QKt3 is White's best move. Black, however, need
not go in for the continuation given above. He has a stronger line in
20. .... Kt×B; 21. Q×Kt, and now—

Not *(1)* 21. .... B×Kt; 22. Q×B, and Black does not recover his
    pawn, as his QB pawn is unguarded;
still less *(2)* 21. .... Q—K4; 22. Kt—R4, and White's position is
    secure;
but *(3)* 21. .... R—R6; and now Black can capture the QR pawn at
    his leisure by driving away the Knight (22. KR—K1, Q—K4; 23.
    R—K3?, B—R3). Black will still have to find the best moves, even
    though his Bishop is stronger than White's Knight.

20. P—QR4

This move can be good only if it can be followed up at once by
P—QKt3. But that is not the case in this position.

20. ....   Kt×B   21. Q×Kt   Q—B5

Hitting the nail on the head. White is tied up, he can no longer
play P—QKt3, his QR pawn is doomed, and his QKtP also stands
a poor chance.

22. KR—Q1

22. Q—Q3, Q—B4 ch brings no relief.

22. ....   KR—Kt1

Note the extreme care with which Black sets about the recovery of
his pawn and, in particular, avoids a premature exchange at White's
QB3.

23. Q—K3

Black's threat was 23. .... R×KtP; 24. R×R, B×Kt, coming out
himself a pawn to the good.

23. ....   R—Kt5

Threatening 24. .... B—Q5.

24. Q—Kt5   B—Q5 ch   25. K—R1   QR—Kt1
(*No. 34*)

White's game now collapses like a house of cards. He is threatened with the loss of a piece by 26. .... B×Kt. If he moves the Q Rook, his QKt pawn falls as well as the QB pawn without slackening of the attack. The white Knight has no move!

26. R×B

With this move White can put up the longest resistance. In view of this possibility it seems that it would have been better for Black to withhold the check 24. .... B—Q5 ch, and to play 24. .... QR—Kt1

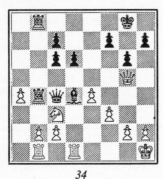
34

35

first. But it does not signify, the game is won for Black in any event. There followed: 26. .... Q×R; 27. R—Q1, Q—B5; 28. P—R4, R×KtP; 29. Q—Q2, Q—B4; 30. R—K1, Q—KR4; 31. R—R1, Q×P ch; 32. K—Kt1, Q—R4; 33. P—R5, R—R1; 34. P—R6, Q—B4 ch; 35. K—R1, Q—B5; 36. P—R7, Q—B4; 37. P—K5, Q×KP; 38. R—R4, Q—R4 ch; 39. K—Kt1, Q—B4 ch; 40. K—R2, P—Q4; 41. R—R4, R×RP. White resigns.

Impressive and convincing as was the last example, our Queen's side attack need by no means be aimed exclusively at opposing pawns. The objective can also be, and frequently is, to obtain command of vital squares in the hostile position and concurrently to hamstring the opponent's normal development, etc.

This is well illustrated by the following example:

ELISKASES—LANDAU, *Noordwijk*, 1938

1. P—Q4, P—Q4; 2. P—QB4, P—K3; 3. Kt—QB3, Kt—KB3; 4. B—Kt5, B—K2; 5. P—K3, Castles; 6. Kt—B3, QKt—Q2; 7. Q—B2, P—B3; 8. R—Q1, P—QR3; 9. P—QR3, R—K1; 10. B—Q3, P×P;

11. B×P, Kt—Q4; 12. B×B, Q×B; 13. Kt—K4, Kt (Q4)—B3; 14.
B—Q3, Kt×Kt; 15. B×Kt, P—R3; 16. Castles (*No. 35*).

White stands better according to Fine.

The first impression is that there is not much to choose between the
two camps. Black is not fully developed, but his position gives a solid
impression. But on closer examination, matters do not appear to be
too easy for Black, particularly as far as the development of his Q Bishop
is concerned. An ingenious conception of what constitutes development will not suffice here: 'Black plays .... Kt—B3, followed by ....
B—Q2, and all is well!' The fact is that the Bishop is well placed,
but not mobilised. The course of the game will make this line of
thought clear.

16. ....   P—QB4

The idea underlying this move is: when presently the Bishop reaches
Q2, there will be an outlet in the direction of QR5.

17. R—B1   P×P   18. P×P   Kt—B3
19. Kt—K5

White need not fear the exchange at his K5 because it would not
solve for Black the problem of his Q Bishop.

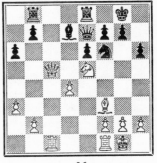
36

19. ....   R—Kt1

With the unmistakable determination
to bring his Bishop *coûte-que-coûte* into
play.

20. B—B3   B—Q2
21. Q—QB5 (*No. 36*)

An excellent move, preventing Black
from occupying the QB file with his
Rooks, which would quickly lead to
equality. If now 21. ....QR—B1; 22.
Q×Q, R×Q; 23. Kt×B, and White wins
a piece. Furthermore, the exchange of Queens would be to White's
advantage, for after 21. .... Q×Q; 22. P×Q, White has the famed
Q-side majority (the subject of our preceding article), which here
would be particularly effective because of his well-posted K Bishop.

21. ....   B—Kt4   22. KR—Q1   K—B1

With an eye on the fast approaching end-game stage, Black plays
his King nearer to the centre. Preferable, however, would be 22. ....
Q—Q1, followed by 23. .... R—K2, with a congested but solid
position for Black.

23. P—QKt3

The black Bishop, having barely tasted the joys of freedom, is already threatened with encirclement. After 24. P—QR4, there is nothing else but 24. .... B—Q2. It would not be so bad now if Black could clear his K1, but he would not escape scot-free: 23. .... KR—Q1; 24. Q×Q ch, K×Q; 25. R—B7 ch costs at least a pawn. In this connection, we would point to the preceding note (.... Q—Q1 and .... R—K2), according to which K1 would now be available to the Bishop and Black would have to contend with far fewer difficulties.

23. ....   P—QKt3

Creating a weakness, but he has nothing better.

24. Q—B7 (*No. 37*).

Black is in difficulties. For instance, if he continues, as intended with the last move, 24. .... P—QR4, followed by 25. .... P—R5, in order to withdraw the Bishop to R3, White would exchange Queens

37

38

and play Kt—B6, winning the exchange; nor would 24. .... Q×Q; 25. R×Q, R—K2; 26. KR—QB1 bring any relief. The actual continuation (24. .... KR—B1) leads to an entirely different type of game in which White also has the better chances.

The Queen's side attack has thus been successful. To recapitulate, the main points in the attack were:

1. Mastering the QB file.
2. Hindering the development of Black's Q Bishop through pressure on QKt7.
3. Command, and eventually occupation, of important points in the hostile position (Q7, QB5, and QB7).
4. Chasing the black Bishop (P—QKt3, and P—QR4).

There followed:

24.	KR—B1	25. Q×R ch	R×Q
26. R×R ch	B—K1		

As a general rule two Rooks are stronger than a Queen, and especially so when, as here, a hostile piece can be pinned. The defence incurs liabilities which put serious limitations on the Queen's mobility; and it is just this mobility on which the defence has to rely as a compensation for the massive strength of the two Rooks.

27. P—QKt4	P—QR4	28. P×P	P×P
29. P—QR4	Q—Q3		

The Queen wanders abroad, which quickly proves fatal. Essential was 29. .... P—Kt4; providing the King with a flight square

30. B—B6	K—K2	31. R—Kt1	Q×P
32. B×B	Q—K5		

32. .... Kt×B; loses the Queen by 33. Kt—B6 ch, and equally so 32. .... Q×Kt; 33. R—Kt7 ch, K—Q3; 34. R—Q8 ch, K—B4; 35. R—Kt5 ch, etc.

33. Kt—B6 ch, K—Q3; 34. R—Q1 ch, Kt—Q4; 35. R—Q8 ch, K—B4; 36. R—B1 ch, K—Kt3; 37. Kt—Kt8, Kt—B6; 38. R—Q6 ch, K—R2; 39. Kt—B6 ch, K—Kt3; 40. Kt—K7 dis ch, K—R2; 41. R—Q7 ch, K—R3; 42. Kt—B8, resigns.

We shall conclude this chapter by giving two examples of an entirely different type, in which the attacker pays no attention to pawns and squares, but is after bigger game. Before doing so however, we give a short account of what frequently happens when Black accepts the Queen's Gambit and attempts to hold the gambit pawn.

In its simplest form, this runs as follows:
1. P—Q4, P—Q4; 2. P—QB4, P×P; 3. Kt—KB3, Kt—KB3; 4. P—K3, P—QKt4 (*No. 38*).

As is well known, this continuation is unfavourable for Black, as White, by the following typical manœuvre, always recovers his pawn.

5. P—QR4

White intends to isolate Black's outpost and then to capture both pawns: 5. .... P×P; 6. B×P, or, a more direct method, 5. .... P×P; 6. Q×P ch, B—Q2; 7. Q×BP.

5. ....   P—B3

It is clear that 5. .... P—QR3; would be no protection at all (6. P×P, etc.), and that 5. .... B—Q2; is equally useless after 6. P×P, B×P; 7. Kt—R3, or 7. B×P, B×B; 8. Q—R4 ch.

6. P×P   P×P   7. P—QKt3

This is the point of White's manœuvre. Black cannot prevent White from recovering his pawn, e.g.—

1. 7. .... P×P; 8. B×P ch, B—Q2; 9. Q×P.

2. 7. .... B—R3; 8. P×P, P×P; 9. R×B, Kt×R; 10. Q—R4 ch, gaining material.

3. 7. .... B—K3; 8. P×P, P×P, and now—

Not (a) 9. B×P, B×B; 10. Q—R4 ch, QKt—Q2; 11. Q×B, R—B1, and Black wins;

but (b) 9. Kt—K5, Q—B2; 10. Q—R4 ch (or 10. Kt—R3, or 10. B×P), 10. .... QKt—Q2; 11. B×P, B×B; 12. Kt×B, R—B1; 13. QKt—Q2.

As a rule White has the better position after recovering his pawn, for Black's is saddled with an isolated QR pawn, while White's pawn formation is excellent.

There are, however, variations in which it is possible for Black either to maintain the gambit pawn or to give it back in return for a satisfactory position. The following examples illustrate this contingency:

1. P—Q4, P—Q4; 2. P—QB4, P—K3; 3. Kt—QB3, P—QB3; 4. Kt—B3, P×P; 5. P—K3, (a stronger continuation is 5. P—QR4,) 5. .... P—QKt4; 6. P—QR4, B—Kt5; 7. B—Q2, Q—Kt3, etc. (not .... P—QR3; 8. P×P, BP×P; 9. Kt×P, or 8. .... B×Kt; 9. B×B, BP×P; 10. P—QKt3, P×P; 11. B×P ch, etc.).

1. P—Q4, P—Q4; 2. P—QB4, P—QB3; 3. Kt—KB3, Kt—B3; 4. Kt—B3, P×P; 5. P—K3, P—QKt4; 6. P—QR4, P—Kt5; 7. Kt—R2, P—K3; 8. B×P, B—Kt2, and Black has a satisfactory game, as White's Q Knight is out of play.

We have now seen the kind of attack which is at White's disposal against a hostile pawn-chain at Black's QKt4 and QB5, or at QR3, QKt4, and QB5.

Here is the first of two examples mentioned above:

CAPABLANCA—SPIELMANN, *New York*, 1927

1. P—Q4, P—Q4; 2. Kt—KB3, P—K3; 3. P—B4, Kt—Q2; 4. Kt—B3, KKt—B3; 5. B—Kt5, B—Kt5; 6. P×P, P×P; 7. Q—R4, B×Kt ch; 8. P×B, Castles; 9. P—K3, P—B4; 10. B—Q3, P—B5; 11. B—B2, Q—K2; 12. Castles KR, P—QR3; 13. KR—K1, Q—K3; 14. Kt—Q2, P—Kt4; 15. Q—R5 (*No. 39*).

The theory's verdict is: White has the better game. The reasons: he has chances of attack on the Q side, firstly because of the possibility of P—QR4, with a weakening of Black's pawn formation, and secondly, because of the advanced and fully secure position of his Queen.

Over and above these remarks we must add:

1. Compared with the preceding illustration, White's action against the
pawns at Black's QR3, QKt4, and QB5
is far less incisive for the following
reasons:

(*a*) The move P—QKt3 is not available;
(*b*) The black QB pawn is doubly
guarded by pawns, so that after a
possible P—QR4, P × P, the Q B pawn
is not left hanging and is in no need
of support.

39

Against this we have the fact that—

(*c*) White has an equal number of pawns, and so whatever action he takes need not in itself be aimed at winning a pawn.

2. The Queen, the strongest piece, can develop enormous power from a suitable outpost. She is at the same time the most valuable, but she is safe in this position and, in the absence of a black Bishop, out of the reach of Black's minor pieces. Therefore the white Queen here can take a leading part in the attack on the Q side.

There followed:

15. ....   Kt—K5

The following exchange weakens Black's QB5, and the text move therefore is to be rejected. Black plays for an apparently safe position, but his plan is refuted by White in the nick of time by an attractive combination. Better would have been 15. .... B—Kt2; and if 16. Q—B7, Q—B3; although White remains with a slight advantage for the end-game.

16. Kt × Kt   P × Kt   17. P—QR4

As was to be expected—

17. ....   Q—Q4

With this intermediary move, Black has apparently improved his defence, as White's Q Bishop is *en prise*. If now 18. B—B4, B—Kt2, Black has a satisfactory game.

18. P × P

A fatal surprise. White offers a piece, and rightly so, as the sequel shows.

18. ....   Q×B

Of course not 18. .... Q×KtP; 19. Q×Q, and White wins a Rook.

19. B×P (*No. 40*)

The real point of the combination becomes manifest if Black plays
19. .... R—R2, e.g. 20. P—Kt6, Q×Q; 21. P×R, and now—

1. 21. .... B—Kt2; 22. R×Q, and White, with a Rook and three
pawns (a strong one at R7) against two minor pieces, has an easy win.

40

41

2. 21. .... Q×R; 22. R×Q, Kt—Kt3; 23. P—R8 (Q), Kt×Q; 24.
B×Kt, and White has an extra pawn and must win Black's Q side
pawns as well.

19. ....   R—Kt1

Equally insufficient.

20. P×P, R—Kt4; 21. Q—B7, Kt—Kt3; 22. P—R7, B—R6 (a last
attempt!); 23. KR—Kt1, R×R ch; 24. R×R, P—B4; 25. B—B3, P—
B5; 26. P×P, resigns.

And finally, the second example, in which once more the Queen plays
the vital part and in which White, sacrificing two pawns, succeeds in
hemming in a whole cluster of hostile units. It was again Capablanca
who produced this work of art.

CAPABLANCA—VIDMAR, *London*, 1922

1. P—Q4, P—Q4; 2. Kt—KB3, Kt—KB3; 3. P—B4, P—K3; 4. Kt—
B3, B—K2; 5. B—Kt5, QKt—Q2; 6. P—K3, Castles; 7. R—B1, P—B3;
8. Q—B2, P×P; 9. B×P, Kt—Q4; 10. B×B, Q×B; 11. Castles, P—
QKt3 (*No. 41*).

Bilguer rightly remarks that the development of the Q Bishop in fianchetto aims at the exchange of Knights at White's QB3. But, after the text-move and White's reply, White obtains an overwhelming position.

12. Kt×Kt

Now White exchanges Knights, and this exchange is particularly strong, because—

1. The white long diagonal will be closed so that Black's last move fails in its purpose and, in fact, creates a serious weakening of the White squares in Black's Q side.
2. The QB file is opened, which White will soon occupy with Queen and Rooks, so that he will speedily break into Black's position.

We shall observe again and again the great effect these two factors will have on the course of the game.

12. ....   BP×Kt

Black must recapture with the QB pawn, as otherwise he would lose a pawn after 13. B—Q3.

13. B—Q3   P—KR3

Black refrains from playing 13. .... Kt—B3, as he wishes, for the time being, to use the Knight for the defence of his Q side. After 13. .... Kt—B3 there might have followed 14. Q—B7, and now—

1. 14. .... Q×Q; 15. R×Q, P—QR4 (15. .... B—Q2; 16. Kt—K5,) 16. KR—B1, B—R3; 17. B×B, R×B; 18. R (B1)—B6, with 19. R—Kt7 to follow, winning a pawn.
2. 14. .... B—Q2; 15. B—R6, Q—Kt5; 16. Kt—K5, B—Kt4; 17. P—QR3, Q—R5; 18. B×B, Q×B; 19. R—B2, trebling major pieces on the QB file.
3. 14. .... Q—Kt5; 15. P—QR3, with much the same sequel as in the game.

14. Q—B7

The white Queen invades enemy territory and occupies an advanced but entirely secure post. There she completely frustrates all Black's attempts at development.

14. ....   Q—Kt5

As Black is quite unable to develop his forces along normal lines, he tries, with this sally by the Queen, to obtain some counterplay—an attempt which the first player refutes in exemplary fashion.

15. P—QR3 (*No. 42*)

A very fine move—White offers one or two pawns in order to win
the Queen or, failing that, a Q side piece.

Let us investigate some of the contingencies:

1. 15. .... Q×KtP; 16. R—Kt1, Q×RP; 17. B—Kt5, and now—
(*a*) 17. .... Kt—B3; 18. R—R1, Q—Kt5; 19. KR—Kt1, winning
the Queen.
(*b*) 17. .... Q—K2; 18. B—B6, R—Kt1; 19. Kt—K5, R—Q1 (19.

42

43

.... Q—Q1; 20. Q×RP, Kt×Kt; 21. P×Kt, etc.); 20. B×Kt,
B×B; 21. Kt—B6, and wins.
2. 15. .... Q—Kt6; 16. R—B3, Q×KtP; 17. R—Kt1, Q—R7; 18.
R (B3)—B1, Kt—B3 (18. .... Q×P; 19. B—Kt5, etc.); 19. B—Kt5,
again threatening 20. R—R1 and 21. KR—Kt1, winning the Queen,
or 20. B—B6, winning a piece.

15. ....   Q—R5   16. P—R3 (*No. 43*)

Again an excellent move, and not merely intended to safeguard his
King. For if we examine the position more closely, we find that Black
can no longer proceed with his proper development, e.g. 16. .... R—
Kt1; 17. Kt—K5, R—Kt2 (17. .... Kt×Kt; 18. B—B2, followed by
19. Q×R); 18. Q—B6, Q×Q (otherwise 19. Kt×Kt, R×Kt; 20.
Q×B); 19. Kt×Q, K—R1; 20. Kt—K7, R—QKt1; 21. Kt×B, QR×Kt;
22. B—R6, and White must win the ending, thanks to the command
of the only open file which Black can no longer wrest from him. This
variation clearly shows the far-reaching consequences of the weakening move 11. .... P—QKt3. Even at this stage it has made it possible
for White to secure possession of the QB file by 22. B—R6!

White's last move ensures that Black will not long be able to withstand his opponent's severe positional pressure.

16. ....   Kt—B3

Black makes a heroic attempt to complete his development, cost what it may. After, say, 16. .... P—Kt3; 17. R—B3, Black would still have to go in for the variation shown in the preceding note.

17. Kt—K5   B—Q2

17. .... B—R3; 18. P—QKt3, Q—R4; 19. Kt—B6 would also cost a piece. Black literally has no move.

18. B—B2   Q—Kt4   19. P—QR4

Decisive; Black must leave his Bishop to its fate.

19. ....   Q×KtP   20. Kt×B

Stronger still would have been, first, 20. R—Kt1, Q—R7; 21. Kt×B, QR—B1; 22. Kt×Kt ch, P×Kt; 23. Q—Kt3 ch, and as the Bishop can move freely, White remains a piece ahead. As it is, White only wins the exchange, but this also Capablanca speedily and soundly turns into a win, as follows:

20. .... QR—B1; 21. Q—Kt7, Kt×Kt; 22. B—R7 ch, K×B; 23. R×R, R×R; 24. Q×R, Kt—B3; 25. R—B1, Q—Kt5; 26. Q—B2 ch, K—Kt1; 27. Q—B6, Q—R6; 28. Q—R8 ch, K—R2; 29. R—B7 (we have seen in our first article, how to take advantage of a superiority in material, the result of a successful attack. Here this superiority consists in the exchange only, but with the Rook on the seventh rank taking a powerful part in the attack on Black's pawns, the ascendency of Rook over Knight in an ending is well illustrated), 29. .... Q×RP; 30. R×BP, Q—Q8 ch; 31. K—R2, Q—R4; 32. Q×RP, Q—Kt3; 33. R—B8, Q—B4; 34. R—B7, Q—Kt3; 35. R—Kt7, Kt—K5; 36. Q—R2, P—K4; 37. Q×P, P×P; 38. R—Kt8, Kt—B3; 39. Q×P, Q—B4; 40. R×P, Q×P; 41. Q—Q3 ch, K—Kt1; 42. R—Kt8 ch, resigns.

CHAPTER IV

KNIGHT AGAINST 'BAD' BISHOP

WHEN discussing the game Botvinnik-Konstantinopolsky (see p. 15), we came to the position shown in *No. 44*, which position we undertook to investigate on a subsequent occasion.

We have already stated that White has the better game, without, however, discussing very closely the reasons on which we base our

44

45

opinion. As we pointed out, White's pawn majority on the Q side has lost its significance. The fact that White can obtain a passed QB pawn after P—QR4 and P—QKt4—Kt5 is certainly of no greater import than the fact that Black already has a passed pawn at his Q4.

Why then is White's position superior? It is because Black has a 'bad' Bishop. Let us examine more precisely what this means. Black's Bishop at Q2 is bad because its own pawns at QB3, Q4, and KB4 are hampering its mobility. The other pawns have no part in it which would lead one to ask: where does the 'inferiority' of a Bishop begin, is it with one, two, or three pawns? There is no definite answer to this question, but it can be said that the most serious hindrance of the Bishop's mobility would be provided by centre pawns, the QBP, QP, KP or KBP. It follows that the term 'bad Bishop' is not a sharply-defined conception, there are degrees of 'badness'; if, for instance, there were no black pawn on KB4 in this position, the Bishop's value would be much improved, and in the absence of a Q pawn as well, the appellation 'bad' would hardly apply at all.

This indicates at the same time what kind of position White must aim at, first and foremost, on this occasion: *in order to keep the Bishop as 'bad' as possible, the obstructive pawns must not be allowed to leave their respective squares.* In this case it means that .... P—KB5 and .... P—Q5 must be prevented.

We shall now give the further course of the game, from which we shall be able to derive additional directives.

20. P—B4

In the light of what we have said before, the object of this move is quite obvious. Black's KB pawn is now blocked, and the Bishop's mobility permanently crippled in this direction.

20. .... R—K2

He cannot play 20. .... R—K6; for after 21. K—B2, P—Q5 leads to the loss of a pawn after 22. KR—Q1.

21. KR—K1

As a rule, an exchange of Rooks increases the superiority of the Knight over the 'bad Bishop.'

21. .... KR—K1

He cannot give up the open file without a fight, as his opponent would penetrate into the heart of his position.

22. R×R   R×R   23. K—B2 (*No. 45*)

In order to exchange the second Rook as well, after which the ending Knight *v.* Bishop would be won for White. It is important first of all to examine this statement. Let us assume that Black, in this position, plays .... B—B1—R3—B5, where its obstruction by pawns would

be less—much less—taking it all in all, a sound plan. The game can develop as follows: 23. .... B—B1; 24. R—K1, R×R (practically forced); 25. K×R, B—R3; 26. P—QKt3 (preventing 26. .... B—B5) 26. .... K—B2; 27. K—Q2, K—K3; 28. K—K3, B—B8; 29. P—Kt3, P—Kt3; 30. K—Q4.

We have now reached the position shown in *No. 46.*

Up to now the moves on either side were by no means forced, and it would lead too far to undertake a detailed inves-

46

tigation of the tangle of possible complications. Our main object is first to give an idea of existing winning chances without paying over-much attention to *finessing* and detail.

The black pawn-position is now fixed, mainly on account of the

strong position of White's King, but the Bishop has escaped outside
its own pawn-chains and is not hindered by them to the same extent as
before.   The drawback of the 'bad Bishop' is now indirect, and is
based on the fact that all the black pawns as well as the Bishop occupy
white squares, so that the black squares are vulnerable and easily fall
into White's control.   The important square at Q4 is already occupied
by White, and Black's King must keep guard over White's K5.   Black
cannot undertake anything, and must remain on the defensive.   On
the other hand, what is there for White to do?   More than appears
at first sight.

From QKt4 the white Knight can attack the QB pawn, which cannot
be defended by .... B—Kt4 because of White's P—QR4.   On the
other hand, if the King guards the pawn by .... K—Q2, the way to
Black's K-side pawns is free *via* K5, KB6, KKt7.   It follows that Black,
reasonably enough, tries to prevent White's Kt—QKt4 by .... P—
QR4; but then White has the opportunity of obtaining a passed R pawn
by P—QKt4, etc.   We perceive how much care is required in the handling of such an ending.

An early advance of P—QKt4, in itself quite a normal move, nevertheless reduces White's chances to a minimum.

Let us work out the above by means of two illustrative variations:

(A) 30. .... B—R3; 31. Kt—R2, B—K7; 32. Kt—Kt4, K—Q2; 33.
K—K5, B—Q8; 34. K—B6, B×P; 35. K—Kt7, P—QR4; 36. Kt—Q3,
K—K3; 37. Kt—K5, P—Q5; 38. Kt×BP, K—Q4; 39. Kt×QP, K×Kt;
40. P—B6, P—R5; 41. P—B7, B—K3; 42. K×P, K—B6; 43. K×P,
K—Kt6; 44. P—R4, K×P; 45. P—R5, K—Kt6; 46. P—R6, P—R6;
47. P—R7, P—R7; 48. P—R8 (Q), and wins.

(B) 30. .... P—QR4; 31. Kt—R2, B—K7; 32. P—QKt4, P×P; (32.
.... B—B5; 33. P×P, winning, but if 32. .... P—R5, then quite
simply 33. Kt—B3,) 33. Kt×P, B—Kt4; 34. Kt—R2, B—B5; 35. Kt—
B3, B—R3; 36. P—QR4, B—B8; 37. Kt—R2, B—B5; 38. Kt—Kt4,
K—Q2; 39. K—K5, K—B2; 40. K—B6, P—Q5; 41. K—Kt7, P—Q6;
42. Kt×QP, B×Kt; 43. P—R4, (not 43. K×P, P—Kt4); 43. .... B—
B5; 44. K×P, B—B2; 45. K—Kt7, B—K1; 46. K—B8, K—Q1; 47.
P—QR5, etc.

These were, in truth, break-neck excursions by which the win was
finally secured, and we can well imagine that the reader may not be
entirely convinced of the forced nature of the variations shown.   But
this does not really affect our point.   The chief thing is—

(*1*) That it was seen that Black could not, on the whole, undertake
anything so that it was in fact established that the Knight is to be pre-
ferred to a 'bad Bishop.'

(*2*) That a general idea was given of the way in which attempts should
be made in order to win the game: a combination of the Knight-

manœuvres Kt—QB3—R2—Kt4 (attacking QB6), Kt—R2, and P—
QKt4 (forcing through a passed pawn), and K—K5 (penetration by
the King).

Let us revert to *No. 45*, in order to continue our discussion of the
game in question; it has now become clear that Black has to avoid
the exchange of Rooks, at least in present circumstances. There
followed:

> 23. ....   K—B2

A cunning move! Should White nevertheless play for an exchange
of Rooks, failure awaits him after 24. R—K1, R × R; 25. K × R, P—
Q5; 26. Kt—K2, K—K3; 27. Kt × P ch, K—Q4, and Black wins back
his pawn with a satisfactory position: the blockade is lifted and all
danger is past. Generally speaking, it can be stated that Black can
save the game if he can play P—Q5 without immediately fatal consequences.

> 24. R—Q1

Forcing the black pawns to remain on white squares.

> 24. ....   R—K1

It is impossible to bring the Bishop into the open without making
some equivalent concession, e.g. 24. .... B—B1; 25. Kt—K2, P—Kt3;
26. Kt—Q4, R—B2; and now the Rook is immobilised.

> 25. R—Q2

Guarding the QKt pawn and preparing the exchange of Rooks.

> 25. ....   P—KR3   26. R—K2   R—QKt1

If instead, 26. .... R × R ch; 27. Kt × R, and White controls the
square Q4, which is the key to winning the game.

> 27. K—K3

More obvious is 27. P—QKt4, but there are two objections:
(*1*) After exchanging Rooks eventually, White can no longer play
Kt—R2—Kt4, and, more important still, he has no further opportunity of obtaining a passed pawn.
(*2*) Black can start a counter-action with 27. .... P—QR4.

> 27. ....   R—Kt6

This fixes White's Queen's side, but at best only temporarily.

> 28. K—Q4

The King has reached the desired strong point and already threatens
K—K5—Q6, etc.

28. ....   K—B3   29. Kt—R2   R—Kt1

After 29. .... P—QR4 there follows 30. Kt—B1, R—Kt1; 31.
P—QKt3, when P—QKt4 must follow sooner or later; the text
move is preferable, even though White can still force a passed R pawn
through.

30. P—QKt4 (*No. 47*)

The crucial moment, for with this move White forgoes the opportunity to carry out the manœuvre indicated before (Kt—R2—Kt4), so
that the ending Knight *v.* Bishop assumes a different aspect.

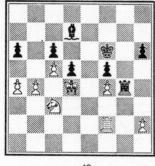

47   48

Let us investigate: 30. .... R—K1; 31. R×R (31. R—K5 also
deserves consideration), 31. .... B×R; 32. P—QR4 (32. P—Kt5
fails against 32. .... P×P; 33. K×P, B—B2 ch), 32. .... P—R3; 33.
P—Kt5, and now—

1. 33. .... RP×P; 34. P—R5, B—Q2; 35. P—R6, B—B1; 36. Kt—
Kt4, K—K3; 37. P—R7, B—Kt2; 38. Kt—R6, K—Q2; 39. K—K5,
P—Kt3; 40. K—B6, and once again White has the whip hand.
2. 33. .... BP×P; 34. P—R5, K—K3; 35. Kt—Kt4, and wins. If
Black omits 32. .... P—R3; and substitutes 32. .... K—K3 (after
30. .... R—K1; 31. R×R, B×R; 32. P—QR4); White likewise has
excellent prospects after 33. P—R5, B—Q2; 34. P—Kt5, P×P; 35.
Kt—Kt4.

30. ....   P—Kt4

Here 30. .... P—QR4 would play into White's hand: 31. P×P,
R—Kt6; 32. Kt—B3, R×P; 33. R—R2, or 31. .... R—QR1; 32.
Kt—B3, R×P; 33. P—QR4. In either case White has a strong passed
pawn.

31. P—Kt3	P×P	32. P×P	P—R3
33. Kt—B3	R—Kt1		

Black decides to leave the Rooks on the board, which, in fact, is his best chance.

34. P—QR4	R—Kt5	35. R—KB2

Now the white Rook fulfils the task of safeguarding the King's side. Meanwhile the remaining white forces carry out the winning plan on the opposite wing (*No. 48*).

There is an interesting winning continuation here, should Black try 35. .... B—K1; e.g. 36. P—Kt5, RP×P; 37. P×P, P×P; 38. Kt×P ch, K—K3 (38. .... K—B2; 39. Kt—K3, winning a pawn); 39. R—K2 ch, K—B2; 40. R×B, K×R; 41. Kt—B6 ch, K—K2; 42. Kt×R, P×Kt; 43. P—B5, P—R4; 44. P—B6, P—R5; 45. P—B7, and White queens first.

35.	B—K3	36. P—Kt5

The break-through, which has been impending for some time.

36.	RP×P	38. Kt×P	R—Kt8
37. P×P	P×P	39. Kt—B3	

First safeguarding the position before he can reap the benefit of his break-through.

39.	K—B2

An indirect defence of his Q4 (40. Kt×P, R—Q8 ch).

40. R—QKt2	R—KB8	41. Kt—K2

Alternatively, 41. K—K5, R—K8 ch; 42. Kt—K2 (as in the game), but not 42. K—Q6, because of 42. .... P—Q5. White must still exercise care before lifting the blockade of Black's Q pawn.

41.	R—K8	42. K—K5	P—Q5

Giving up the pawn is Black's best chance. If 42. .... K—K2, the following line is conclusive: 43. P—B6, P—Q5; 44. R—Kt7 ch, K—Q1; 45. K—Q6, R×Kt; 46. R—Kt8 ch, B—B1; 47. P—B7 ch, etc.

43. K×P

White's strategy has resulted in the gain of a pawn, and the rest is no longer of interest as far as our subject is concerned. There followed 43. .... K—Kt3; 44. Kt—B3, K—R4; 45. R—K2, R×R; 46. Kt×R, K—Kt5; 47. K—K5, B—B1; 48. Kt—Q4, P—R4; 49. Kt×P, B—Q2 (not 49. .... B×Kt; 50. P—R3 ch); 50. Kt—Kt7, B—R5; 51. P—B5, K—Kt4; 52. Kt—K6 ch, resigns.

Let us sum up in short the conclusions derived from this example:

Assessment. White has the better game because Black has a 'bad Bishop,' and White is in a position to fix the hostile pawns which obstruct the Bishop.

Plan.

1. Fix the obstructing pawns (20. P—KB4 and 24. R—Q1).

2. Occupy the blockading square, for preference by the King (28. K—Q4).

3. Sum up the various possibilities of a break-through, and try to combine these (analysis of *No. 46*).

4. Unassuming moves may have important consequences, e.g. 30. P—QKt4, which, for a well-defined period of time, prevents a number of possibilities.

5. Calculate accurately when to lift the blockade and allow the hostile passed pawn to advance. In such situations the smallest variation may make all the difference between a win and a loss.

Our next example illustrates a Knight *v.* Bishop ending in which the Rooks have already been exchanged (*No. 49*).

49

This is another position from Chapter II (*No. 25*, Eliskases-Flohr), in which the main subject, the pawn majority on the Q side, plays a subordinate part. This illustration also is instructive although, we might even say because, both players are guilty of some inaccuracies. Here again we have a Knight against a 'bad Bishop.' The Rooks have already disappeared. White's pawns at K4 and Q5 hinder their own Bishop, and the unguarded K pawn ties the Bishop for the time being to KB3, KKt2 or KR1.

The *verdict* on the position is: Black has the better game but, as will be seen, a win cannot be forced against best play.

The *plan* consists again in a combination of possible continuations:

1. Advance of the Q-side pawns.

2. March of the black King to QB4, Q5, etc.

3. Establishing and reinforcing the pressure on White's K4.

Let us examine the sequel.

28. ....   P—B4

Black loses no time in increasing his pressure on White's K4. In addition he need no longer be anxious about White's P—B4, which might be the reply to the text-move if played later. At the moment 29. P—B4 would be satisfactorily met by 29. .... K—B3.

29. P—B3

A difficult decision for White. Another system consists in 29. P×P, P×P; 30. P—B4, P—K5, after which White controls his Q4 and has by no means a bad position. Black has a better continuation against 29. P×P, namely 29. .... Kt×P; 30. K—Q2, K—B3; 31. K—Q3, K—K2, and now—

1. 32. K—K4, K—Q3;
  (*a*) 33. B—B1, Kt—K2; 34. B—B4, Kt—Kt1, followed by 35. .... Kt—B3 ch, winning a pawn;
  (*b*) 33. P—B4, P×P; 34. P×P (34. K×P, Kt—K2, etc.); 34. .... P—QKt4; 35. B—B1, P—Kt5; 36. B—B4, Kt—K2; 37. K—Q4, Kt—B1; 38. B—Kt3, Kt—Kt3, followed by .... P—QR4—R5.
2. 32. K—B4, K—Q3;
  (*a*) 33. B—B1, Kt—K2; 34. B—Kt2, Kt—B1, followed by 35. .... Kt—Kt3 ch, winning a pawn;
  (*b*) 33. P—QR4, P—QR3; with various possibilities for Black, e.g. 34. P—R5, Kt—K2; 35. P—B4, P×P; 36. P×P, Kt—B1; 37. B—K4, P—Kt4 ch; 38. P×P e.p., Kt×P ch; 39. K—Q4, P—QR4.

These variations are far from exhaustive, but they will serve to show that the continuation 29. P×P, leads to a different type of game, without, however, satisfactorily solving White's problems.

29. ....   P×P   30. P×P

Black has obtained one of his target-positions: permanent pressure on White's K4 whereby at least one of the white pieces (King or Bishop) is tied to its defence.

30. ....   P—QKt4
Mobilising the Queen's side.

31. K—Q2   P—QR4   32. K—Q3
The King guards the K pawn so that the Bishop may be free to move.

32. ....   K—B3   33. B—B3   K—K2
Bringing the black King into action

34. P—KR4 (*No. 50*)

White's last move leads to a decisive weakening of White's K-side pawns, because he thereby abandons the possibility of keeping the KKt pawn guarded by a pawn. It will become clear why this factor is of importance when we come to discuss Black's 36th move.

Correct would be at once 34. B—Q1, K—Q1; 35. P—QR4, and now—

50   *51*

1. 35. .... P×P; 36. B×P, K—B2; 37. B—B2, K—Kt3; 38. K—B3, etc.

2. 35. .... P—Kt5; 36. B—Kt3, K—B2; 37. B—B2, K—Kt3; 38. B—Kt3, Kt—Kt2; 39. K—B4, Kt—B4; 40. B—B2, which brings us to the position given in *No. 51*.

It is now essential for White to obtain this position with Black to move, or else he will be in *Zugzwang*. As White, however, has sufficient moves with his Bishop, he can effect this at all times.

Let us examine the position in *No. 51*.

1. 40. .... P—Kt4; 41. P—Kt4, P—R3; 42. P—R3, P—Kt6 (otherwise Black is at a standstill); 43. B—Kt1 (after 43. B×P, Kt×KP, the ending is won for Black); 43. .... P—Kt7; 44. K—B3, Kt×RP ch; 45. K—Kt3, Kt—B4 ch; 46. K×P, K—Kt4; 47. K—B3, etc.

2. 40. .... P—R4; 41. P—R4, P—Kt6; 42. B—Kt1, P—Kt7; 43. K—B3, Kt×RP ch; 44. K—Kt3, Kt—B4 ch; 45. K×P, Kt—Q2; 46. B—Q3, Kt—B3; 47. K—Kt3, Kt—Kt5; 48. B—K2 (otherwise 48. .... Kt—B7, followed by .... Kt—R8, winning the KKtP), 48. .... Kt—B7; 49. B—B3, etc.

All these variations lead to positions of the type which actually occurs in the game later on after 36. .... P×P. With correct play White draws the game, while the slightest inexactness spells disaster.

We have gone more deeply into the position shown in *No. 51*, so that we could clearly diagnose Black's winning chances, whatever continuation he selects up to his 36th move. With the text-move 34. P—KR4 (*No. 50*), White intended to continue with P—R5, and in reply to .... P—Kt4 to advance P—R6, blockading Black's KR pawn, after which the black King could not safely move to the Q side. But Black can easily thwart this plan.

Carrying from the position given in *No. 50* (p. 48), the game went on—

      34. ....   P—R3

Simple, for, if now 35. P—R5, Black plays 35. .... P—Kt4.

52   53

      35. B—Q1   K—Q1

Note that 35. .... P—R5, in order to prevent 36. P—R4, is inadequate because of 36. B—B2 (in order to free the King), 36. .... K—Q2; 37. K—B3, K—B2; 38. K—Kt4, K—Kt3; 39. B—Q3, etc., and White is practically out of danger.

      36. P—R4 (*No. 52*).

White now does hit on the right plan: he may by no means adopt a waiting policy for, once the black King reaches the centre of the battle, the advance of his Q-side pawns will prove decisive.

      36. ....   P×P

Here Black misses his opportunity. With 36. .... P—Kt5, and by manœuvring his King to QKt3 and his Knight to QB4, he could win in an interesting manner, e.g.

1. 37. B—Kt3, K—B2; 38. B—Q1, K—Kt3; 39. B—B2, Kt—Kt2;
    40. K—B4, Kt—B4.

2. 37. B—Kt3, K—B2; 38. B—Q1, K—Kt3; 39. B—Kt3, Kt—Kt2;
    40. K—B4, Kt—B4; 41. B—B2. (*No. 53*—for analysis)

Here again White has the option of reaching the position in question with or without the move, as his Bishop can at will gain or lose a *tempo*.

We shall now demonstrate that Black has a win no matter who has the move—

1. White to play: 41. P—Kt4, P—Kt4; and now—

(*a*) 42. P×P, P×P; 43. P—Q6 (otherwise he loses either the R pawn or the K pawn), 43. .... K—B3, and wins.

(*b*) 42. P—R5, P—Kt6 (here this move wins nicely); 43. B—Kt1 (43. B×P, Kt×KP also wins for Black), 43. .... P—Kt7; 44. K—B3 (or 44. B—B2, Kt×RP, followed by Kt—B4—Q2—B3, winning the KKt pawn, alternatively 45. K—Kt3, P—Kt8 (Q) ch; 46. B×Q, Kt—B4 ch, etc.); 44. .... Kt×RP ch; 45. K—Kt3, Kt—B4 ch; 46. K×P, Kt—Q2; and again .... Kt—B3 wins a pawn.

2. Black to play 40. .... P—R4 and wins, for either the QR pawn or the K pawn must fall (41. P—Q6, K—B3, etc.). The same picture keeps on recurring: White drifts into *Zugzwang*, and White must pay dearly for allowing his KKt pawn to become weak, for it has lost the support of the KR pawn against an attack by the black Knight. We perceive also the difference between the positions shown in *Nos. 51* and *53*. In *No. 51*, P—KR3, for White is still available. A fine example which teaches how very carefully such endings must be conducted!

Let us return to the game proper from *No. 52* after 36. P—QR4.

| 36. .... | P×P | 38. B—B2 | K—Kt3 |
| 37. B×P | K—B2 | 39. K—B3 | K—Kt4 |

The attack on White's KKt pawn no longer wins: 39. .... Kt—K1; 40. K—B4, Kt—B3; 41. B—Q3, Kt—R4; 42. P—Kt4, Kt—B3; 43. P—Kt5, P×P; 44. P×P, Kt—R2; and White just draws after 45. P—Q6, K—B3; 46. P—Q7, K×P; 47. K—Q5, etc.

| 40. K—Kt3 | K—B4 | 41. K—R4 | Kt—B5 |

Black makes the last attempt which still has some chance of success (*No. 54*).

42. B—Kt3

Now White loses after all. Correct was 42. B—Kt1, Kt—Q7; 43. B—Q3 (stopping the black Knight from reaching its KB8), and now 43. .... K—Q5 fails against 44. P—Q6. Black can, then, undertake nothing more, and must be content with a draw.

| 42. .... | Kt—Q7 | 43. B—B2 | Kt—B8 |

Winning the KKt pawn (44. P—Kt4, Kt—K6). Now Black obtains a passed pawn on the K side which wins in the nick of time. It is remarkable that White's weak KKt pawn should thus turn the scale in Black's favour through White's own fault (42. B—Kt3).

44. K×P   Kt×P   45. K—R4

It makes no difference whether the white King moves up the board or down, e.g. 45. K—R6, Kt—R4; 46. K—Kt7, Kt—B3; 47. K—B7, P—Kt4, etc.

45. ....   Kt—R4   46. K—Kt3   K—Q5

47. K—Kt4, Kt—B3; 48. P—Q6, P—Kt4; 49. P×P, P×P; 50. K—Kt5, P—Kt5; 51. B—Q1, P—Kt6; 52. B—B3, K—K6; everything works out now to within a *tempo*; 53. B—R1, K—B7; 54. K—B6, P—Kt7; 55. B×P, K×B; 56. P—Q7, Kt×P; 57. K×Kt, K—B6. White resigns.

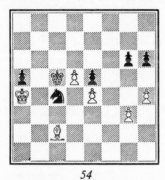

54   55

A difficult ending, which establishes the fact that exact calculation is required before anything of a definite nature is undertaken. A new element in this ending is the '*tempo*-squeeze' which can arise (see analysis, *No. 53*). This additional weapon in an ending 'Knight *v.* bad Bishop' is illustrated in greater detail in the simple example above (*No. 55*).

The black Bishop is definitely bad—all the pawns are on squares of the same colour as the Bishop—yet this would not in itself necessarily mean a loss for Black. If it is White's move, he cannot win. But if it is Black's move he must lose by *Zugzwang*. The Bishop cannot move as Black would lose a pawn, and after 1. .... K—B3; 2. K—K5, followed by 3. Kt—Kt3, 4. Kt—Q4, and 5. Kt×P, would be decisive.

Here are a few variations of this position showing some additional possibilities:

1. Add another black pawn at his Q4. The situation is altered, and the game is drawn no matter who has the move, e.g. 1. Kt—Q3, B—K3; 2. Kt—B5, B—B1; or from the new position with Black to move, 1. .... K—B3; 2. K—K5, P—Q5; 3. K×P, K—Q3; etc.

2. In *No. 55* place the white King on Q3 and the black King on his **B2**. This is drawn irrespective of 'the move,' e.g. 1. K—Q4, K—Q3, or 1. .... K—B3; 2. K—Q4, K—Q3.

3. With the white King at K3 and the black King at K2, White wins his whether he has the move or not—
1. .... K—Q3; 2. K—Q4, or 1. K—Q3, K—Q3; 2. K—Q4.

The characteristics of the 'bad Bishop' play an important rôle and are an easy guide to the correct procedure, not only when the Knight is opposed to a bad Bishop, but also in a contest between a 'good' and a 'bad' Bishop. In this case the advantage is far less clear-cut, and in this chapter we shall therefore restrict ourselves to the study of Bishop *v.* Knight.

We conclude with two examples, both important for the theory of the openings.

ALEKHINE—EUWE, London, 1922

1. P—Q4, Kt—KB3; 2. Kt—KB3, P—KKt3; 3. B—B4, B—Kt2; 4. QKt—Q2, P—B4; 5. P—K3, P—Q3; 6. P—B3, Kt—B3; 7. P—KR3, Castles; 8. B—B4, R—K1; 9. Castles, P—K4; 10. P×P, Kt×P; 11. B×Kt, P×B; 12. Kt—Kt5, B—K3?; 13. B×B.

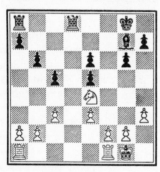
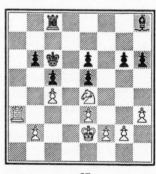

56   57

White has a decisive advantage. This is clear because Black remains with a doubled pawn, and that this advantage is decisive arises from the fact that, before long, White will reach the end-game with a Knight against a bad Bishop.

| 13. .... | P×B | 15. Q×Q | KR×Q |
| 14. QKt—K4 | Kt×Kt | 16. Kt×Kt | P—Kt3 (*No. 56*) |

17. KR—Q1	K—B1	19. P—QB4	P—KR3
18. K—B1	K—K2	20. K—K2	R×R
	21. R×R	R—QKt1	

The end-game is reached and White wins by careful play. We give the rest of the game without much comment.

| 22. R—Q3 | B—R1 | 23. P—QR4 | R—QB1 |
| | 24. R—Kt3 | | |

The last preparation for the important break-through by P—R5.

| 24. .... | K—Q2 | 26. P×P | P×P |
| 25. P—R5 | K—B3 | 27. R—R3 (*No. 57*) | |

White has succeeded in opening the way into Black's position *via* the QR file.

| 27. .... | B—Kt2 | 28. R—R7 | R—B2 |
| | 29. R—R8 | | |

The white Rook is much more active than its counterpart, and an exchange would be unwise.

| 29. .... | R—K2 | 31. R—KKt8 | K—B3 |
| 30. R—B8 ch | K—Q2 | 32. P—R4 | |

Strengthening his position on the K side; there is nothing that Black can undertake.

58

32.	K—B2
33. P—KKt4	K—B3
34. K—Q3	R—Q2 ch
35. K—B3	R—KB2
36. P—Kt3	K—B2
37. K—Q3	R—Q2 ch
38. K—K2	R—B2
39. Kt—B3	

After stumbling, White now finds the right course: the Knight makes room for the King—the changing of the guard.

39.	R—K2	41. P×P	K—B3
40. P—Kt5	P×P	42. K—Q3	R—Q2 ch
	43. K—K4 (*No. 58*)		

The ideal set-up! The King on the blockade square.

| 43. .... | R—Kt2 | 44. Kt—Kt5 |

The beginning of the end.

44. ....   R—K2   45. P—B3

Careful throughout.

45. ....   K—Q2

Against 45. .... K—Kt2; 46. Kt—Q6 ch, followed by 47. Kt—K8, is conclusive.

46. R—Kt8   K—B3   48. R—B7 ch   K—Q1
47. R—B8 ch   K—Q2   49. R—B6

Winning a pawn.

49. ....   R—Kt2   50. R×KP

Black resigns.

Note that in this example the black Bishop was so 'bad' that throughout the ending Black was playing practically a piece down.

BLUMIN—FINE, *New York*, 1939

1. P—Q4, Kt—KB3; 2. P—QB4, P—K3; 3. Kt—QB3, B—Kt5; 4. Q—B2, Kt—B3; 5. Kt—B3, P—Q4; 6. P—K3, Castles; 7. P—QR3, B×Kt ch; 8. Q×B, B—Q2.

The course of the game provides an explanation of this, at first sight, mysterious move. Black wishes to exchange this Bishop for White's K Bishop in order to come out with a Knight against a bad Bishop.

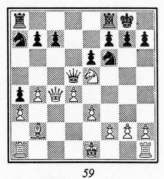

59   60

9. B—Q3   P—QR4   10. P—QKt3   P—R5

The sequel to the foregoing, as will soon become clear.

11. P—QKt4   P×P   12. B×P   Kt—R2

The point! White cannot prevent .... B—Kt4 (if 13. Q—Q3, Q—K1), and this practically forces the desired exchange.

13. Kt—K5   B—Kt4   14. B—Kt2   B×B
15. Q×B   Q—Q4 (*No. 59*)

The verdict of the theory that Black has the better game now needs no explanation; it is the preponderance of the Knight over the 'bad Bishop.'

There followed:

16. Q×Q
(16. Q×P, Q×KtP)

16. ....   P×Q   17. R—QB1   Kt—Kt4

Blockade of the pawns on the black squares.

18. Castles   Kt—K5   20. B—B1   KR—K1
19. R—B2   KKt—Q3   21. R—Q1   P—KB3
22. Kt—Q7

A blunder which costs a piece. He should have played 22. Kt—Q3, after which, however, 22. .... Kt—B5; follows, with a definite advantage to Black.

22. ....   P—QKt3

Cutting off the Knight's retreat

23. R—B6   R—K2

And Black won easily.

The last example shows particularly well the significance of the 'bad Bishop's' characteristics. The 'bad Bishop' is no match for the Knight, and stands helpless against such strange-looking moves as 8. .... B—Q2; 9. .... P—QR4; and 12. .... Kt—R2. That the Knight is superior to the 'bad Bishop' was made sufficiently clear in the various examples given.

Here again—as in preceding chapters—it must be conceded that it is easier, though no less important, to formulate a judgment than to evolve a plan.

Finally, a recent and instructive example from grand-master practice. Here the player having the Bishop comes to grief because his opponent —disregarding all the rules—forces him into the unpleasant necessity to reduce his good Bishop to the status of a bad one.

AVERBACH—LILIENTHAL, *Moscow*, 1949

The white pawns are placed (*No. 60*) on squares of the same colour as the opposing Bishop; in other words, the Bishop is 'good.' It follows that with correct play, Black should in no circumstances lose the game. On the other hand, he has no winning chances as White has full compensation in his Knight's strong position and in his advantage in space.

A normal development would now be: 25. .... R—K1; 26. K—B2, R×R ch; 27. K×R, K—K2; 28. K—K3, K—B3; 29. K—K4, and neither side could do much more than play a waiting game.

It is remarkable that Black should neglect this simple drawing method, taking chances which hold out no prospects, as White is enabled to transfer his Q-side pawns to black squares. As a result the advantage of Bishop against Knight is entirely nullified.

      25. ....   P—QB4   26. P×P e.p. P×P

Now Black's Q pawn is seriously weakened, and the consequence will be that, before long, he will be tempted to push his Q pawn on to Q4, so that the whole of Black's strategy will in the end lead to for him, unfortunate results.

      27. R—Q2

Aiming at the weakened Q pawn.

      27. ....   K—K2   28. Kt—K2

In preparation for manœuvres such as Kt—B3—R4 or K4, with the alternative threat of advancing P—QB5 or of attacking the Q pawn a second time.

      28. ....   B—K3   29. K—B2

He could also have played 29. Kt—B3, but he would clearly not wish to prevent Black's next move. It is important to note that after 29. .... P—QR4 White can still play 30. Kt—B3, for 30. .... P—R5; 31. Kt×P, B×BP fails against 32. Kt—Kt6.

      29. ....   P—Q4 (*No. 61*)

The position for Black is a difficult one, but with the text-move he practically throws in his hand. He should have adopted a waiting policy and played .... P—QB4 at the appropriate moment. In either case White still had an advantage, but not a decisive one.

      30. P—B5

After 30. P×P, B×QP, White's position still is preferable, but the text-move which makes for a 'black' pawn formation on the Q side is much stronger, as the Bishop will become 'bad.'

      30. ....   K—Q2   31. Kt—Q4

The Knight occupies an excellent square and, while it holds Black's Q pawn, it is practically unassailable.

31.	P—B3	33. P—B4	R—KKt1
32. R—K2	B—B2	34. P—Kt3	P—KR4
	35. R—K3	R—K1	

While White quietly proceeds with his preparations, Black loses patience; he exchanges Rooks, which makes the winning procedure considerably easier.

36. R×R   B×R (*No. 62*)

Compare this diagram (*No. 62*) with the original position in *No. 60*, and you will notice that Black is in the process of turning his good Bishop into a bad one. We see further that the Bishop in this case is

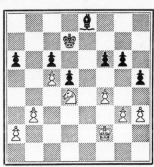

61   62

particularly bad because it has no chance at all of getting into the open; the journey to QR3 is too long and too complicated, and the black K-side pawns would in the meantime have become an easy prey for White's King and Knight. The rest is not difficult:

37. P—KKt4

. With the object of establishing a white pawn at KKt5, and thus forcing Black's K-side pawns also on to white squares. Black cannot prevent this, for 37. .... P—Kt4; 38. P×KtP, BP×P; 39. Kt—B3 costs him a pawn.

37. ....   P×P   38. P×P   K—B2

Preparing for B—Q2—B1—R3, but Black gets there much too late.

39. K—Kt3   B—Q2   40. P—Kt5

Now Black failed to put up the best defence—he was probably convinced that his task was hopeless—and gave up after 40. .... P×P; 41. P×P, B—B1; 42. K—B4, as he could not avoid material loss (42. .... K—Q2; 43. K—K5).

He had in fact two continuations, each of which would have set White a problem not at all easy to solve.

They are: 40. .... P—B4; (*No. 63*) and 40. .... P×P; 41. P×P, K—Q1; 42. K—B4, K—K2; (*No. 64*).

Let us now work out the position in these two diagrams:
No. 63 (after 40. .... P—B4; instead of 40. .... P×P).

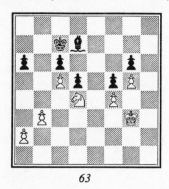

63   64

41. Kt—B3

With the intention of placing the Knight at K5, thus tying the Bishop permanently to Black's K1.

41. ....   B—K1   42. Kt—K5   K—Q1

An attempt at action on the other wing must fail, as White, in reply to .... P—R4, always has the reply P—R4.

43. K—B3   K—K2   44. K—K3   K—K3

Black is condemned to utter inactivity, for his King must carefully watch the possibility of the white King invading black territory *via* Q4 and K5.

45. K—Q4   K—K2   46. P—R4

A systematic winning process. White intends to tie up Black's R pawn, as will be seen immediately.

46. ....   K—K3

If Black plays 46. .... P—R4 to cut across White's plan, White wins by 47. Kt—Q3 and 48. P—Kt4, without any difficulty, thanks to his passed R pawn and the possibility of breaking in *via* K5.

47. P—R5   K—K2   48. Kt—Q3

And Black can no longer prevent the loss of either his R pawn or QB pawn.

Now, from the position of *No. 64*—

43. K—K5   B—K1

Again Black has nothing else, because, as before, he cannot allow

the white King to penetrate to Q6 or KB6, e.g. 43. .... K—Q1; 44.
K—Q6, B—K1 (44. .... K—B1; 45. K—K7, and 46. K—B7, or 44.
.... K—K1; 45. K—B7, and 46. K—Kt6); 45. Kt—K6 ch, K—B1;
46. K—K7, B—Q2; 47. Kt—Q4, and 48. K—B7.

44. P—R4
The same method of winning as in *No. 63*.

44. .... B—Q2
If 44. .... P—R4, the reply again is 45. Kt—B2, and 46. P—Kt4.

45. P—R5   B—K1   46. Kt—B2 and wins
For after 47. Kt—Kt4, White wins the R pawn or B pawn.

CHAPTER V

WEAKENING THE KING'S SIDE

ALEKHINE—BRINCKMANN, *Kecskemet*, 1927

1. P—K4, P—K4; 2. Kt—KB3, Kt—QB3; 3. B—Kt5, P—Q3; 4. P—Q4, B—Q2; 5. Kt—B3, Kt—B3; 6. B×Kt, B×B; 7. Q—Q3, P×P; 8. Kt×P, P—KKt3; 9. B—Kt5, B—Kt2; 10. Castles QR, Q—Q2; 11. P—KR3, Castles KR; 12. KR—K1, KR—K1; 13. Q—B3, Kt—R4; 14. P—KKt4, B×Kt; 15. R×B, Kt—Kt2; 16. B—B6 (*No. 65*).

| 65 | 66 |

According to 'theory,' White has a definite and considerable superiority. In what does this superiority consist? Has White a mating attack? The answer is: White has latent threats which reduce Black to a strict defensive and which eventually will force him to give way in some other and important direction.

Suppose for instance it were White's move and he could play 1. Q—KR6, threatening mate, matters would quickly come to a head after 1. .... Kt—K3; 2. P—B4, and Black has no reply to 3. P—B5, winning a piece, as the Knight cannot give up the protection of Black's KKt2. How has this possibility arisen? It is a consequence of the weakened pawn formation in front of Black's King. With the K-side pawns on their original square, Black would have little to fear. The serious weakness is his pawn at KKt3 or, to be more precise, the fact that White has been able to occupy KB6 with a Bishop, while Black no longer has a defending Bishop at his Kt2.

The *verdict* then is: White has the advantage because Black's King's field is weakened. For the appropriate *plan* let us first examine the further course of the game.

16. ....   R—K3

Intending .... Kt—K1, driving off the Bishop.

17. QR—Q1

Making room for the Bishop so that it can continue to watch the important squares KB6 and KKt7.

17. ....   Kt—K1   18. B—Q4   Q—K2 (*No. 66*)

Here the defender could have chosen another course: 18. .... P—B3, in order to close the Bishop's diagonal, whereupon White plays 19. Kt—Q5, and Black cannot exchange the Knight without losing a pawn (19. .... B×Kt; 20. P×B, R×R; 21. R×R, Q—B2; 22. R—K6, K—Kt2; 23. P—Kt5). He must therefore play 19. .... Q—B2, leading to the position in *No. 67*.

Now Black is tied to the defence of his KB pawn, while the Knight merely obstructs his game, and the Bishop has lost in effectiveness; the result has been an additional weakness at Black's KB3 which hamstrings the whole of his forces. Thus 18. .... P—B3 provides no satisfactory solution of Black's difficulties; White has a free game and can improve his position in various ways, e.g. P—KR4—R5, or Q—KKt3, and P—KB4—B5.

67

Let us return to the actual game: (*No. 66*)

19. R—K3   Kt—Kt2

Again an important moment. Black seizes the first opportunity to get the Knight away from K1 so that his other Rook can take part in the fight. The line selected by Black must be considered with care for since the Knight at Kt2 has no square available except K1, he has to reckon with the possibility of a direct attack on his King's field.

20. Q—B4

Threatening 21. Q—R6.

20. ....   Q—R5

The correct counter. 20. .... P—KKt4 would create an irreparable weakness which would enable White to open new lines of attack by 21. Q—Kt3 and 22. P—B4.

21. QR—K1   QR—K1 (*No. 68*)

This is the position which Black had in view when he played 18. .... Q—K2. All immediate danger is past, and Black need not be afraid of 22. Kt—Q5, because, after 22. .... B×Kt; 23. P×B, R×R; 24. R×R, R×R; 25. Q×R, the position has become so simplified that a decision can no longer be reached.

It remains to point out that a direct attack by 22. R—B3 (threatening both 23. Q×P ch and 23. B—B6) leads to nothing. After 22. ....

68

69

P—B4; 23. B×Kt, K×B; 24. KtP×P, Q×Q ch; 25. R×Q, P×P; 26. R—Kt1 ch, R—Kt3; 27. R×R ch, P×R; 28. P×P, P—KKt4, Black has sufficient counter-play.

Thus we see that in *No. 68* not only have White's main threats been parried, but Black has, besides, some compensation in the pressure on White's K pawn.

Nevertheless, Black's troubles are not yet at an end, for his King's field is still weakened and the Bishop maintains an unpleasant leverage on Black's Kt2, which causes such an important piece as Black's Queen to remain misplaced. Furthermore, although all the black pieces are in action, they are limited in their movements. For instance, ... R—KB1 would lead to a swift *débâcle* after the reply Kt—Q5.

We may sum up: while the defence, for the time being, is adequate, it is a little cramped.

22. P—Kt3

A procedure typical of this kind of position. Black can do nothing worth while, and so White proceeds to improve the positions of his pawns and of his King.

22. ....   P—QR4   23. P—R4   P—Kt3
            24. K—Kt2   R—(K1)K2

Played not only to fill up a *tempo* but also to vacate K1 for his Knight.

25. Q—R2 (*No. 69*)

Striking out in a new direction and preparing P—B4.

25. ....   Kt—K1

A serious mistake. This new interference with the mobility of the black Rooks gives White the chance of a quickly decisive turn.

Equally insufficient would be 25. .... P—B4 (to take advantage of the temporary absence of the white Queen), because of 26. KP×P, followed by—

1. 26. .... R×R; 27. R×R,

(a) 27. .... R×R; 28. P×R, P×P; 29. B×Kt, K×B; 30. P×P, and White is a healthy pawn ahead;

(b) 27. .... P×P; 28. B×Kt,

(i) 28. .... R×B; 29. Q—B4, and wins because of the threat 30. Q—B4 ch.

(ii) 28. .... K×B; 29. Q—B4, P×P; 30. R—Kt3, etc.

2. 26. .... P×P; 27. B×Kt, R×R; 28. R×R.

Black's best defence in *No. 69* is 25. .... B—Kt2; for then 26. P—B4, leads to nothing after 26. .... P—QB4; 27. B×Kt, K×B; 28. P—B5, R—K4, and White's attack has petered out.

White must therefore go to work in a more subtle manner, beginning with 26. Kt—Kt5, providing a line of retreat for the white Bishop, after which 26. .... R×P; 27. R×R, R×R; 28. R×R, B×R; 29. Kt×BP leads to a decisive advantage for White.

Less clear, however, is the position if, in answer to 26. Kt—Kt5, Black plays 26. .... Kt—K1, for now Black threatens to strike in earnest at White's K4, so that White has to play the defensive 27. P—KB3 before embarking on further schemes.

An exhaustive analysis of the position thus reached would lead too far, but it is worth while to establish the following points: (*1*) The black King's field is still weak (pawn at KKt3), which weakness is demonstrated by the full control over the black squares exercised by the white K Bishop. (*2*) Any attempt to break up the black position quickly must fail, because Black's defence is working at full strength.

26. P—B4

With the obvious threat 27. P—B5.

26. ....   Kt—B3

If 26. .... R—Q2 (making room for the K Rook); 27. P—B5, KR—K2; 28. Q—K2, threatening 29. Kt—Q5, e.g. 28. .... B—Kt2; 29. Kt—Q5, B×Kt; 30. P×B, K—B1; 31. P—B6, R×R; 32. Q×R, Kt×P; 33. P—Kt5, wins. Black could meet this threat with 28. .... K—B1 (not 28. .... P—B3; 29. Q—B4 ch), but in this position he is faced with a hopeless task—his pieces are badly placed, and White can break through in a number of ways.

27. P—B5   R×P

Despair! But 27. .... Kt×KtP, as intended after the preceding move, fails against 28. Q—B4.

| 28. Kt×R | Kt×Kt | 30. Q—B1 | P—Q4 |
| 29. Q—B4 | P—KKt4 | 31. P—B4 | |

White finishes up with some hefty blows.

| 31. .... | Q—R3 | 33. P×P | B×QP |
| 32. P—B6 | R—K1 | 34. Q—B5 | Resigns |

The salient points of the plan followed by White in the above game were:

1. Maintaining the Bishop on its lifeline, the long black diagonal.
2. Utilising the Bishop either directly with the help of the Queen or indirectly in a break-through.
3. Consolidation of his position as a preliminary to further action.

Here is a more forcible example, which shows that the weakness at KKt3 can quickly become fatal:

1. P—K4, P—QB3; 2. P—Q4, P—Q4; 3. P×P, P×P; 4. P—QB4, Kt—KB3; 5. Kt—QB3, Kt—B3; 6. B—Kt5, P×P; 7. P—Q5, Kt—K4; 8. Q—Q4, Kt—Q6 ch; 9. B×Kt, P×B; 10. Kt—B3, P—KKt3; 11. B×Kt, P×B; 12. Castles KR, B—K2; 13. QR—Q1, Castles; 14. R×P, B—KB4; 15. R—Q2, B—Q3 (*No. 70*).

70   71

A variation recommended by Botvinnik. The position now shows various characteristics: White has a passed pawn as against Black's doubled pawn, but Black has the two Bishops. The essential feature, however, is the weakness in Black's King's field, which will lead to the pawn at his KB3 becoming indefensible.

The sequel is—

16. P—KKt4

The object of this move is to clear his K4 so that the Knight can take an active part in the fray.

16. ....   B—B1

Thus runs Botvinnik's analysis, but he takes no account of the following variant, which prevents an immediate *débâcle*: 16. .... B—K4. Now, after 17. Kt×B, P×Kt; 18. Q×KP, B×P; 19. Kt—K4, P—B3; 20. Q—B4, White no doubt has the better game, but it still has to be won.

17. Kt—K4

Now, suddenly, the weak KB pawn cannot be saved, *e.g.* 17. .... K—Kt2; 18. P—Kt5, or 17. .... B—K2; 18. P—Q6. It is self-evident that 17. .... P—B4 will not work because of 18. Kt—B6 ch, etc. In this case it is not the pawn but the square at KB6 which White has captured.

17. ....   B—K4

Relatively the best.

18. Kt×B   P×Kt   19. Q×KP   P—B3
                20. Q—B4

And White remains a valuable pawn ahead.

We have seen in the preceding examples that the move .... P—KKt3 produces a weakness in so far as the squares at KB3 and KKt2 can easily and, as it were, of their own accord, fall into the opponent's power. This possibility is lessened and even rendered practically non-existent if there is a defending Bishop at KKt2. But even then all danger is not eliminated, for there is yet another aspect to be considered: the adversary can, in certain circumstances, force open the KR file, as can be seen in the following example:

KATETOV—GOLOMBEK, *Prague*, 1946

1. P—K4, P—QB4; 2. Kt—KB3, P—Q3; 3. P—Q4, P×P; 4. Kt×P, Kt—KB3; 5. Kt—QB3, P—KKt3; 6. P—B3, B—Kt2; 7. B—K3, Castles; 8. Q—Q2, Kt—B3; 9. Castles, Kt×Kt; 10. B×Kt, B—K3; 11. P—KKt4, P—QR3 (better is 11. .... Q—R4). White obtains before long an irresistible attack (*No. 71*).

White has four lines of attack to Black's three, but Black has compensation in his mobility on the Q side, where he has available such moves as .... Q—R4 and .... P—QKt4, and moreover, he has an open QB file and a well-placed Bishop at K3. Nevertheless, it is clear that, on account of Black's weakness at his KKt3, the balance will weigh heavily in favour of White, as he will have the opportunity of opening the KR file by the advance of his KR pawn.

Let us examine the further course of the game:

12. P—KR4

Speaking generally, Black has a choice of two methods which he can apply against the advance of the KR pawn. But here it is a question whether the cure is not worse than the ill, for in this position either method is wholly inadequate:

1. 12. .... P—R3 (in order to reply to 13. P—R5 with 13. .... P—KKt4).

Here this loses a pawn after 13. B×Kt, B×B; 14. Q×RP, or 13. .... P×B; 14. Q×QP.

2. 12. .... P—KR4 is refuted by 13. B×Kt, B×B; 14. P×P, P×P; 15. Q—R6, etc.

12. ....   P—QKt4   13. Kt—Q5

Unexpectedly White delays his advance. He could have played 13. P—R5, to be followed by 14. P×P, but he first undertakes preparatory manœuvres so that he can open the KR file under favourable conditions. We shall soon see in which way this is accomplished.

13. ....   B×Kt

Practically forced: White threatened to weaken the Q pawn by an exchange at KB6, while Black could evidently not move his Knight away, as the exchange of his K Bishop would seriously embarrass his defence of the King's field.

14. P×B   Q—B2

Clearly not 14. .... Kt×P, because of 15. B×B, winning a piece.

15. P—R5   QR—B1

15. .... P×P would definitely not lighten Black's burden. After 16. P×P, threatening P—R6, or equally after 16. B×Kt, B×B; 17. R×P, White would have a quick and easy win.

16. P×P   BP×P (*No. 72*)

It is mostly better to recapture with the R pawn, but in this particular instance it would reduce Black's already meagre chances of successfully defending himself, e.g. 16. .... RP×P; 17. B—Q3 (so that the Queen can manœuvre freely), 17. .... KR—Q1; 18. R—R3,

K—B1; 19. QR—R1, K—K1 (in no other way can Black parry the mate threatened by 20. R—R8 ch, etc.); 20. P—Kt5, Kt—R4; 21. B×B, Kt×B; 22. R—R7, and now—

1. 22. .... Kt—B4; 23. B×Kt, P×B; 24. Q—Q3, or
2. 22. .... Kt—R4; 23. R (R1)×Kt, P×R; 24. B—B5, etc.

White has much the better game, because he controls the KR file, where his Rooks will threaten vital points in Black's position, while his other pieces also have a good range of activity.

72

17. B—Q3
Attacking and defending at the same time.

17. .... R—B2
Here 17. .... Kt×QP; also was insufficient, because Black's best defensive piece, the K Bishop, would be eliminated. After 17. .... Kt×QP; 18. B×B, K×B; 19. Q—R6 ch, and White wins comfortably, as can be seen from the following: 19. .... K—B2; 20. Q×RP ch, K—K1; 21. B×P ch, followed by 22. R×Kt (or 20. .... K—K3; 21. Q×KtP ch), or 19. .... K—B3; 20. P—Kt5 ch, K—K3; 21. Q—R3 ch, K—B2; 22. Q×P ch, and wins.

18. Q—Kt5 Kt—K1
Hastening his defeat. A slightly better defence would be 18. .... Q—Kt2. In reply White can play 19. B×KKtP. After 19. .... P×B; 20. Q×P, White has various threats, first and foremost 21. R—R8 ch, K×R; 22. Q×R, etc. Other preparatory moves such as 21. R—R2 and 21. P—Kt5 also lead to mate after 21. .... Kt—K1; 22. Q—R7 ch, K—B1; 23. Q—R8 ch, etc. Against all these strong threats Black has no adequate defence (for instance, 20. .... Q×P fails against 21. B×Kt), and we can conclude that the open KR file which White has been able to conquer because of Black's weakness at his KKt3 is a deciding factor.

19. R×P
Very strong, if fairly obvious.

19. .... K×R
Other replies are no better.

20. Q×P ch K—Kt1 21. R—R1
Threatening mate in two by 22. R—R8 ch, K×R; 23. Q—R7 mate.

21. ....   Kt—B3   22. B×Kt   Resigns

For after 22. .... R or P×B there is again a mate by 23. R—R8 ch, etc.

So much for the weakness at KKt3, which is particularly awkward in the absence of the K Bishop at KKt2 as long as the opposing Bishop of the same colour is still on the board, and an advance P—KR4—5 together with the forcing open of the KR file is to be expected.

Curiously enough, in such cases the plan is easy but the judgment is complicated. In almost every case where the conclusion is that there is in fact a weakness at KKt3 (even if there still is a Bishop at KKt2), the plan indicated—P—KR4—R5 and an exchange of pawns at KKt3 —is the one to adopt.

But it is necessary, before embarking on this manœuvre, to take the following into account:

1. Frequently it is a preliminary necessity to play P—KKt4, to provide against .... P—KR4.

2. The parry .... P—KR3, followed by .... P—KKt4, which, on tactical grounds, was not playable in the last example, is, generally speaking, not so doubtful for Black, because the original pawn formation—KR2, Kt3, and B2—is in itself vulnerable, whether to P—KB4, or to some action at KKt5.

3. The exchange at KKt3 (see note to move 15, above) usually aggravates the defender's position.

4. It is of great importance for White to force the exchange of Black's K Bishop, as this piece plays a big part in the defence.

In the example under review the opening up of the KR file is decisive because White has castled on the Q side and Black on the K side. Where both players have castled KR the advance of the KR pawn is hardly feasible against KKt3. It follows that the instances in which KKt3 represent a weakness are in the minority, and that is why such positions are difficult to assess accurately.

Still more difficult is the case of .... P—KR3, which move represents a weakness only in certain well-defined circumstances.

We give three such examples. In the first two, each with the weakness at KR3, the attack is carried out by pieces, while pawns play the chief part in the third.

BOTVINNIK—SZABÓ, *Groningen*, 1946

1. P—Q4, P—Q4; 2. Kt—KB3, Kt—KB3; 3. P—QB4, P—K3; 4. Kt—B3, P—B4; 5. BP×P, Kt×P; 6. P—K3, Kt—QB3; 7. B—B4, Kt×Kt; 8. P×Kt, P×P; 9. KP×P, B—K2; 10. Castles, Castles; 11. B—Q3, P—QKt3.

12. Q—B2

This move forces Black to weaken his King's field, but in which way: .... P—KKt3 or .... P—KR3? Speaking generally, KKt3 is the more serious weakness, but not, as will be seen, in this particular instance. Now after 12. .... P—KR3 we reach the position shown in *No. 73*. (In the game Szabó played 12. .... P—Kt3.)

13. Q—K2

With the threat to win a piece by 14. Q—K4. The normal reply—

73

74

13. .... B—Kt2

loses a pawn:

14. Q—K4

Threatening mate. Black now has the choice between 14. .... P—Kt3; 15. B×P and 14. .... P—B4; 15. Q×P ch.

It can be seen why KR3 here constitutes a weakness; in parrying the attack on R2 by .... P—KKt3, the R pawn is left in the air. KR3 can also be accounted a weakness when it provides greater possibilities of a sacrifice, as for instance in the following well-known variant of the Scotch Opening:

1. P—K4, P—K4; 2. Kt—KB3, Kt—QB3; 3. P—Q4, P×P; 4. Kt×P, Kt—B3; 5. Kt—QB3, B—Kt5; 6. Kt×Kt, KtP×Kt; 7. B—Q3, P—Q4; 8. P×P, P×P; 9. Castles, Castles; 10. B—KKt5, P—B3; 11. Q—B3, B—K2; 12. QR—K1, P—KR3? (*No. 74*).

Here is the refutation of Black's last move:

13. B×P   P×B   14. Q—K3

Attacking pawn and Bishop.

14. ....   B—Q3

Not 14. .... B—K3; 15. Q×KRP, and Black has no defence against the double threat R—K3—Kt3 and R—K5—Kt5.

15. Q×KRP   R—Kt1

Intending .... R—Kt5. If Black plays 15. .... P—Q5 to prevent R—K3, the reply is 16. Kt—K4, Kt×Kt; 17. R×Kt (threatens 18. R—Kt4 ch, and 19. Q—R7 mate) 17. .... P—KB4; 18. R—KR4 and wins.

16. P—B4

Black is defenceless against the double threat of 17. R—B3 and 17. R—K5, e.g. 16. .... B—KKt5; 17. R—K5, B×R; 18. P×B, followed by 19. P×Kt and mate.

In most cases in this type of combination, the disposition of the Rooks plays a very important part. As soon as the pawn screen in front of the King is scattered, the Rooks will get busy on the third, or perhaps on the fourth and fifth rank.

The weakness at KR3 can be still more serious on different grounds:

BLAU—VAN SCHELTINGA, *Hilversum, 1947*

1. P—K4, P—K4; 2. Kt—KB3, Kt—QB3; 3. B—Kt5, Kt—B3; 4. Castles, B—B4; 5. P—B3, Castles; 6. P—Q4, B—Kt3; 7. R—K1, P—Q3; 8. P—KR3, Q—K2; 9. B—Kt5, P—KR3; 10. B×KKt, Q×B; 11. Kt—R3, Kt—K2; 12. Kt—B4, Kt—Kt3; 13. Kt×B, RP×Kt (*No. 75*).

 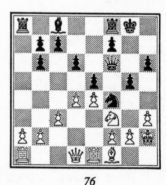

75   76

Black has the advantage because White's King's field is weakened by P—KR3. It may be objected that Black also has played .... P—KR3! The point is that, unlike White, Black is able to exploit·his adversary's weakness. We shall see how:

14. B—B1

Intending P—KKt3.

14. .... Kt—B5

Thus P—KR3 also means weakening his KB4, for he cannot play P—KKt3 without losing his KR pawn.

15. K—R2

Intent on forcing P—KKt3.

15. .... P—KKt4 (*No. 76*)

This is another method of exploiting the weak point at Black's KR3, an advance .... P—KKt4—5, with the opening of the KKt file.

Observe the similarity of the procedure adopted against KKt3, the advance P—KR4—5, and opening of the KR file.

16. Kt—Kt1

Evidently intended to prevent .... P—Kt5.

It is important to note that 16. P—KKt3 would not have the desired effect, e.g. 16. P—KKt3, P—Kt5; and now—

1. 17. Kt—Kt1, as in the game.

2. 17. P×Kt, Q×P ch; 18. K—Kt2, after which Black can choose between a small advantage in the end-game after—

(*a*) 18. .... P×Kt ch; 19. Q×P, Q×Q ch; 20. K×Q, P—KB4; or a continuation of his attack by—

(*b*) 18. .... K—R2; 19. Kt—R2, R—KKt1; 20. K—R1, P—Kt6;

  (i) 21. P×P, Q×P, etc.;

  (ii) 21. Kt—Kt4, P×P; 22. R—K2, B×Kt; 23. P×B, Q×P, etc.

3. 17. P×KtP, B×P; 18. P×Kt, Q×P ch; 19. K—Kt2, K—R2; 20. B—K2, R—KKt1, etc.

16. .... P—Kt5   17. P—KKt3

If 17. P×KtP, Q—R5 ch; 18. Kt—R3, B×P; 19. Q—Q2 (19. P—KKt3, Q—R4;) 19. .... B×Kt; 20. P×B, K—R2, with a strong attack. Black has fully carried out the appropriate plan against White's weakness, and has gained the following two advantages: (*a*) an invulnerable Knight at KB5, and (*b*) an open KKt file for his Rooks.

The text-move constitutes a pawn sacrifice, and has the object of slowing down Black's attack.

17. .... Kt×P   18. Kt×Kt   P×Kt
         19. Q—Q2

The KB pawn was *en prise*.

19. .... Q—Kt3

Again 20. B×P is not feasible because of 20. .... Q—R4.

20. P—KB4   B—Kt5   21. P—B5   Q—R4

Black has maintained his extra pawn, and the forward march of the KKt pawn has in addition provided him with an open line of attack. Indeed, he won without any great difficulty. We refrain from giving the rest of the game, as it has no relation to our subject.

The plan by which the attacker will attempt to exploit the weakness at KR3 will, as shown above, contain the following elements:

1. Attack along the long diagonal Q3—KR7
2. Posting a Knight at KB5
3. The charge P—KKt4—Kt5
4. Sacrifice at the defender's KR3

But the success of this plan will depend primarily on whether P—KR3 has in fact created a weakness, in other words, only then can the assessment of the position be conclusive.

The move P—KR3 can also have advantages, the most frequent being (*a*) preventing B—KKt5 pinning the KKt, and (*b*) providing the King with a flight square at R2.

RESHEVSKY—SANTASIERE, *New York*, 1939

1. P—Q4, P—Q4; 2. P—QB4, P—QB3; 3. Kt—KB3, Kt—B3; 4. Kt—B3, P×P; 5. P—QR4, B—B4; 6. P—K3, P—K3; 7. B×P, B—QKt5; 8. Castles, Castles; 9. Q—K2, B—Kt5; 10. P—R3, B—KR4; 11. R—Q1, QKt—Q2; 12. P—K4, Q—K2; 13. P—K5, Kt—Q4; 14. Kt—K4, P—KR3; 15. Kt—Kt3, B—Kt3; 16. Kt—K1, P—B3; 17. P×P, Q×P; 18. Kt—Q3, B—Q3; 19. Kt—K4, Q—K2; 20. Kt×B, Q×Kt; 21. R—R3, QR—K1; 22. Kt—K5 (*No. 77*).

77

'White stands better,' says the book. Black's position is weakened in several respects, and the white pieces are so deployed that the dangers arising from these weaknesses stand out clearly. The white Knight controls the important squares at Black's KKt3 and KB2.

The white Rook posted on the third rank adds to the chances of a sacrifice at KR6, while the diagonal from White's QKt1 to KR7, at present held by Black's Q Bishop, is in fact vulnerable. White has in consequence many possibilities of attack, and Black will have a difficult, though not an impossible task.

22. ....   B—R2

Black fails to tackle the difficulties that beset him, and straight away makes the decisive mistake.

How difficult it is in such positions to hit on the right move is shown by the fact that the obvious move 22. .... Kt×Kt, which eliminates the powerful white Knight, is equally insufficient.

A few variations: 22. .... Kt×Kt; 23. P×Kt, and now:
1. 23. .... Q—B4; 24. R—KKt3, K—R2; 25. P—Kt4;
(*a*) 25. .... Q×P; 26. Q—Kt4, Kt—K2; 27. B—R3, and wins.
(*b*) 25. .... Kt×P; 26. R×B, K×R; 27. Q—K4 ch;
   (i) 27. .... R—B4; 28. B—B4, and Black has no defence against 29. P—Kt4, while 28. .... K—B2 fails against 29. Q×R ch;
   (ii) 27. .... K—B2; 28. R—Q7 ch, R—K2; 29. B—K3, Q—R4; 30. Q—B5 ch, K—K1; 31. R×R ch, K×R; 32. Q×P ch, K—Q1; 33. Q—Q6 ch, K—K1; 34. B—B5, and wins;
(*c*) 25. .... Q—K2; 26. R×B, K×R; 27. B—Q3 ch, K—B2; 28. Q—R5 ch, K—Kt1; 29. Q—Kt6, and wins.
2. 23. .... Q—B4; 24. R—KKt3, Kt—B5; 25. B×Kt, R×B; 26. R×B, R×B; 27. R—Q7, R—B8 ch; 28. K—R2, R—K2; 29. R—Q8 ch;
(*a*) 29. .... K—B2; 30. R—B6 ch, P×R; 31. Q—R5 ch, K—Kt2; 32. Q—Kt4 ch, etc.;
(*b*) 29. .... K—R2; 30. R×RP ch, P×R (.... K×R; 31. R—R8 ch, etc.); 31. Q—K4 ch, K—Kt2; 32. Q—Kt4 ch, and again mate by 32. Q—Kt8.
3. 23. .... Q—B2; 24. R—Kt3;
(*a*) 24. .... K—R2; 25. R×B, transposing to *1.* (*c*);
(*b*) 24. .... Q—B2; 26. R—Q4, B—R4 (preventing 27. R(Q4)—Kt4); 27. Q—B2, with a strong attack.

It is clear from this analysis that on move 22 Black should move his Bishop and, indeed, he can put up a stronger resistance with 22. .... B—B4. White's best reply is then (*No. 77*): 22. .... B—B4; 23. R—KKt3, K—R2; 24. R—Kt3, and now:
1. 24. .... Kt (Q2)—Kt3; 25. B—Q3, with the powerful threats 26. P—Kt4 and 26. P—R5.
2. 24. .... P—QKt3; 25. P—Kt4, B—Kt3; 26. Kt×B, K×Kt; 27. Q—B2 ch, K—B2; 28. B×P, and wins.
3. 24. .... Kt×Kt (best); 25. P×Kt, and White has the advantage.

To revert to the actual course of the game after 22. .... B—R2:

23. R—KKt3

Threatening to win a pawn by 24. B×P, and Black can parry the threat neither by 23. .... R—B3; 24. Kt—Kt4, nor by 23. .... Kt—B5; 24. Q—Kt4.

      23. ....   K—R1   24. B×Kt

A surprising exchange, the meaning of which at once becomes clear.

      24. ....   BP×B

The recapture by the QB pawn is forced, as 24. .... KP×B fails against 25. Kt—B7 ch, and 24. .... Q×B against 25. B×P, P×B; 26. Kt×Kt, etc.

      25. B×P   R—K2

If 25. .... P×B, there follows 26. Kt×Kt, Q×Kt; 27. Q—K5 ch, with mate to follow. Thus the exchange at Q5 had the object of preventing Black's Knight from settling at KB3.

      26. B—Q2   Kt×Kt

Else Black loses at least another pawn after 27. R—Kt3.

      27. P×Kt   Q—Kt3   28. B—K3   Q—R4
                        29. R—Q4

White must win, for he has a sound extra pawn and can continue his attack with undiminished energy.

      29. ....   R—B4

If 29. .... B—B4; 30. Q—R5, K—Kt1; 31. R—R4, and wins.

      30. R—R4   Q—B2   31. Q—Kt4

Threatening 32. Q—Kt6.

      31. ....   K—Kt1   32. B—Kt5   R (K2)—B2
                        33. B—B6

The participation of the Bishop heralds a decisive intensification of the attack.

      33. ....   P—R3   34. P—R5   Q—Q2

Black no longer has any adequate moves at his disposal. For instance: 34. .... R—Q2; 35. K—R2, P—Q5; 36. R—R6, P—Q6; 37. Q—R4, and wins.

      35. R—R6   K—R1   36. Q—Kt6   Resigns

So far we have examined weakened King's positions only in which the King had castled KR. If we widen our field of observation, we can include positions in which the King is still in the centre, when he is exposed to attack. This occurs chiefly when the attacker has by some means succeeded in confining the opposing King to his original position.

Normally this can be achieved only by means of sacrifices. Thus it becomes necessary to weigh up the material sacrificed against the prospects of the resulting attack, and straight away the *assessment of the position* becomes complicated. The *plan* depends on the degree of insecurity of the hostile position.

All this is illustrated in the following two characteristic examples. In the first, the attacker prevents the opponent from castling KR *via* the diagonal QR3—KB8; in the second, he effects this by means of the open K file at the cost of much material.

MIKENAS—FEIGIN, *Kemeri-Riga*, 1939

1. P—Q4, P—Q4; 2. P—QB4, P—QB3; 3. Kt—KB3, Kt—B3; 4. Kt—B3, P×P; 5. P—QR4, B—B4; 6. Kt—K5, P—K3; 7. P—B3, B—QKt5; 8. Kt×P (B4), Kt—Q4; 9. B—Q2, Q—R5 ch; 10. P—Kt3, Q×QP; 11. P—K3, Q—B3; 12. P—K4, Kt×Kt; 13. Q—Kt3, Kt×KP; 14. B×B (*No. 78*).

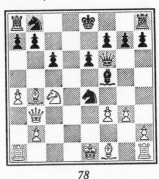

78   79

According to theory White has a winning attack. If we ask ourselves why this attack should be a winning one, the answer is not so easy to find, for we are in the midst of a combination which White has initiated with his 13th move.

Let us look at what follows;

14. ....   Q—Q5

Black has no option but to fall in with White's combination. If 14. .... Kt—Kt4; 15. P—R4, wins a piece.

15. P×Kt   Q×P ch   16. K—B2   Q×R (*No. 79*)

The combination has run its course, and we notice that, at the cost of the exchange and three pawns, White has succeeded in keeping the hostile King in the centre.

What is even more important, all the white pieces without exception are so placed that the final assault can be launched at once. On the other hand, Black has no pieces available for the defence; his most important unit, the Queen, is cut off and in danger of being trapped. When assessing positions of this type, it is essential to take into account the potentialities of attack and defence.

17. Kt—Q6 ch
The beginning of the hunt.

17. ....   K—Q2

Black has little choice. If 17. .... K—K2, or 17. .... K—B1, there follows, of course, 18. Kt×B dis ch, and 17. .... K—Q1 is refuted, as follows:

17. .... K—Q1; 18. Kt×B, P×Kt; 19. R—Q1 ch, K—B1 (19. .... K—K1; 20. B—Kt2, and 21. Q—K3 mate, unless Black gives up his Queen); 20. B—Kt2, Q×P; 21. Q×P, and now:

1. 21. .... P—QKt3; 22. B—Q6, Kt—Q2; 23. B—B4, R—Q1; 24. Q—K6, and wins.

2. 21. .... R—Q1; 22. R×R ch, K×R; 23. Q—K7 ch, K—B1; 24. B—Q6, and mate next move.

18. Kt×B   R—Q1
If 18. .... P×Kt, we again have the variations given above.

19. B—K7
With a two-fold attack on the Rook and the QKt pawn.

19. ....   Kt—R3   20. Q×KtP ch Kt—B2
                 21. R—Q1 ch   Resigns
After 21. .... K—K1; 22. Q×Kt, leading to mate.

1. P—Q4, P—Q4; 2. P—QB4, P×P; 3. Kt—KB3, Kt—KB3; 4. Q—R4 ch, QKt—Q2; 5, Kt—B3, P—K3; 6. P—K4, P—B4; 7. P—Q5, P×P; 8. P—K5, P—QKt4; 9. Q×KtP, R—QKt1; 10. Q—R4, P—Q5; 11. P×Kt, P×Kt; 12. B×P, BP×P (better 12. .... R—Kt5); 13. B×P ch, K×B; 14. Q—B4 ch, K—K1; 15. P—B7 ch, K—K2; 16. B×P, R×B; 17. Castles KR (*No. 80*) (Keres' analysis).

White has a strong attack, so avers the 'theory.' But in this case, unlike the preceding example, it is not clear that the attack is necessarily a winning one. Indeed, although White's attack is very dangerous and, especially in practice, exceptionally full of promise, accurate defensive play should see Black through.

Here are a few variations which throw a light on White's attacking chances and the possibilities of Black's defence.

80

1. 17. .... K—Q3; 18. KR—Q1 ch, K—B2; 19. Q—B4 ch,
(*a*) 19. .... K—Kt3?; 20. QR—Kt1, R—Kt5; 21. P—QR3, R×R; 22. R×R ch, K—B3; 23. Q—R4 ch, K—Q3 (23. .... K—B2; 24. Q—R5 ch, etc.); 24. R—Q1 ch, and White wins;
(*b*) 19. .... K—Kt2; 20. Q—K4 ch (if 20. Kt—K5, Q—B3), 20. .... K—Kt1; 21. Kt—K5, Q—B2, and Black can hold out.

2. 17. .... Q—Kt3 (best); 18. QR—K1 ch, K—Q1; 19. Q—B4,
(*a*) 19. .... B—Q3?; 20. Q—Kt5 ch, K—B2; 21. R—K8 (threat: 22. Q—Q8 ch, and White wins);
(*b*) 19. .... B—K2, and White's attack has come to a standstill.

These few variations, selected from a great many, show how very difficult it is to judge a position in which it is necessary to assess the relative values of material against attacking chances.

CHAPTER VI

THE ATTACK ON THE KING'S FIELD

THIS chapter is closely connected with the preceding one, in which it was shown how advantage can be taken of *weaknesses in the hostile King's field*. In order to exploit such weaknesses it becomes necessary to start a King's side attack, and so the subject of this chapter has already been touched upon in what has gone before. We shall therefore in the main examine attacks on positions as yet unweakened, and in order clearly to define the field of our investigations, let us begin with the following typical example:

MATCH, RUBINSTEIN—TEICHMANN, 1908

After 1. P—Q4, P—Q4; 2. P—QB4, P—K3; 3. Kt—QB3, Kt—KB3; 4. B—Kt5, B—K2; 5. P—K3, QKt—Q2; 6. Kt—B3, Castles; 7. Q—B2, P—QKt3; 8. P×P, P×P; 9. B—Q3, B—Kt2; 10. Castles QR, P—B4; 11. P—KR4, P—B5; 12. B—B5, R—K1 (better, 12. .... P—Kt3); 13. B×KKt, Kt×B; 14. P—KKt4, B—Q3; 15. P—Kt5, Kt—K5; 16.

81

P—R5, Q—K2; 17. QR—Kt1, P—QR3 (*No. 81*).

White has a great advantage in space on the King's side; most of his pieces are aimed directly or indirectly at Black's King's position, with the advanced KKt and KR pawns as a spearhead. However—and here is the difference from the examples of the preceding chapter—on the black K side the pawn formation is intact; his pawns there are on their original squares, and Black's powers of defence are greatly increased. For instance, against 18. P—R6 Black replies simply 18. .... P—Kt3, while 18. P—Kt6 is answered by 18. .... BP×P; 19. P×P, P—R3. In either case the avenues of attack against the black King's position are closed, and it has become extremely difficult to carry on the attack. The precept advocated in analogous conditions against a weakened King's side—advance of the pawns in order to open lines of attack—does not work automatically in this case, and we must look for other and more trenchant methods. But at the same time greater responsibilities will be incurred which will demand more intricate and accurate calculation: *as a rule an unweakened King's field can be overcome only by means of sacrifices.* This makes both assessment and plan more difficult. White stands better because he has a preponderance on the K side—but, is his preponderance so great thàt he can force a decision without offering a sacrifice? The answer to this question is of particular importance whenever the defender has some compensation of some sort in another field. Thus in *No. 81*, for instance, Black has a pawn majority on the Q side which would play an important and perhaps decisive part, should White fail to force his attack home fairly soon. In many of these cases, it is a question of weighing up the pros and cons, for the expert in combinative play, a question of intuition. He knows whether his attack will just succeed or just fail.

However, in the present position this knowledge is no longer important; the die has already been cast on the 10th move, when White, by castling on the Q side, challenged his opponent to the race on opposite wings. From that moment only the *plan* came in question. White has brought his border pawns forward (the exchange at KB6, making room for the KKt pawn, is worthy of special notice). All is ready for the climax, the Rooks behind the pawns, the Bishop at KB5 fully active, the Queen ready in the background, and the Knights prepared to intervene.

Rubinstein has made all preparations for the decisive combination which now follows.

18. B×P ch

The same general idea was shown in the preceding chapter, but here it costs material so that the consequences must be calculated to a nicety.

18. ....   K×B   19. P—Kt6 ch

The logical continuation, but one may perhaps ask whether, after 19. .... P×P; 20. P×P ch, K—Kt1, the open R file is really worth a piece. Patience! Rubinstein did the combining for us, but his plans were rather different: after 19. .... P×P he intended to win quickly by 20. Kt×Kt, P×Kt; 21. Kt—Kt5 ch, and now:

1. 21. .... K—Kt1; 22. Q×P ch, etc.
2. 21. .... K—R1; 22. P×P dis ch, etc.
3. 21. .... K—R3; 22. Kt—B7 ch, etc.

19. ....   K—Kt1   20. Kt×Kt   P×Kt

Not 20. .... Q×Kt; 21. P×P ch, K×P; 22. Kt—Kt5 ch, etc.

21. P—R6 (*No. 82*)

This is the critical position on which the success of White's attack depends. It is one of the situations which White had visualised a few moves before and on which he passed judgment, partly after calculation and partly intuitively. Most great players rely on instinct when they play, though they do analyse one or two variations as a kind of control. We will now attempt to outline the basis of this intuition;

in other words, let us try to establish whether there were solid grounds for the great master's, possibly subconscious, decision that this position can be won for White. And now we come to minor features, of which we must be aware, and which constantly occur whenever the success of a sacrificial combination is at stake:

1. The vertical action of the Rook on the KKt file.

2. The vertical action of the Rook on the KR file.

82

3. The horizontal action of a Rook established at KKt7.

4. The horizontal action of a Rook established at KR7.

5. The power of a guarded pawn at KKt7 with the support of a Rook on the KR file.

6. The possibility of the Queen intervening at QB4.

7. Possible action by the white Queen along the diagonal QB2—KR7 if Black captures at White's KB3.

If we wish to examine the position systematically, the first step is to take stock of the material on either side. The basis of this reckoning is the distribution of forces at the relevant time.

In this position, with an equality in material on either side, there can be no two opinions: White has no need for exact calculations to know that he can win in 10 to 20 moves. But White is a piece down, and so he must be on the look-out for any possible chances of material gain to redress the balance. In *No. 82* the question is: Does the move 22. P×P ch constitute a threat of material gain? Let us examine:

1. 22. .... K×P; 23. R×P ch, K—B1; 24. R×Q, R×R; 25. Kt—Kt5, and White has Queen and pawn for Rook and minor piece.

2. 22. .... Q×P; 23. R×P ch, Q×R; 24. P×Q, P×Kt; 25. Q—R7 ch, etc.

Thus the answer is quite clear: 22. P×P ch does constitute a threat, and this makes it superfluous to examine such moves by Black as .... QR—B1 or .... P—Kt4. Other ineffective measures such as .... P×Kt and .... Q—B3 can likewise be ignored, so that practically

speaking only four pawn moves are left for consideration (....
P×KtP, ... P×RP, ... P—B4, and .... P—B3).

However, for the sake of completeness, let us pass in review all
reasonable moves:

1. 21. .... P×Kt; 22. P×P ch,

   (*a*) 22. .... Q×P; 23. P×P, Q×P; 24. Q—R7 ch, etc.;

   (*b*) 22. .... K×P; 23. Q—Kt6 ch, K—Kt1; 24. P×P, etc.

2. 21. .... B—Q4; 22. P×P ch, B×P; 23. P×P, B—Q4; 24. R—R8
ch, K—B2; 25. P—Kt8 (Q) ch, R×Q; 26. R—R7 ch, etc.

3. 21. .... R—KB1; 22. P×P, K×P; 23. P×P dis ch, K—B3; 24.
R—R6 ch, etc.

4. 21. .... Q—B3; 22. P×P ch, K×P; 23. R×P ch,

   (*a*) 23. .... Q×R; 24. P×Q, P×Kt; 25. Q—B5 ch, K—K2; 26.
P—Kt8 (Q), etc.;

   (*b*) 23. .... K—B1; 24. Kt—Kt5, etc.;

   (*c*) 23. .... K—K3; 24. R×B, Q×Kt; 25. Q×BP ch, etc.

5. 21. .... P×RP; 22. P×P db ch, K×P; 23. R×P, R—R1;
24. Q×P ch, etc.

6. 21. .... P×KtP; 22. Kt—R4, P—KKt4; (22. .... B—Q4; 23.
R×P, or 22. .... K—R2; 23. P×P, K×P; 24. Kt—B5 ch,)
23. Kt—Kt6, Q—K3; 24. P—R7 ch, K—B2; 25. P—R8(Q), R×Q;
26. Kt×R ch, etc.

7. 21. .... P—B4; 22. P×P;

   (*a*) 22. .... P×Kt; 23. Q×P, B—K5; 24. R—R8 ch, K×P; 25.
R—R7 ch, K—Kt1; 26. Q—KR5, etc.;

   (*b*) 22. .... Q×P; 23. R—R7, etc.;

    (i) 23. .... P×Kt; 24. Q×P, etc.;

    (ii) 23. .... Q—B3; 24. R—KB7, Q—K3; 25. Kt—Kt5, Q—Q4;
26. Q—Q1, R—K2; 27. Q—R5, etc.

8. 21. .... P—B3 (as played in the game); 22. P×P,

   (*a*) 22. .... P×Kt; 23. R—R8 ch, K×P; 24. R—R7 ch, K—Kt1;
25. Q—B5, and wins.

   (*b*) 22. .... Q—K3; 23. R—R8 ch, K×P; 24. R—R7 ch,

    (i) 24. .... K—Kt1; 25. R (Kt1)—R1, and wins;

    (ii) 24. .... K—B1; 25. R×B, P×Kt; 26. P—Kt7 ch, K—Kt1;
27. Q—R7 ch, etc.

Taken as a whole, a complicated set of variations which it would
be hardly possible to calculate in detail over the board, so that instinct
must play an important part. On the other hand, it must never be
forgotten that instinct and intuition do not rest on exact foundations,
and as far as possible should be supplemented by calculation.

Reviewing all we have seen in this position, we arrive at the following *judgment*: White has a (winning) advantage, thanks to the advanced

position of his K side pawns and the mobility of his pieces, especially his Rooks. The *plan* is to find the winning combination, which by means of the sacrifice of a Bishop opens lines of attack for the Rooks.

If, however, we go through the same process a little earlier in the game, say after the 10th move, we arrive at the following conclusion:

Assessment: White's chances on the K side and those of Black on the Q side are approximately equal.

Plan (for White): Advance the K side pawns, the pieces taking up action stations.

The standing rule not to hesitate in bringing pawns forward to strengthen a King's side attack is of course always valid when the players have castled on opposite wings. For instance, in *No. 83* White

83   84

can bring his pawns forward without any special risks, but where both sides have castled on the same wing, the advance of pawns in an attack on the hostile King involves a weakening of the attacker's own King's field, and therefore requires careful deliberation.

Let us now examine the position in *No. 84*, which occurs after the following moves:

ALEKHINE—H. JOHNER, *Zürich*, 1934

1. P—K4, P—K4; 2. Kt—KB3, Kt—QB3; 3. B—Kt5, P—QR3; 4. B—R4, P—Q3; 5. Castles, Kt—B3; 6. P—B3, B—Q2; 7. P—Q4, B—K2; 8. P—Q5, Kt—QKt1; 9. B—B2, B—Kt5; 10. P—B4, QKt—Q2; 11. P—KR3, B—R4; 12. Kt—B3, Castles; 13. P—KKt4, B—Kt3; 14. Q—K2.

White has brought his King's side pawns forward, thereby making room for the effective posting of his attacking units (thus, after B—Q2 and K—Kt2, Rooks to KR1 and KKt1). Black has no such opportunities, one of the reasons being that the Bishop at Kt3 stands in the way. It follows that the white position deserves preference, unless Black finds in *No. 84* some way of developing an active defence. Black's only chance is 14. .... P—KR4, which, however, does not seem to work because of 15. Kt—KR4, exchanging Knight for Bishop, and weakening Black's pawn formation. 15. .... B—R2 loses a pawn after 16. P—Kt5, and the well-known combination 15. .... B×P fails against 16. Kt×B, Kt×Kt; 17. Q×Kt, because of the mating threat. But on examining the position more closely, it becomes evident that Black need not fear the exchange in question, and that he can continue with 15. .... P×P; 16. P×P, Kt—R2; and now, after—

1. 17. Kt×B, P×Kt, Black threatens to immobilise White's game by 18. .... B—Kt4, obtaining the mastery over White's KB4. White must play 18. P—B4, and after 18. .... P×P; 19. B×P, B—B3, Black controls White's K5.
2. Also unsatisfactory for White is 17. Kt—B5, B—Kt4, as shown in a game v. d. Bosch-Kmoch, *Baarn*, 1941 (18. K—Kt2, B×B; 19. QR×B, Q—Kt4; 20. R—KR1, B×Kt; 21. KP×B, P—KKt3, etc.).

The point in both cases is that Black gains the control of a number of black squares, whereby the white pawn complex loses its elasticity and the Bishop at QB2 is out of action. Accordingly the advance of the K side pawns has proved unfavourable, and White's 13th move, P—KKt4, deserves a question mark. White should have made careful preparations for this advance, e.g. with B—Q2, K—R2, and R—KKt1. Although it is by no means certain that his attack would then prove successful, at any rate he would not incur any disadvantage.

It will be well worth-while continuing the game Alekhine-H. Johner from the position in *No. 84*, because it illustrates the disastrous consequences of a passive defence, and also because White's handling of the situation can truly be called a model of what such treatment should be.

14. ....   Kt—K1   15. B—Q2   P—R3

A weakening move which, in view of Black's passive policy, must ultimately mean trouble for the Bishop and help White's attack. Therefore the active continuation 15. .... P—KR4 is still preferable (16. Kt—Q1, KKt—B3). In this case Black, although he has lost *tempi*, has nevertheless some counter-chances.

16. K—Kt2   B—R2   17. R—R1   P—KKt4

This enables White, at any given moment, to open the KR file, but in fact the consequences of White's P—KR4, and eventually P—KKt5 (after thorough preparations), would have been no less serious.

18. P—KR4   P—KB3   19. Kt—Q1   R—B2
20. Kt—K3   Kt—B1

Intending to bring this Knight to KB5 *via* KKt3.

21. Kt—B5   B×Kt

Compulsory, but now his KKt3 will be out of bounds.

22. KtP×B   R—KR2   23. QR—KKt1   Kt—Kt2
24. K—B1

White has everything neatly tied up.

24. ....   Q—K1

This allows a Knight to reach KB5 after all.

25. Kt—R2   Kt—R4   26. Kt—Kt4   Kt—B5
27. Q—B3 (*No. 85*)

85

86

Threatening to win beautifully by 28. B×Kt, KP×B; 29. Q×P, P×Q; 30. Kt×RP db ch, with mate to follow.

27. ....   K—Kt2   29. R×R ch   Kt×R
28. P×P   RP×P   30. R—R1

By simple means White has gained control of the KR file, and now threatens to win quickly by 31. B×Kt, and 32. Q—KR3.

30. ....   K—R1   31. R—R6   Q—B2
32. B—Q1   R—KKt1

Black has to face a difficult task: he has no counter-play and must defend himself against any number of threats. Thus, for example, there are these impending threats: 33. Q—R1, 34. B×Kt, and 35. Kt—K5 (after 34. .... KP×B) besides 36. B—R5 and 37. B—Kt6. The text-move deals with this manœuvre, as .... R—Kt2 can follow;

on the other hand, it leaves Black's Q side bare, and White exploits this circumstance without loss of time.

33. Q—QKt3

Instructive, and particularly strong; the attacker must never ignore the possibility of some deflecting manœuvres. Here, for instance, unless the black Rook returns in time, the white Queen will penetrate Black's position, and Black would at least lose some pawns.

33. ....   P—Kt3

After 33. .... R—Kt1; 34. B×Kt, KtP×B (or .... KP×B), there can follow either 35. Q—KR3 (35. .... R—Kt1; 36. Kt×KP, BP×Kt; 37. B—KR5, or 35. .... Q—Kt2; 36. R—Kt6, Q—B1; 37. Kt—R6) or 35. R—Kt6.

34. Q—R4

With the double threat 35. Q×P and 35. Q—Q7.

34. ....   B—B1   35. Q×P   B×R
36. Kt×B   Q—Kt2

Note how important it is for White that his Bishop at Q1 should prevent the black Queen from reaching her KR4.

37. Kt×R   K×Kt   38. Q—B8 ch   Kt—B1
39. B×Kt

At last this last outpost is eliminated, and at a time when Black cannot take advantage of the open files resulting from this exchange.

39. ....   KP×B

After 39. .... KtP×B, White wins in the simplest manner by 40. B—B3, and the advance of his QR and QKt pawns.

40. Q—K8   P—Kt5

Black's last chance, which is not to be underestimated.

41. Q—R5   P—B6   42. B—R4   Kt—R2
43. B—B2

After 43. B—K8, Black has counter-chances by 43. .... Kt—Kt4.

43. ....   Kt—B1 (*No. 86*)

In the tournament book Alekhine explains why 43. .... Kt—Kt4 now leads to nothing: 44. Q×P, Q—R3; 45. K—Kt1, and now:
1. 45. .... K—B1; 46. B—Q1, Kt—R6 ch; 47. K—B1, Q—B8 (or Q7); 48. Q×P, etc.
2. 45. .... Q—Kt2; 46. Q—Kt3, etc.

44. P—K5

White was faced with difficult problems, because his Bishop could develop little activity, but the text-move solves all difficulties. White's offer of a pawn has two aspects. One is positional (44. .... BP×P; 45. P—B6, Q×P; 46. Q×P ch, K—B2; 47. B—K4) and the other combinative, as shown by the further course of the game.

| 44. .... | QP×P | 45. P—Q6 |

Now 45. .... P×P will not do because of 46. P—B5, e.g.:

1. 46. .... KtP or QP×P; 47. B—Kt3 ch, and wins.

2. 46. .... Q—QB2; 47. B—Kt3 ch, K—Kt2; 48. Q×P ch, K—R3; 49. Q—Kt8, Q—K2; 50. P—B6, etc.

3. 46. .... Q—Q2; 47. P×QP, Kt—R2; 48. B—Kt3 ch, K—R1; 49. Q—Kt6, and wins.

| 45. .... | P—B4 |

Not, of course, 45. .... P—B3; 46. P—B5, etc.

| 46. B—K4 | Q—Q2 | 47. Q—R6 |

Black resigns because 47. .... Kt—R2 fails against 48. B—Q5 ch, K—R1; 49. Q—Kt6, Q—Q1; 50. P—Q7.

Assessment of the position after move 16: in favour of White, because he controls greater space on the K side.

Plan: effective disposition of forces (Rooks at KKt1 and KR1, one Knight at KB5 and, above all, one at KKt4, later on a Bishop at Q1), careful preparation for opening up lines of attack (28. P×KtP), at the same time not forgetting the opposite wing (33. Q—QKt3).

White's attack was made possible by Black's passive policy, and helped by the unfortunate position of the black Q Bishop. Without the presence of this Bishop at Black's KKt3, it would have been far more difficult for White to secure an open file for his attack. This problem is much in evidence in some important variations of the Ruy Lopez; we give here a particularly representative example:

ALEXANDER—PACHMAN, *Hilversum*, 1947

1. P—K4, P—K4; 2. Kt—KB3, Kt—QB3; 3. B—Kt5, P—QR3; 4. B—R4, Kt—B3; 5. Castles, B—K2; 6. R—K1, P—QKt4; 7. B—Kt3, P—Q3; 8. P—B3, Castles; 9. P—KR3, Kt—QR4; 10. B—B2, P—B4; 11. P—Q4, Q—B2; 12. QKt—Q2, B—Kt2; 13. P—Q5, B—B1; 14. Kt—B1, R—K1; 15. K—R2, P—Kt3; 16. Kt—K3, B—B1; 17. P—KKt4 (*No. 87*).

White has the better game. The situation here is better for White than in *No. 84*, as Black has not the opportunity himself to become active on the K side (in *No. 84*, 14. .... P—KR4).   Neither can he set up an entirely satisfactory defensive position with pawns at KB3 and KKt3, Knights at KB2 and KKt2, as, in consequence of his 9th move, ... Kt—QR4, his Q Knight is too far away.

17. ....   B—KKt2   18. R—KKt1 K—R1
                  19. Kt—Kt5

| 87 | 88 |

With the idea of provoking 19. .... P—R3.   Should Black fail to respond, then Black's important KR and KB pawns remain under fire.

19. ....   R—B1   20. P—KR4
The object is to allow the white Knight, if attacked, to retire to KR3, from where it can assist the advance P—KB4.

20. ....   Kt—Kt1   21. Q—K2   B—Q2
                  22. B—Q2 Kt—K2
This gives White the opportunity for a surprising combination. Correct is 22. .... P—B3; 23. Kt—R3, and only then 23. .... Kt—K2.

23. Kt—B5 (*No. 88*)
White offers a Knight in order to open the KKt file and give his Queen access to KR5.   As in our first illustration, intuition also plays an important part in this case, for the consequences could not be calculated accurately.

23. ....   P×Kt
A convincing proof of how difficult it is, even for a master, to assess the offer of a sacrifice at its true value.   After its acceptance here, White's attack gathers decisive strength.   Black's only chance is 23. .... B—KB3, when White must choose between:

1. The solid continuation 24. Kt×Kt, B×Kt(K2); 25. P—KB4, etc.
2. The promising sacrificial turn 24. Kt×RP, K×Kt; 25. P—Kt5, etc.

24. KtP×P (*No. 89*)

24. ....　　　P—B3
Other possibilities do not hold out any better prospects, e.g.:

1. 24. .... P—R3; 25. Q—R5, B—K1 (or 25. .... P—B3; 26. Kt—
B7 ch, or 25. .... K—Kt1; 26. P—B6); 26. P—B6, and wins.

89　　　　　　　　　　90

2. 24. .... Kt—Kt1; 25. Kt×P, K×Kt; 26. Q—R5 ch, B—R3 (or
26. .... Kt—R3; 27. R×B ch, etc.); 27. R×Kt, and wins.

25. Kt×P
A second sacrifice, and a logical complement of the first. If now
25. .... K×Kt; 26. Q—R5 ch, K—Kt1; 27. R×B ch, K×R; 28.
R—Kt1 ch, and mate follows.

25. ....　　　B—K1
There is nothing better; Black must hold his KR4. If 25. .... R—
KKt1, White's simple continuation then is: 26. Kt×P, or if 25. ....
R—B2, White wins after: 26. Q—R5, K—Kt1; 27. B—R6, B—K1;
28. R×B ch, R×R; 29. Kt×P ch, K—B1 (or R1); 30. B×R ch, K×B;
31. Kt×B ch, etc.

26. R×B
A last surprise. If instead, 26. Kt×R, Black still has some defensive
chances.

26. ....　　　K×R　　　27. Kt×R　　　K×Kt
Black must recapture; otherwise the Knight finds refuge at K6.
Note: 27. .... B—B2; 28. Kt—K6 ch, B×Kt; 29. R—Kt1 ch, etc.

28. B—R6 ch   K—B2

Not 28. .... K—Kt1; 29. Q—Kt4 ch, etc.

29. Q—R5 ch   Kt—Kt3   30. P×Kt ch   K—Kt1
              31. Q—B5   Q—K2

With two powerful extra pawns, to say nothing of further attacking chances, White has a clear win, and we therefore give the concluding moves without comment:

32. R—KKt1, Kt—B5; 33. B—B1, B—Q2; 34. Q—B3, R—KB1; 35. P—Kt3, Kt—Kt3; 36. P—R5, P—B4; 37. B—Kt5, P×P; 38. Q—K2, Q—K1; 39. B×P, B—B4; 40. B—R6, R—B3; 41. Q—B3, and Black resigns.

To conclude, let us return to the question of judging and planning in the position of *No. 87*.

Assessment: White has the better game, since his advantage in space gives him attacking chances on the K side.

Plan: Place the attacking pieces in the most favourable positions, provoke the creation of weaknesses (19. Kt—Kt5), and eliminate the protective pawn formation in front of the King (23. Kt—B5 and 25. Kt×P).

Sometimes a pawn advance on the K side has no other object than to establish strong points or to drive·off well-posted enemy units, when the advance of the pawns is of only secondary importance. In such cases great care has to be exercised by the attacker in seeing to the security of his own King. Here is one pertinent example:

1. P—K4, P—QB3; 2. P—QB4, P—K4; 3. Kt—KB3, P—Q3; 4. P—Q4, B—Kt5; 5. Kt—B3, Kt—Q2; 6. B—K2, KKt—B3; 7. Castles, B—K2; 8. B—K3, Castles; 9. Kt—Q2, B×B; 10. Q×B, Q—R4; 11. P—KKt4 (*No. 90*).

Why this last move? Does White intend a forward push by his K side pawns, threatening Black's King's field? Evidently not, for the white pieces are entirely unprepared for such an attack. But it may well be that, after this preliminary advance, White will be able to move his pieces into the required battle formation.

Generally speaking, however, it is very risky to start an attack with K side pawns, as long as the centre is not secure; which leads to a simple maxim: an open centre gives the defender too many chances of counter-action. Here the centre is still open, but White can well, at a given moment, play P—Q5 and thereby create more favourable conditions for a general advance of the pawns.

The move P—KKt4 must therefore be looked upon in the light of the following considerations:

(a) White reserves for himself the possibility to play P—Q5, followed eventually by P—KB3, K—B2, R—KR1, and QR—KKt1.
(b) The white KKt pawn commands the squares KB5 and KR5, making it impossible for the black Queen to whip over to the K side.
(c) White has a latent threat of P—Kt5, driving Black's K Knight to an unfavourable square.

Assessment: White has the greater mobility, and therefore the better game.
Plan: Preserving his preponderance by judicious distribution of his pieces, while the transition to a general attack (see (a)) must be kept in view.

    11. ....   P×P
Black releases the tension in order to eliminate the danger of a general attack. But 11. .... P—KR3 with 12. .... Kt—R2 is preferable.

    12. Kt—Kt3
Much stronger than the immediate recapture 12. B×P, to which the reply is 12. .... Q—KKt4.

    12. ....   Q—R3   13. Kt×P   Kt—K4
Attacking White's KKt pawn and QB pawn. White's next move is compulsory.

    14. P—Kt5   Kt—K1   16. P—B4   Kt—Kt3
    15. P—Kt3   B—Q1   17. P—KR4
It gradually begins to look very much like a general assault. But the difference lies in its real purpose. In such an attack, the first objective is to occupy the sixth rank, in order to carry out a direct threat to the hostile King. This procedure would, in the present case, have little chance of success, because the white pieces are not effectively deployed. The advance of the pawns here serves a different object, and is in the first place intended to gain space and obtain the command of important squares.

    17. ....   B—Kt3
Of course not 17. .... Kt×RP, because of 18. P—KB5, and the Knight is cut off.

    18. Kt—B5
Now White threatens to win a piece by 19. P—R5, as 19. .... Kt—R1 is not feasible because of 20. Kt—K7 mate. Note that Black's

awkward situation is the consequence of the advance of the white pawns, which has driven the Knights to unfavourable squares.

18.	Q—R4	19. QR—B1	B × B ch
20. Q × B	Q—B2		

Guarding his K2, which parries White's threat indicated above.

21. Kt—K2	Kt—K2	22. Kt—Q4	Kt × Kt
23. Kt × Kt (*No. 91*)			

91

Upon closer examination we see that White has succeeded in bringing his whole front forward, but not without creating some weaknesses in his own camp, which Black, however, is not in a position to turn to his own advantage. His pieces are inactive and badly placed. While it is thus clear that White has suffered no damage in advancing his pawns, one may well ask what advantage he has gained in doing so. This can be answered as follows:

(*a*) The squares in front of Black's King's field are inaccessible to his defending pieces (both Knights have had to retreat).

(*b*) The advanced pawns are available as supports for attacking pieces (Knights at KB5).

(*c*) The advanced pawn formation is a potential weapon of attack, as soon as Black attempts to use his own K side pawns (e.g. 23. .... P—KKt3; 24. Kt—R6 ch, K—Kt2; 25. Q—B3 ch, P—B3; 26. Kt—Kt4, and Black is in great difficulties).

It follows that Black is compelled to remain passive, which explains why he plays for an exchange of Queens with 23. .... Q—Kt3, although, contrary perhaps to his expectations, it will not ease the situation. After 24. P—R5, Kt—B2; 25. Q × Q, P × Q; 26. R—QB2, KR—Q1; 27. R—Q1, Black labours under the disadvantage of a weak Q pawn which he finally lost, a factor in his defeat being the power of White's K side, which prevents any sort of counteraction by Black on that wing.

An instructive but dangerous example: instructive because it shows that the attacking value of an advancing pawn formation increases as it gets further forward, dangerous because there is always a tendency to underestimate the risk entailed in the advance of K side pawns. It must always be borne in mind that pawns do not satisfactorily fulfil their defensive functions once they have left their original squares, and

it is particularly difficult to gauge when a pawn advance just succee
or just fails in its purpose.

Here is an example which demonstrates one of the many dangers
which a King's side is exposed when weakened by a pawn advance:

ALEKHINE—DR. EM. LASKER, *New York*, 1924

1. P—Q4, P—Q4; 2. P—QB4, P—K3; 3. Kt—KB3, Kt—KB3;
Kt—B3, QKt—Q2; 5. P×P, P×P; 6. B—B4, P—B3; 7. P—K3, Kt
R4; 8. B—Q3, Kt×B; 9. P×Kt, B—Q3; 10. P—KKt3, Castles; 1
Castles, R—K1; 12. Q—B2, Kt—B1; 13. Kt—Q1, P—B3; 14. Kt
K3, B—K3; 15. Kt—R4, B—QB2; 16. P—QKt4, B—Kt3; 17. Kt—E
B—KB2; 18. P—Kt5 (*No. 92*).

92   93

There followed:

    18. ....   B—KR4
Attacking the K Knight and indirectly the Q pawn, so that anoth
pawn advance is practically forced.

| 19. P—Kt4 | B—KB2 | 21. Q—Kt2 | P×P |
| 20. P×P | R—B1 | 22. P—B5 | |

In order to prevent Black's Knight from re-entering the field *via* Q
but the move still further weakens White's K side.

    22. ....   Q—Q3
Threat: 23. .... Q—B5.

23. Kt—Kt2	B—B2	26. R×R ch	R×R
24. KR—K1	P—KR4	27. R—K1	R—Kt1
25. P—KR3	Kt—R2	28. Q—B1	Kt—Kt4

Conclusive. The exchange of Knights is compulsory, and ther
follows a fatal check at White's KR2, e.g.: 29. Kt×Kt, Q—R7 ch

30. K—B1, P×Kt; 31. Kt—K3, Q×RP ch; etc.   The game went on:
29. Kt—K5, P×Kt; 30. Q×Kt, P—K5, with a speedy decision.

These two examples show that it is essential to weigh up advantages
and dangers when deciding on a pawn advance.   But these considerations do not count when the players have castled on opposite wings,
as we have pointed out before in this chapter.

SPIELMANN—MARÓCZY, Göteborg, 1920

1. P—K4, P—K4; 2. Kt—KB3, Kt—QB3; 3. B—Kt5, P—Q3; 4.
P—Q4, B—Q2; 5. Kt—B3, Kt—B3; 6. B×Kt, B×B; 7. Q—Q3, P×P;
8. Kt×P, B—Q2; 9. B—Kt5, B—K2; 10. Castles QR, Castles; 11.
P—B4, Kt—K1; 12. B×B, Q×B; 13. Kt—Q5, Q—Q1; 14. P—KKt4
(*No. 93*).

The advance of the KKt pawn hardly requires any calculation.   The
simple consideration that the capture of this pawn gives White an open
KKt file is all-sufficient: the attack on that file is worth more than a
pawn.   The justification for this intuitive decision would be quite an
undertaking, and would require the examination of variations such as:
14. .... B×P; 15. QR—Kt1, B—Q2; 16. P—B5, P—KB3; 17. Kt—
B4, or 15. .... B—K3; 16. Kt—K3, P—QB4; 17. Kt (Q4)—B5.   The
nature of the contest is simple for both players.   If Black misses the
right method of defence, or White fails to find the most incisive line
of attack, a quick defeat is the probable result.

When there is a considerable difference in the playing strength of
the adversaries, the stronger player seldom hesitates to offer such a
pawn sacrifice, but the weaker player should not refrain from doing
the same when occasion arises: one cannot learn to play chess by
attempting nothing.   You should stand firmly by the maxim: *After
castling on opposite wings, and with the forces reasonably well placed
for attack, an open KKt or KR file is well worth a pawn.*

The game went on:

14. ....   Kt—B3   15. Kt—B5 (*No. 94*)

He holds to our principle that the open KKt file outweighs the sacrifice of a pawn.   In this case the proof of its soundness is less involved:
15. .... Kt×KtP; 16. KR—Kt1, B×Kt; 17. P×B, and now:

  1. 17. .... Kt—B7; 18. Q—KKt3, etc.
  2. 17. .... Kt—B3; 18. Q—QB3;
    (*a*) 18. .... K—R1; 19. R×P;
      (i) 19. .... Kt×Kt; 20. R—Kt8 db ch, with mate to follow;
      (ii) 19. .... K×R; 20. R—Kt1 ch, K—R1; 21. Kt×Kt, etc.;
    (*b*) 18. .... Kt—K1; 19. P—B6, P—KKt3; 20. Kt—K7 ch, K—R1;
    21. P—B5, Q—Q2; 22. P×P, RP×P; 23. Kt×P ch, P×Kt; 24.
    R×KtP, Q—R2; 25. QR—Kt1, etc.

3. 17. .... Kt—R3; 18. P—B6, P—KKt3; 19. Q—KR3, and wins.

Note that the advance, P—KKt4, in the first place is intended to act as a support for a white Knight at KB5. If Black eliminated this Knight by exchanging it, White obtains an open KKt file with all that this portends. Driving away the Knight is not in question, as 15. .... P—KKt3 is at once refuted by 16. Q—Q4 (16. .... Kt×Kt; 17. Kt—R6 mate).

15.	Kt×Kt	16. Q×Kt	B—B3
	17. Q—Q4	Q—B3	

Black submits to a weakening of his pawn formation because, after 17. .... P—B3, he fears the continuation of White's attack by 18. P—Kt5 and 19. KR—Kt1, and no doubt he is right.

94

95

The game went on: 18. Q×Q, P×Q; 19. Kt—Kt3, K—R1; 20. KR—K1, with a considerable superiority for White in the end-game.

If we review the examples given in this chapter, we find that the positions in *Nos. 81, 84* and *87* are dynamic in character and in *Nos. 91* and *93* static.

However, it can of course happen that a King's side attack is initiated without any pawn advance, but even then in most cases one or the other of the wing pawns will finally play an important part.

Here is an example:

SPIELMANN—PETROV, *Margate*, 1938

1. P—K4, P—K3; 2. P—Q4, P—Q4; 3. Kt—QB3, P×P; 4. Kt×P, Kt—Q2; 5. KKt—B3, KKt—B3; 6. Kt×Kt ch, Kt×Kt; 7. B—Q3, P—B4; 8. P×P, B×P; 9. B—Kt5, B—K2; 10. Q—K2, Castles; 11. Castles QR (*No. 95*).

Assessment: White undoubtedly has the better game, not only because he threatens to win the Queen (B×P ch), but above all because all his pieces are so well posted that they almost without exception can take part in a King's side attack.

Plan: See the further course of the game.

| 11. .... | Q—R4 | 12. K—Kt1 | Q—Kt3 |

13. P—KR4

The important pawn, indispensable in this case. After this there will sooner or later be a threat of a combination, characteristic of such positions: 14. B×Kt, B×B; 15. B×P ch, K×B; 16. Kt—Kt5 ch, and now 16. .... B×Kt would open the R file for White. This combination does not work at once on account of the mating threat at White's QKt2 (after 14. B×Kt, B×B), and so White must first lose a *tempo*. Therefore it is best for White first to play 14. P—B3, interrupting the black Bishop's action on the long diagonal and only then the combination shown above. Black, practically powerless against White's designs, now makes a blunder which alters the logical course of events.

13. ....   B—Q2

In the assumption that White cannot take advantage of the fact that his Q Rook and the black Q Bishop are both on the Q file because, after 14. B×Kt, B×B; 15. B×P ch, K×B; 16. R×B, there is a mate on by 16. .... Q×P. But White has a more subtle version of the same theme: 14. B×P ch, K×B; 15. R×B, Kt×R; 16. B×B, followed by 17. Q—Q3 ch. And so White remains a pawn ahead. This is what occurred in the game: 14. B×P ch, Kt×B; 15. B×B, B—Kt4; 16. P—B4, KR—K1; 17. B—Q6, B—B3; 18. B—K5, and White won.

An attack by pieces only is illustrated in the following game:

SPIELMANN—HÖNLINGER, *Vienna*, 1929

1. P—K4, P—QB3; 2. P—Q4, P—Q4; 3. Kt—QB3, P×P; 4. Kt×P, Kt—B3; 5. Kt—Kt3, P—K3; 6. Kt—B3, P—B4; 7. B—Q3, Kt—B3; 8. P×P, B×P; 9. P—QR3, Castles; 10. Castles, P—QKt3; 11. P—Kt4, B—K2; 12. B—Kt2, Q—B2 (*No. 96*).

96

White has a considerable advantage: the Bishops are aimed at Black's K side; the Knights are ready to co-operate. There followed:

13. P—Kt5

He wishes to secure K5 for his Knight.

13. ....   Kt—QR4   14. Kt—K5   B—Kt2
15. Kt—Kt4

Entirely logical; he wants to get Black's best defensive piece out of the way.

15. ....   Q—Q1

The best defence. Any other move would lead to a weakening of Black's King's field, e.g.:

1. 15. .... Kt×Kt; 16. Q×Kt, P—Kt3.
2. 15. .... Kt—Q4; 16. Kt—R6 ch.
3. 15. .... Q—KB5; 16. Kt×Kt ch, B×Kt; 17. Kt—R5.

16. Kt—K3

Reculer pour mieux sauter. Exchanges at Black's KB3 lead to nothing after 16. Kt×Kt ch, B×Kt; 17. Q—R5, P—Kt3. With the text-move White retains a choice of continuations.

16. ....   Kt—Q4

Very careless. Black should never of his own free will have withdrawn this Knight from the defence.

17. Q—R5   P—Kt3

Note that 17. .... P—KR3 fails after 18. B×P, K×B; 19. Kt (K3)—B5 ch, etc.

18. Kt—Kt4 (*No. 97*)

97   98

A well-known turn: Black cannot capture the Queen because 19. Kt—R6 mate.

18. ....   B—KB3

After 18. .... P—B3 White sacrifices at his KKt6, and after

18. .... Kt—KB3 White wins by 19. Q—K5, K—Kt2; 20. Kt—R5 ch, P×Kt; 21. Q—Kt5 ch.

19. Kt×B ch   Kt×Kt   20. Q—R6

Stronger here than 20. Q—K5, which would be answered by Q—Q4.

Now that Black has had to weaken his King's field and moreover no longer has a K Bishop to guard the black squares, the win for White is a question of only a few though, of course, strong moves.

20. ....   R—B1   21. QR—Q1   Q—K2
              22. KR—K1 (No. 98)

The effective disposition of the pieces is now all that is required. He threatens 23. Kt—B5 (23. .... P×Kt; 24. Q—Kt5 ch, etc.).

22. ....   Kt—K1   23. Kt—B5   Q—B4

Or 23. .... KtP×Kt; 24. B×P.

24. R—K5   B—Q4   25. Kt—K7 ch

Black resigns, because mate in three follows: 25. .... Q×Kt; 26. Q×RP ch, K×Q; 27. R—R5 ch, K—Kt1; 28. R—R8 mate.

It is difficult to give general directions on the conduct of a King's side attack without the help of pawns. It is always a case of the pieces achieving the greatest possible mobility and accuracy in combining. In addition it is essential to be conversant with known stratagems. The following therefore holds good for the position in No. 96:

Assessment: White has attacking chances because he has a great advantage in space, and further because he has command of a great number of good squares for his pieces.

Plan: Effective deployment of pieces and sound combinations.

To conclude, here is an example in which the King's side attack becomes possible because an advanced centre pawn hinders the most effective disposition of the defending forces, incidentally a frequently recurring situation.

DR. EUWE—BOGOLJUBOFF, 6th Match Game, 1928

1. P—Q4, Kt—KB3; 2. P—QB4, P—K3; 3. Kt—QB3, P—Q4; 4. B—Kt5, QKt—Q2; 5. P—K3, B—K2; 6. Kt—B3, Castles; 7. R—B1, P—B3; 8. B—Q3, P—QR3; 9. P×P, BP×P; 10. Castles, P—Kt4; 11. Kt—K5, Kt×Kt; 12. P×Kt, Kt—Q2; 13. B—KB4, B—Kt2; 14. Kt—K2, Q—Kt1; 15. Kt—Q4 (No. 99).

White has the greater freedom of movement on the K side, thanks to the position of his pawn at K5, which prevents a black Knight or Bishop from moving to Black's KB3. In addition White's Knight is firmly posted at Q4, which again is due to the pawn at K5.

15. ....   P—Kt3

A compulsory weakening of the King's field, intended to intercept the action of White's K Bishop.

16. B—R6   R—B1   17. R×R ch   Q×R
                    18. P—B4

The K pawn is now solidly guarded.

99

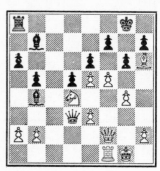

100

18. ....   Kt—B4   19. P—KKt4

The intention is to play P—B5. After the opening of the KB file the Knight at Q4 and Bishop at KR6 will reach their maximum efficiency.

19. ....   Kt×B   21. Q—Q2   B—Kt5
20. Q×Kt   Q—B5   22. Q—KB2   Q—Q6
                    23. P—B5 (*No. 100*)

23. ....   Q—K5   24. Q—Kt3

After 24. P×KP, Q×P ch; 25. K—R1, Q—K5 ch; White can avoid perpetual check only by the exchange of Queens.

24. ....   KP×P   26. B×B   R×B
25. P×P   B—KB1   27. P—B6

With the threat of 28. Q—Kt5 and 29. Q—R6.

27. ....   P—KR4   28. Q—Kt5   Q—Kt5 ch

Or 28. .... K—R2; 29. Kt—B5. However, the exchange of Queens does not ease the situation.

29. Q×Q   P×Q   30. P—K6

The point is that Black cannot take this pawn because of 30. ....
P×P; 31. Kt×P, R—B2; 32. Kt—Q8, R—Q2; 33. P—B7 ch, etc.

| 30. .... | K—R2 | 32. R—B1 | K—R3 |
| 31. P—K7 | R—K1 | 33. Kt—K6 | |

Black resigns.

Reverting to *No. 99*:

Assessment: White has strong attacking chances on the K side, because his advanced K pawn hamstrings the defence.

Plan: Bringing all the forces on to the field of battle, culminating in the advance of the KB and KKt pawns.

CHAPTER VII

WEAK PAWNS

KAN—BONDAREVSKY, *Tiflis*, 1937

AFTER 1. P—K4, P—K3; 2. P—Q4, P—Q4; 3. Kt—Q2, P—QB4; 4. P×QP, KP×P; 5. B—Kt5 ch, B—Q2; 6. Q—K2 ch, Q—K2; 7. B×B ch, Kt×B; 8. P×P, Q×Q ch; 9. Kt×Q, B×P; 10. Kt—QKt3, B—Kt3; 11. QKt—Q4, KKt—B3; 12. B—Kt5, Castles KR; 13. Castles QR (*No. 101*). Fine assesses the position as being in White's favour, which will surprise nobody, for it is common knowledge that an isolated pawn constitutes a weakness. White has six united pawns, Black has five, plus one lone pawn at Q4. Has Black some compensation in space? Scarcely; at most can it be said that he has a promise of possible better things in the fact that his K Knight can get to K5, where it can hardly be driven off by P—KB3, because this move may perhaps spell a weakening of White's position. But this line of play, depending as it does on a 'perhaps,' is of great importance.

Thus Black has a weak Q pawn, which is held fast. But White must not imagine that the ultimate capture of this pawn is a mere matter of technique and accuracy. On the contrary, in practice it is seen that in nine cases out of ten the isolated pawn holds out. In view of this, the isolated pawn would not appear to constitute such a serious weakness. This conclusion is, however, equally fallacious; the drawback of the isolated pawn lies not so much in the danger of its being lost as in the commitments which it entails and the constant thought and attention required. The units which are necessary for the defence of the pawn will not as a rule be less in number than those concerned in the attack, but while the attacker can at any time switch over and concentrate on some other object, the defender has no such discretion; he is wholly dependent on his opponent's course of action. Thus, although in most cases the defence of the weak isolated pawn will be successful, it will usually be impossible to avoid damage on other fronts.

Let us first continue the game from the position given in *No. 101*. There followed:

13. ....   Kt—Kt5

He prefers the text-move to 13. .... Kt—K5, the difference being that the Knight, which can be maintained neither at Kt5 nor at K5, can now retire *via* Black's K4 instead of Q3. There is little to choose between the two methods. The text-move results from the following

considerations. Black's Q pawn is difficult to defend as long as he
has a Knight at Q2, nor can this Knight move away at present, because
B×Kt would give Black an awkward doubled pawn. Clearly there
is nothing else to do than first to move the K Knight. Black, on

101   102

account of his weak Q pawn, is acting under slight but continuous
pressure.

14. B—R4   B—Q1

Black takes advantage of the opportunity to vacate his QKt3 for
his Q Knight. The text-move gains a *tempo*, as White's Bishop must
keep guard over his KB2.

15. B—Kt3   B—B3   16. Kt—KB3

The first of a series of moves which gradually force Black into a
less favourable situation. The Q pawn is now attacked by the Rook;
the Knight at KB3 commands K5, with the result that the black K
Knight's retreat through that square is no longer feasible.

16. ....   Kt—Kt3   17. P—KR3   Kt—R3
                  18. Kt—B4   KR—Q1

Attack and *riposte*.

19. R—Q3   R—Q2

A characteristic part of the action against the isolated pawn. White
prepares for the doubling of his Rooks, and Black, *nolens volens*, must
do the same.

20. KR—Q1   QR—Q1 (*No. 102*)

Thrice attacked and thrice defended. For the time being White is
unable to increase the pressure and must now think out something
else. Let us see what can be done:

21. Kt—R5, B—K2; 22. Kt—K5, R—Q3 (22. .... R—B2 does not work because of 23. Kt×BP); 23. Kt—Kt4, R—QB3 (to prevent B—B7); 24. Kt—B4, B—Kt4, and White has achieved nothing. No advantage is to be gained for White from this line of play, but it is important for the attacker carefully to check any sequence of moves, provided it appears to have a forcing character as this one certainly does. Such a forcing character is mostly present when a threat occurs to a defending unit, such as 22. Kt—K5, attacking a black Rook. Burdened with the anxious task of protecting that problem child, his Q pawn, Black finds his freedom of action much restricted.

21. B—R2
Excellently thought out. Now White threatens the advance of the KKt pawn, creating fresh disturbances in the enemy lines, not so much because of the threat itself, but because once White obtains command of his KB5, Black's Knight on the KR file will be completely immobilised.

21. ....   P—Kt3
Undoubtedly better is 21. .... Kt—B4, freeing the Knight in the nick of time from its confined position. It is true that—according to the Russian Tournament book—the Knight has no great future after 21. .... Kt—B4; 22. P—KKt4, Kt—KR5; 23. Kt—R5, B—K2; 24. Kt—Q4, but in the game itself the Knight suffers a worse fate.

22. P—KKt4   B—Kt2   23. B—Kt3   P—B3
With the idea of giving the Knight a new lease of life via KB2, but there is now a fresh weakness at his K3, and this is more than the position can stand.

It is difficult, however, to think of another move which Black could have tried. The Knight at QKt3 and both his Rooks are tied up, the Knight at KR3 is locked in, and the Bishop practically so. The alternative therefore must be a move by the King or a pawn. Now 23. .... K—B1 (instead of 23. .... P—B3) fails against 24. B—R4, P—B3; 25. Kt—K6 ch, and 23. .... P—Q5 loses a pawn after 24. Kt—K2. Black therefore must try 23. .... K—R1 or 23. .... P—R3, neither of which is at all attractive. It is easy to see that Black can hardly undertake anything, and this has a damaging psychological effect, which results from the pressing commitments imposed by the presence of the weak isolated pawn.

24. Kt—Q4 (No. 103)
With obvious threats. White wishes to drive away one of the defending Rooks by 25. Kt (Q4)—K6, after which Black's Q pawn is one

guard short. As a matter of course, playing the other Knight to K6 would not work, as this Knight is wanted for the attack on the Q pawn.

24. ....   Kt—B2

Black thinks that he has found an active defence in .... Kt—K4; but the result is that he still loses a pawn, although it is not the weak brother at Q4. Let us examine whether there is, after all, a method by which Black could avoid the loss of a pawn:

1. 24. .... R—QB1; 25. Kt (Q4)—K6, and the Q pawn falls (25. .... R—B3, then first 26. Kt × B).

2. 24. .... R—K1; 25. Kt (Q4)—K6,
(*a*) 25. .... P—Kt4; 26. Kt × B, P × Kt; 27. Kt × R, etc.;
(*b*) 25. .... B—R1 (else there follows 26. Kt × B and 27. Kt × QP); 26. Kt—B5, R—QB2; 27. Kt—Kt3, etc.

103

3. 24. .... P—B4; 25. Kt (Q4)—K6, R—K1; 26. Kt × B,
(*a*) 26. .... K × Kt; 27. Kt × QP, Kt × Kt; 28. R × Kt, R × R; 29. R × R, P × P; 30. R—Q7 ch, etc.,
(*b*) 26. .... R × Kt; 27. P × P, Kt × P; 28. Kt × QP.

4. 24. .... P—Kt4; 25. Kt (B4)—K6,
(*a*) 25. .... R—K1; 26. Kt—QB5, R (Q2)—K2; 27. Kt—Kt5, P—R3; 28. Kt—B7, etc.;
(*b*) 25. .... R—QB1; 26. Kt—Kt5, P—R3; 27. Kt—B3.

In every case White wins a pawn with an excellent position; Black's weak pawn cannot be defended.

| 25. Kt (Q4)—K6 | Kt—K4 | 27. Kt × Kt | R × Kt |
| 26. Kt × R | Kt × R ch | 28. Kt—B5 | |

The QKt pawn must fall. This particular case is of course accidental, but the fight in the open depends on such accidental happenings, which are bound to occur in this type of position. When they do occur, the defender who is faced with a host of difficulties always bears the cost.

Let us revert to the original position in *No. 101*. The *assessment*, as can easily be seen, must be: White has the advantage, because Black has an isolated pawn.

The attacker's *plan*, based on this consideration, comprises the **following** elements:

1. Direct threats to the Q pawn, e.g. by 18. Kt—B4, and more so by doubling the Rooks on the Q file.

2. Indirect attacks on the weak pawn by threats to the defending pieces (see, for instance, 25. Kt (Q4)—K6, and in addition various other contingencies shown in the analysis to Black's 24th move).

3. Subsidiary operations on fields away from the weak pawn. Of course only a limited number of pieces takes part in these operations, in this particular case three white against two black pieces. It is to be noted that Black's Knight at his QKt3 takes no part in these manœuvres, while White's Knight at his KB4 is active both in the attack on Q5 and in the subsidiary action.

A plan for the defender is difficult to devise. He depends entirely on the measures taken by his opponent, and he can generally do nothing else but adopt a patient waiting policy, hoping for a period of rest and calculating exactly when and where the blow is going to fall. This compulsory and rather unpromising suspense has a depressing effect on the defender, who more often than not decides on some violent counter-action which leaves the situation for him rather worse than better. That, however, the attacker must keep an eye on the possibilities of such counter-play is self-understood.

At the beginning of this chapter it was said that, although a weak isolated pawn is a source of worry to its owner because of the various commitments it implies, it by no means follows that its loss is more or less forced.

Let us examine this question in connection with the simple position in *No. 104*.

Black's QB pawn is isolated and weak. Two white Rooks are attacking it, and it is defended by two black Rooks. White cannot in any way strengthen the attack, so that there is no question of capturing the pawn by direct means. Therefore, if White still wishes to play for a win, he will have to find some indirect means of taking advantage of the constrained position of the black Rooks. For instance, White moves his pawn up to KR5 in order to fix Black's K side pawns. If then Black plays .... P—Kt3, White exchanges pawns and obtains a passed K pawn. If at some time or other Black plays .... P—B3, then White should be able to move his King to KB5 and, with the help of a *Zugzwang*, force his way through to K—Kt6. If, however, Black plays neither .... P—Kt3 nor .... P—B3, White can try to force him to play one of these moves by attacking the Kt pawn and playing a Rook to KKt4. All this is rather vague, and there is little doubt that White's plan is doomed to failure if Black hits on the correct defensive manœuvre. This consists in bringing his King to his Q3 without delay, giving the QB pawn additional support, thus liberating one of the Rooks, which will be well able to frustrate any possible plan of attack by White.

Nevertheless, it is clear that, even at this advanced stage in the game, the isolated pawn constitutes a weakness which demands careful handling.

If we now transfer White's K pawn to QKt2 as in *No. 105*, then

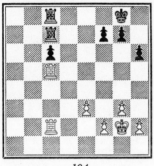

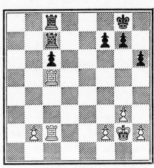

104   105

White has a different method of attack on Black's isolated pawn, which is quickly successful.

    1. P—QKt4

Now Black cannot parry the threat 2. P—Kt5, which forces the gain of the QB pawn, for both against .... R—Kt1 and .... R—Kt2, P—Kt5 still wins. However, Black has here another continuation, which defeats the consequence of his loss, but this is purely accidental and hardly likely to occur frequently.

    1. ....   K—B1   2. P—Kt5   K—K2

And now—

1. 3. P×P, K—Q3; 4. R—B5, P—B3, and White's QB pawn must fall.

2. 3. R×P, R×R; 4. P×R, K—Q3, etc. (or 4. R×R, R×R; 5. P×R, K—Q3, etc.).

3. 3. P—Kt6, R—Kt2; 4. R×P, R×R; 5. R×R, K—Q2, etc.

Even some small alterations in Black's pawn formation cannot give any positive chance to win, e.g. the Kt pawn at his Kt4 instead of Kt2, or pawns at KB4, KKt3 and KR2 instead of KB2, KKt2 and KR3.

But suppose that in *No. 105* it were Black's move, then all danger of loss could be obviated: 1. .... R—Kt1.

Black abandons his isolated pawn and attacks the white QKt pawn instead. Now White has no means of preparing the advance P—QKt4 effectively, and it is no longer possible. With 2. .... R (B2)—

Kt2 Black can in any event win the white QKt pawn in exchange for his own QB pawn. In such cases counter-attack always is the best defence.

Let us now place the white Rook in *No. 105* at QB4 instead of QB2, and suppose it is White's move.

      1. P—QKt4

Now Black has a curious loophole:

      1. ....   R—Kt1   2. P—Kt5

Capturing the pawn leads to an easy draw.

      2. ....   P×P   3. R×R   P×R

Draw.

It is to be noted here that 1. .... R—Kt2 is insufficient because, after 2. P—Kt5, P×P, White captures at QB8 with a check.

Now let us add a white pawn at White's QR2, and a pawn for Black at his QR2; the position does not appear to be different to any material extent (*No. 106*).

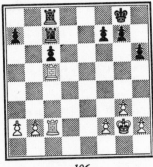
106

107

There follows:

      1. P—QKt4   P—R3   2. P—QR4

and now White can force the gain of a pawn by 3. P—Kt5. But we must remember that here again Black can obtain a draw by bringing up his King, and so White must look for an improvement in his method of attack, and, indeed, there is a way:

      1. P—QKt4   P—R3   2. R—QR5   R—R1
                    3. P—Kt5

Winning a pawn (3. .... P—QB4; 4. P×P, P—B5; 5. R—R4, P—B6; 6. R—R3, and after a general liquidation White remains with an extra QR pawn, a winning advantage).

If Black plays differently, say 1. .... K—B1 (instead of 1. ....
P—R3), there follows 2. P—Kt5, K—K2; 3. P×P, K—Q3; 4. R—QR5,
and this attack on the QR pawn enables White to preserve his extra
pawn at QB6. The win is still difficult, but with patience and accurate
play it can be achieved.

How did White get these additional chances? They are a consequence of the presence of the two QR pawns. Black's QR pawn
constitutes a second weakness on which White can fasten because of
his greater mobility. This is shown even more clearly in the example
No. 107, opposite.

Black has *two* weak pawns, and this quickly proves fatal.

1. R—QR4   R—R1   2. R (Q5)—QR5 R (Q2)—R2
3. P—QKt4

and Black is helpless against the threat 4. P—Kt5. Moreover, White
has an alternative method of winning:

1. R—QKt4   K—B1   2. R—Kt6

and Black cannot guard both the pawns.

With the black King at his KB1, the second method is not effective
because 1 .... K—K2, guarding the Q pawn, so that in this case White
would have to use the first method. With a black Rook at Black's
QB3 instead of Q1, neither of the lines shown above will lead to anything in a direct way. The Rook at QB3 guards both pawns, and
the attacker's greater mobility, which as a rule is the deciding factor,
is here of no importance. The defender is therefore well advised to
place his pieces so that they guard more than one weakness at one
and the same time.

If we pass under review the positions shown so far in this Chapter,
we find that the weak pawn, round which the play revolves, is held
fast either by the opponent controlling or actually occupying the square
in front of the weak pawn. Occupying this square is called a blockade,
and the square in question is a blockading square. It is much easier
to shoot a sitting bird than a bird on the wing. On the same principle
it is important to immobilise the target, the weak pawn, before starting
on direct action.

So far we have given examples only of isolated pawns which were
weak, but united pawns also can be weak, as can be seen in the
following diagram (*No. 108*):

Black's QR pawn is isolated, but is nevertheless hardly weaker than
the KKt pawn, although it differs in value. We call the KKt pawn
a 'backward' pawn; it can get no support from the KR pawn unless
it succeeds in advancing to KKt4. Let us add that a backward pawn
has all the characteristics of an isolated pawn, and we speak of a

backward pawn also when, as here, it is on an open file. In such circumstances the isolated pawn is at its weakest, because it is easy to attack it. That is why the isolated QR pawn in *No. 108* will not cause Black over-much worry.

Black's QB and Q pawns are united, but cannot guard each other,

108

109

as their advance is hindered by White's QKt and K pawns, and so they are liable to be attacked and in certain circumstances, which we shall specify, these 'hanging pawns,' as they are called, constitute a definite weakness.

What about the white pawns in *No. 108*? The pawns at QR2 and QKt3 are united, as are also those at K3 and KB2, but here the similarity ends. The pawn at KB2 is on an open file, and can be attacked. If it advances to B3 or B4 to take part in an attack, the K pawn is at once vulnerable and in the latter case becomes a backward pawn.

Here is a short review of various examples from practical play, in which weak pawns play a part. The main object of this discussion is a further elucidation of the principles already mentioned and the circumstances in which pawn weaknesses can arise.

DR. EUWE—TYLOR, *Nottingham*, 1936

1. P—Q4, P—Q4; 2. P—QB4, P—K3; 3. Kt—QB3, Kt—KB3; 4. B—Kt5, B—K2; 5. P—K3, Castles; 6. Kt—B3, P—QKt3; 7. P×P, P×P; 8. B—Kt5, P—B4; 9. P×P, P×P; 10. Castles, B—Kt2 (*No. 109*).

Black's hanging pawns at his Q4 and QB4 constitute a weakness here, because White is ahead in development and can attack them before Black's forces are mobilised.

11. R—B1   Q—Kt3   12. Q—K2   P—QR3

There was a threat of 13. B×Kt, B×B; 14. Kt—QR4, winning a pawn, and Black cannot bring out his Q Knight.

13. B—QR4   R—Q1   14. KR—Q1   Q—K3

A critical moment. It is clear that at this point 14. .... Kt—B3 is refuted by 15. B×KKt, B×B; 18. Kt×P, but why does not Black play 14. .... QKt—Q2? The answer is: because White would play 15. B—Kt3, forcing Black to advance the QB pawn, 15. .... P—B5, which would reduce the Q pawn in rank from a hanging to a backward pawn. This last weakness, entirely according to formula, is more serious: Black's Q pawn is immobilised, his Q5 is under White's control, and the black Q Bishop's diagonal is obstructed.

15. B—Kt3   Kt—K5

Black labours under considerable pressure, hoping that a combination may free his game. This is psychologically understandable, and is one of the disadvantages of a weak pawn. *Nolens volens*, Black must play 15. .... P—B5, after which White can begin the assault on Q5.

16. Kt×Kt   Q×Kt   17. R×BP

and White is a pawn ahead with a solid position (17. .... P—B3; 18. R—B7).

ZUKERTORT—TAUBENHAUS, *Frankfurt*, 1887

1. P—Q4, P—Q4; 2. P—QB4, P—K3; 3. Kt—QB3, Kt—KB3; 4. B—Kt5, B—K2; 5. Kt—B3, P—QKt3; 6. P—K3, B—Kt2; 7. R—B1, P—B4; 8. P×QP, KP×P; 9. P×P, P×P; 10. B—Kt5 ch, QKt—Q2; 11. Castles, Castles (*No. 110*).

110

A position of a type similar to the preceding one. White has furnished his opponent with 'hanging pawns' in, for himself, favourable conditions, in that his pieces are safe from any attack by the weak pawns.

12. B×QKt

This exchange, which may strike the reader as a little strange, is intended to gain a *tempo* after 13. Kt—K5, which accelerates the development of White's attack.

12. ....   Q×B   13. Kt—K5   Q—B4
                         14. P—B4

It is true that White's K pawn has now become weak, but Black will have his work cut out to derive any advantage from this fact.

14. ....   KR—Q1   15. P—KKt4   Q—K3
                16. P—B5

Excellent! 16. .... Q×Kt loses the Queen (17. B—B4).

16. ....   Q—B1

Worth considering is 16. .... Q—R3. At QB1 the Queen is in the line of fire of the white Q Rook.

17. Kt—R4   Q—B2   18. B—B4   B—Q3
                19. QKt×P

The liquidation which turns the two hanging pawns into one isolated pawn.

19. ....   B×QKt   20. Kt—Q3   B×P ch
                21. B×B   Q—Q2 (No. 111)

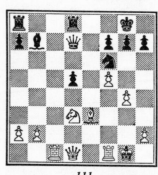

111   *112*

A new phase. Black's isolated Q pawn can easily be defended, but the drawback of the isolated pawn is shown here in a different light: White is the master of his Q4, the strong blockading square in front of the weak pawn. We call Q4 a strong square for White, and it is clear that this is due to the presence of Black's isolated pawn without which it would not be so. We shall deal with the conception of a strong square in our next chapter.

There followed:

22. Kt—B5   Q—K2   23. B—Kt5   B—B3
                24. Q—Q4

From this strong square White controls the whole board.

24. ....   R—K1   26. KR—K1   Q—Q3
25. Kt—Q3   QR—B1   27. B×Kt

Note that White refrains from 27. Q×RP, for there would follow 27. .... P—Q5; and the black Q Bishop comes to life. The isolated pawn remains—displaced from Black's Q4 to Q5—but White's square at his Q4 is no longer strong, and the black Q Bishop is no longer shut in. All this should be well worth a pawn for Black.

27.	R×R ch	30. P—QR3	R—K1
28. R×R	P×B	31. R×R ch	B×R
29. Kt—B4	R—Kt1	32. Kt—R5	

and White wins.

They knew it all seventy years ago!

In 1933, J. H. Wertheim published in the *Tijdschrift voor Schaak* an essay in three languages on the subject of hanging pawns. He arrives at the conclusion that in the middle-game and with minor pieces on the board, hanging pawns in the centre constitute an advantage, unless —as in the examples we have shown—the opponent is ahead in development which enables him to win a pawn or to break up the hanging pawns.

In the end-game, hanging pawns as a rule are a drawback, as we can see in the following example (*No. 112*):

BURN—MARÓCZY, *Vienna*, 1898

Play went as follows:

24.	QR—Q1	26. P—B3	KR—Q1
25. Kt—K3	R—Q3	27. QR—Q1	P—QR4

In order to prevent White from playing P—QR5, at some inconvenient moment, and obtaining a passed B pawn.

28. K—B2	K—B2	31. K—K3	B—R3
29. Kt—B2	Kt×Kt	32. B—Kt3	R—QB1
30. B×Kt	K—K2	33. R—QB1	R (Q3)—B3

Changing the bill of fare; it is now the B pawn's turn.

34. R (Q2)—QB2	K—Q3	38. P—Kt3	K—Q2
35. P—B4	R (B3)—B2	39. R—KB1	K—K2
36. K—Q3	P—R3	40. R (B1)—B1	K—Q3
37. R—K1	P—KKt4	41. R—K1	K—Q2

Black is probably in time trouble.

42. R (K1)—K2	P×P	43. P×P	R—KKt1
	44. R—K1		

If instead, 44. R—KKt2, R (B2)—B1; followed by 45. .... B—Kt2, the KKt file remains likewise in Black's keeping. This is the indirect result of Black's pressure on the QB pawn, which prevents White from taking the necessary defensive measures in time. This is a well-known symptom when there is a weak pawn on the board, the attacker is quicker in transferring his forces to another field.

	44.	R—Kt5	45. R (B2)—K2

At last some counter-action.

	45.	R—B3	47. K—B3	R—B3
	46. R—KB2	R—Q3	48. R—K3

The decisive mistake.

	48.	R—Kt8	49. R—R3	B×P
		50. R×P

50. B×B, R—B8 ch; is about equally disastrous.

	50.	R—Kt8	52. R×P	R(B3)×B ch
	51. B×B	R—Kt5	53. K—Q3	K—K2
		54. R—R6	R×P ch

and Black wins.

KOTOV—KERES, Russian Championship, 1948

1. P—K4, P—K3; 2. P—Q4, P—Q4; 3. Kt—Q2, Kt—KB3; 4. P—K5, KKt—Q2; 5. B—Q3, P—QB4; 6. P—QB3, P—QKt3; 7. Kt—K2, B—R3; 8. B×B, Kt×B; 9. Castles, B—K2; 10. Kt—KKt3, Castles; 11. Q—Kt4, P—B4; 12. P×P e.p., R×P (*No. 113*).

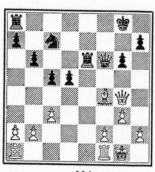

113   114

Black's K pawn has remained backward, and it must be White's aim not only to attack this pawn, but also to prevent Black from eliminating this weakness by forcing .... P—K4 at a suitable time.

	13. Kt—R5	R—Kt3	14. Q—K2	Kt—B2
		15. Kt—B3

White covers the square in front of the weak pawn—the blockading square.

15. ....   B—Q3

Now it would be of no use to White to occupy the blockading square: after 16. Kt—K5, B×Kt; 17. P×B, the K file is closed, which means that the weakness of Black's K3 has considerably diminished; one might even say that for all practical purposes it has disappeared. To put it pithily, the weakness is sealed.

16. P—KKt3   P—K4

Black offers a pawn to relieve the pressure of the besieger (psychological play).

17. Kt×KP

Stronger is 17. P×KP, R—K3; 18. Kt—B4, R—K1; 19. Kt×P, preserving his extra pawn.

17. ....   B×Kt   18. P×B   R—K3

And so Black recovers his pawn.

19. Q—Kt4   P—Kt3   21. P×Kt   Q×P
20. Kt—B6 ch   Kt×Kt   22. B—B4 (*No. 114*)

A fresh situation has arisen. Now Black's Q pawn is weak, at least as long as it cannot advance to Q5.

There followed: 22. .... Kt—K1; 23. QR—Q1, Q—B2; 24. Q—B3, (not 24. R×P, Kt—B3, etc.) 24. .... Kt—B3; 25. P—B4, winning the weak pawn.

KERES—DR. EUWE, *World Championship, Moscow*, 1948

1. P—K4, P—K4; 2. Kt—KB3, Kt—QB3; 3. B—Kt5, P—QR3; 4. B—R4, Kt—B3; 5. Castles, Kt×P; 6. P—Q4, P—QKt4; 7. B—Kt3, P—Q4; 8. P×P, B—K3; 9. Q—K2, B—K2; 10. R—Q1, Castles; 11. P—B4, KtP×P; 12. B×P, B—QB4; 13. B—K3, B×B; 14. Q×B, Q—Kt1; 15. B—Kt3, Kt—R4; 16. QKt—Q2, Kt×Kt; 17. R×Kt, Kt×B; 18. P×Kt (*No. 115*).

Black's QR pawn is isolated on an open file, but his QL pawn, a 'united pawn,' is even weaker, since White can

115

prevent its advance to QB4. At the same time White's QKt pawns are also weak, so that it becomes a question of 'first come, first served,' and in this case it is White. The continuation was:

18. ....   R—B1

To enforce .... P—QB4.

19. R—QB1   P—QB4

Best in the circumstances: after 19. .... Q—Kt5; 20. R—B5 (a positive prevention of the QB pawn's advance), 20. .... QR—Kt1; 21. R—Q3, followed by 22. R (Q3)—B3, 23. Kt—Q4, and White's pawn at QKt3 is solidly held, while, in the long run, Black's QB pawn must fall. Here again it is in fact the weak pawn which has turned the scale; it is incidental that White obtains strong squares at his Q4 and QB5 (see Chapter VIII). With the text-move White exchanges his weak QB pawn for White's weak QKt pawn.

20. R×BP   R×R   21. Q×R   Q×KtP
22. Kt—Q4

It is now clear who stands best; Black has two weaknesses (at his Q4 and QR3), White has only one. White has a strong Knight (on a strong square), Black has a Bishop which works only at half power (along one diagonal instead of two). Finally, White has a majority on the K side of four pawns to three, and after adequate preparations these can go forward, and will develop great offensive powers.

FLOHR—DR. VIDMAR, *Nottingham*, 1936

1. P—Q4, P—Q4; 2. P—QB4, P—K3; 3. Kt—QB3, Kt—KB3; 4. B—Kt5, B—K2; 5. P—K3, Castles; 6. Kt—B3, QKt—Q2; 7. Q—B2, P—B4; 8. P×QP, Kt×P; 9. B×B, Q×B; 10. Kt×Kt, P×Kt; 11. B—Q3, P—KKt3; 12. P×P, Kt×P; 13. Castles KR, B—Kt5; 14. Kt—Q4, QR—B1 (*No. 116*).

White has forced an isolated pawn upon his opponent, but the circumstances are not such that White could within a predictable time threaten its capture. First comes endless manœuvring, the sole object of which is to exchange as many pieces as possible, and so make it easier for White to realise his advantage. He will keep a firm hold on the blockading square Q4, so that Black is unable at any time to get rid of his weakness (by .... P—Q5) or to seal it (by an exchange at Q5 without White being able to recapture with a piece).

15. Q—Q2   P—QR3   16. B—B2   Q—Kt4
17. P—B3

Black has forced a weakness at White's K3, which, however, is of no great importance, as this pawn is close to White's base, and is therefore not difficult to defend.

17.	B—Q2	21.	B×B	Kt×B
18. KR—K1	KR—Q1	22.	R—QB1	Kt—B4
19. QR—Q1	Q—B3	23.	KR—Q1	Q—Kt3
20. B—Kt3	B—R5	24.	Kt—K2	Kt—Q2
	25.	Q—Q4		

White is making considerable progress.

116

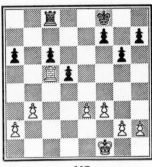

117

25.	Q×Q	27.	P—QKt3	K—B1
26. Kt×Q	Kt—K4	28.	K—B1	R×R
	29.	R×R	Kt—B3	

The point of Black's defensive plan which, however, miscarries.

30. Kt×Kt	R—B1	31. R—B5	P×Kt (*No. 117*)

(Or 31. .... R×Kt; 32. R×P, R—B8 ch; 33. K—K2, R—B7 ch;
34. R—Q2.)

What has Black achieved? His Q pawn is no longer isolated; but against that his QB pawn is backward, while his QR pawn has become a weak pawn and is open to attack. Moreover, two strong squares; Q4 and QB5, are available for White's King. The win for White is now only a question of time.

The game continued:

32. K—K2	K—K2	35.	K—Q4	P—KB4
33. K—Q3	K—Q3	36.	P—QKt4	R—QKt1
34. R—R5	R—QR1	37.	P—QR3	R—QR1

After 37. .... R—Kt3; 38. P—B4, Black gets into a *Zugzwang* position, which means that he will have to leave the white King in command of his K5 and QB5.

38. P—K4	BP×P	40.	K×P	R—R2
39. P×P	P×P	41.	K—B4	

White now turns his attention to Black's K side in order to create some weaknesses there before embarking on decisive action. Black's King and Rook are completely tied up.

41.	P—R3	45. P—Kt3	R—R2
42. P—KR4	K—K3	46. K—B3	R—R1
43. K—Kt4	R—R1	47. K—K4	R—R2
44. P—R5	P—Kt4	48. R—K5 ch	

The beginning of the end. The white Rook is to penetrate Black's position *via* K8, forcing the black King to declare his intentions: King's side or Queen's side.

48.	K—Q3

After 48. .... K—B3; 49. R—K8, Black must lose either the QR pawn or the QB pawn, and after 48. .... K—Q2; 49. K—B5, the white King enters the enemy lines with decisive results.

49. R—K8	P—B4	50. R—Q8 ch

and White wins (50. .... K—B2; 51. R—KR8, or 50. .... K—B3; 51. R—B8 ch).

CAPABLANCA—FINE, *Semmering*, 1937

1. P—Q4, P—Q4; 2. P—QB4, P—QB3; 3. Kt—KB3, Kt—B3; 4. Kt—B3, P×P; 5. P—QR4, B—B4; 6. P—K3, P—K3; 7. B×P, B—QKt5; 8. Castles, Castles; 9. Q—K2, B—Kt5; 10. R—Q1, Q—K2; 11. P—R3, B—KR4; 12. P—K4, QKt—Q2; 13. P—K5, Kt—Q4; 14. Kt—K4, P—B3; 15. P×P, P×P; 16. Kt—Kt3, B—B2; 17. B—KR6, KR—K1 (*No. 118*).

Black's K pawn constitutes a weakness in his formation, although White will, for the present, not be in a position seriously to threaten this pawn, i.e. because Black's K Bishop controls White's K1, preventing the doubling of the white Rooks. Moreover, Black has greater control of the square in front of his weak K pawn. This circumstance must not, however, be overestimated, for the advance .... P—K4 would not liberate the K pawn, but merely displace it, while Black would have to reckon with the fact that this advance might make White's KB5 available for the white Knight, playing from KKt3.

18. Kt—K1
To drive away Black's K Bishop.

18.	K—R1	20. Q—B3	R KKt1
19. Kt—Q3	B—Q3	21. Kt—B4	

The more pieces are exchanged, the easier the task for the attacker—a general rule when there are weak pawns on the board.

21.	Kt×Kt	24. B—Kt3	QR—Q1
22. B×Kt	B×B	25. R—K1	Kt—Q4
23. Q×B	Kt—Kt3	26. Q—R4	B—Kt3
	27. Kt—K4 (*No. 119*)		

118   *119*

White has succeeded in drawing the hostile KB pawn also into the orbit of his attack, so that 28. Kt—B5 threatens the K pawn, but there is another threat to the KBP after 28. B×Kt. Black has now an unpleasant choice of moves:

1. Exchanging at his K5, after which White can concentrate all his forces on K6;
2. Guarding his KB pawn, when White can reply with Kt—B5, strengthening his attack on K6; and, finally,
3. An immediate liquidation which leads to the loss of a pawn.

27.	P—KB4	29. Kt—B5	R×P
28. Q×Q	Kt×Q	30. R×P	Kt—Q4
	31. Kt×P		

and White has a considerable advantage.

When the isolated pawn is, in addition, a doubled pawn, the weakness is even more serious, and this holds good also in the case of a backward doubled pawn (in *No. 115*, in QKt2 and Kt3 we have a doubled backward pawn). Not only can the backward doubled pawn expect no assistance from neighbouring pawns, but it stands in the way of such pieces as have the task of providing for its safety. The rules given for the handling of a single isolated or backward pawn apply in an even greater measure to a doubled pawn.

The case of united doubled pawns (e.g. KB2, KKt2 and KKt3) is different, and, although they also can, in certain circumstances, constitute a weakness, their treatment is entirely different and is outside the scope of this chapter.

Let us conclude with a recapitulation in which the *assessment* of the various forms of pawn weaknesses falls under two heads.

A. Isolated and Backward Pawns

Assessment: These are weaker when they stand on an *open file* and cannot *advance*. Moreover, the weakness gradually and proportionately increases when there are more than one of these pawns.

B. Hanging Pawns

Assessment: These are weak only (*1*) if the attacker is ahead in development, and (*2*) if most of the minor pieces have been exchanged. They are nearly always weak in an end-game.

Plan (valid for both *A* and *B*): Attack on the pawn itself (typical forms of attack: doubling Rooks, advance of a pawn on an adjacent file, see *Nos. 105* and *106*), and on the *square in front of the pawn*, namely the *blockading square*. A piece which occupies this square can, as a rule, develop great activity (see Chapter VIII). Avoid an exchange on this square if the recapturing unit is a pawn, lest the weakness become sealed. *Keep harrying* the pieces which *protect* the weak pawn. Exchanging pieces is usually to the attacker's advantage. If the direct assault is not likely to succeed, make use of the attacker's better opportunities for the quicker transfer of his forces; this is the more important and effective when there are several weak points in the opponent's formation.

The *defender* must above all be armed against the psychological effect which the sustained pressure of the attack is likely to engender.

One more technical hint: the simultaneous guard on several points by one and the same unit can here constitute an economical use of available forces.

CHAPTER VIII

'STRONG SQUARES'

THE characteristic feature, 'strong squares,' which we now propose, to discuss, is in no way less important than what has gone before. It differs, however, in that it appeals less to the imagination, seems of less general application, and mostly occurs in combination with one or other of the themes which we have described in previous chapters. It follows that gains in material or other advantages could easily be ascribed to accidental circumstances, and it will be appropriate to illustrate the subject of this chapter by an example from practical play, in which the reader will be left without any doubt that 'strong squares' alone have been the deciding factor (*No. 120*).

120

In this position we say that White's K4 is a *strong square*. On it he has established a Knight. In the preceding chapter we have already discussed 'strong squares.' To amplify what we said then, a 'strong square' as we understand it must fulfil the following requirements:

1. The square must be safe from attack by hostile pawns.

2. It must be near the enemy position.

3. It must be possible to bring to bear sufficient force on the square in question, so as to lead sooner or later to its effective occupation.

Chess is not a matter of mathematics: it may well be that a square satisfies all three stipulations given above, and yet does not have any real significance, or that it conforms to two of these requirements and fails in the third and yet still is effective. These varying circumstances make it extraordinarily difficult to assess the value of any particular strong square, and we shall let the matter rest at this point and try to obtain from a practical example a satisfactory understanding of the nature of a strong square and its consequences.

White, as we have said, has occupied the strong square K4 with a Knight which commands a number of important squares in the hostile position, namely QB5, Q6, KB6 and KKt5. This is an important point, but more important still is the fact that the Knight cannot be driven from its post. It stands out of the reach of enemy pieces. The black Bishop cannot attack the Knight, nor can the black Knight force an exchange. It can be compared with a gun well posted on a hill, and on which the enemy cannot fire without himself running grave risks.

The position can now be *assessed* clearly: White has an important advantage in his strongly posted Knight. And now the *plan*: in this position the importance of the strong square comes into its own. It is easy to formulate a plan when the elements on which the plan is to be based are of a secure and lasting nature. For at least five moves the Knight will remain at K4, and thus, in formulating a plan, the time factor will not be of the same urgency as in other cases.

Let facts now speak for themselves and, after following the course of the game, we shall have a clear understanding of the type of plan required in such positions.

1. P—QB4

Guarding the passed pawn and blockading the black QB pawn, so that in a possible counter-attack Black cannot play .... P—B5.

1. ....   QR—KB1   2. B—K3

Aimed at Black's QB pawn.

2. ....   P—KR3   3. R—Kt5

Following up the attack on the QB pawn.

3. ....   R—B1   4. Q—Kt4

Threatening both 5. Q×R and 5. B×RP.

4. ....   KR—B1

The alternative 4. .... R—KB2 is fatal, because of 5. R×Kt, etc. The Queen has to guard the Bishop, and therefore has no moves.

5. B×RP   Kt×BP

Black can hold out a little longer; the Queen guards the KKt pawn and the Knight guards the Bishop.

6. R—B1

A typical and instructive example of overloading. As soon as the Knight gives way, the Queen immediately assumes two functions, which she is unable to fulfil at one and the same time: defending the Bishop, and preventing the mate at KKt2. Thus, after 6. .... Kt—Kt3, there follows Kt×B, etc.

6. ....   P—R3   7. R—Kt3

QR—Kt1 also wins, but the text-move is quicker.

| 7. . . . . | P—QKt4 | 8. R—Kt3 | R—QB2 |

9. B×P

and wins. (9. . . . . Q×B; 10. Q—K6 ch.)

A nice example of an attack, but what has it all to do with the strong Knight at K4? The question is not so difficult to answer. In the first place, the control by the Knight of KB6 and KKt5 has made the defence uncommonly difficult; in the second, by attacking the Bishop at Q6 it has seriously curtailed the black Queen's mobility; thirdly, the Knight, by helping in the threat to Black's QB pawn, has tied several black pieces to its defence, and finally the Knight at K4, by guarding White's KB pawn, has prevented any counter-action by Black along the KB file.

It is not a case of inordinately praising the strong square on all possible or impossible grounds, but of assessing objectively its actual performance, which indeed, for a Knight, though it remains passive on its strong square, must not be underestimated.

In examining the course of the game from this point of view, the logic of White's sequence of moves becomes apparent; it is clear on the other hand that Black had no great choice of ideas, and that compulsory marching and counter-marching (. . . . QR—KB1—B1 and . . . . R (KB4)—B1) have cost him invaluable time.

Now as to the *plan*. How can White take advantage of his Knight's strong position? The answer is to start some manœuvre in which the strong piece is the king-pin, and one or two subsidiary actions in which, as a consequence, the attacker has greater freedom of action than the defender, and therefore a greater variety of lines of play from which to choose.

In this example White first of all pursued the scheme by which the QB pawn was attacked by three pieces (the Rook at QKt5, Bishop at K3, and Knight at K4), and subsequently a mating attack was launched (with Q—Kt4, B—KR6, and R—QKt5—QKt3—KKt3). In all these manœuvres the Knight at K4 played an indirect but yet vital part. Were it not for this Knight the defender would have had access to his KB3 and the Queen would not have been tied to the defence of his Bishop at Q3, etc. It is remarkable how the interchange of manœuvres by the Bishop at K3 and the Rook at QKt5 is effected with the gain of *tempi*, while the defender is unable to regroup his forces, and yet the Knight at K4 has no need to take any part in these evolutions but remains steadfast at K4, with effective threats to both wings. Black's defence has failed; he should at least have tried to bring his own Knight to Q3 by . . . . Kt (Kt3)—B1; . . . . B—K2; and . . . . Kt—Q3, to challenge the opposing Knight on the strong square, but it would have taken too much time.

To revert to our initial diagram (*No. 120*, p. 119), in which the three requirements for a strong square are fulfilled: (1) the white square is out of reach of hostile pawns and safe from attack by enemy pieces; (2) the square is close to the opponent's lines; and (3) White has firm control of the said square. This control is based on a number of factors, as for instance the absence of the black Q Bishop commanding white squares, and above all the closing of the K file by Black's pawn at his K4. This pawn is the cause of it all! Without it Black might perhaps succeed in driving off the white Knight—at any rate the Knight would not be nearly so secure, and White would have the task of defending it directly as well as indirectly. But the black K pawn is very much there and White's K4 is thereby a strong square and consequently a weak square for Black. In general it can be assumed that the square in front of an isolated pawn is or can become a strong square for the opposing side (see Chapter VII), but that is only one of many forms of a strong square. If, for example, the unit at Black's Q3 is not a Bishop, but a pawn, so that the K pawn is no longer isolated, even then White's K4 would still remain a strong square. In fact, the 'strong square' is found in all kinds of pawn formations. A glance at the various diagrams in this chapter will show how many variations there are of the same theme.

Strong square—weak square. Are these conceptions reciprocal—does strong for one side mean weak for the opponent? One may well consider it so, but in chess language a difference is made between the two. If we speak of a weak square, we usually refer to a square which may at some future time become a strong square for the opponent; if, on the contrary, we speak of a strong square, then it is generally an accomplished fact, a strong square in being at the time.

Of the three requirements mentioned above, much more could be said, but instead of theorising, let us rather find out about these things with the help of further examples. We would only emphasise the fact that a strong square in itself signifies nothing unless a suitable piece is available for its occupation, which means that effective action will depend on the piece in question.

We shall now give the moves leading to our next example, which will afford us an excellent illustration of the manner in which the *strong square* originates.

BOTVINNIK—BOLESLAVSKY, *Moscow*, 1941

After 1. P—K4, P—K3; 2. P—Q4, P—Q4; 3. Kt—Q2, P—QB4; 4. KP×P, KP×P; 5. B—Kt5 ch, Kt—B3; 6. KKt—B3, B—Q3; 7. Castles, Kt—K2; 8. P×P, B×P; 9. Kt—Kt3, B—Kt3; 10. B—K3, B×B; 11. B×Kt ch, P×B; 12. P×B, Castles (*No. 121*).

Botvinnik considers that the position, for the present, is in favour of White, on account of various theoretical considerations. The situation, and especially the sequence of moves which have brought it about, is truly remarkable. His Q Bishop's singular manœuvre (10. B—K3), which without any ostensible necessity saddles him with an isolated pawn, and particularly the deeply thought-out exchange on his 11th move, bear witness to an outstanding insight into the potentialities of the position.

121

White has the possibility of obtaining two strong squares at Q4 and QB5, as the next diagram (after 19. P—QKt4) clearly demonstrates. A cursory examination indicates that Black can no longer defend his QB4 by direct means: only the Queen can get there, for the black Knight at K2 is four moves away, while the Bishop is of the wrong colour. Against this, White's Queen and his Knight at QKt3 are at hand.

Thus White's QB5 will fall into his hands with absolute certainty, and the command of his Q4 will follow of its own accord. White's control of both squares will form an harmonious whole. Should Black, however, succeed in obtaining command of the square in question, he would be able, at the right moment, to play .... P—QB4, and to challenge White's Q4 as well.

13. Q—Q2   Q—Kt3   14. Q—B3

It is clear that both players aim at the critical square.

14. ....   R—Kt1

Indirectly defending his QB4, as now its immediate occupation by White would lose him the QKt pawn.

15. QR—Kt1

Indirectly attacking QB5! Later on it will be seen that the move not only guards White's QKtP, but, above all, prepares for its advance to Kt4.

15. ....   R—K1

His QB4 cannot now be defended, and so he turns his attention to White's weak K pawn.

16. KR—K1

In the spirit of Nimzowitsch's theory of prevention. The weak K pawn is to be guarded in anticipation. Botvinnik himself criticises this move, by which he places a good half of his advantage in jeopardy. Logical is 16. Kt—B5, Kt—B4; 17. KR—K1.

16. ....   Kt—Kt3

The difference is that now this Knight seeks a better post than KB4. Black intends to occupy his K4 as some compensation for the loss of his QB4 and Q5. Clearly, K4 is a strong square for Black.

17. Kt—B5

The first and more difficult fortress is carried; the second will fall at once. In the meantime 16. R—K1 is clearly shown to have been a wasted move.

17. ....   B—Kt5

In keeping with Black's counter-plan, the command of his K4.

18. Kt—Q4   Kt—K4   19. P—Kt4 (*No. 122*)

122   *123*

White has achieved his strategical objective: both his Knights occupy dominating positions. The question now is, how White can follow up his advantage, while taking well into account the trump card which Black holds in the favourable position of his own Knight. Meanwhile the position of the respective Knights has a static rather than a dynamic value; Black's Knight commands a number of important squares, but it has no dangerous leap at its disposal. The white Knights on the other hand are similarly situated: they are both beautifully posted, but have little chance of any effective sally and no opportunities of co-operating with the other pieces. All this will come later—a psychological advantage conferred by the possession of strong squares: there is plenty of time.

19. ....   QR—Q1   20. P—K4

White seizes the opportunity of getting rid of his weak K pawn,

simultaneously opening the K file, thereby threatening to dislodge
Black's strong Knight. Black has some compensation in the opening
of the Q file and a possibility of weakening White's Q4.

20. ....   P×P

The text-move illustrates one of those unobtrusive faults which frequently occur even among very strong players: capturing instead of
letting the opponent capture. It is clear that effecting the capture
yourself always costs one if not two *tempi*, which, among other things,
means in the present instance that White will be the first to double
Rooks on an open file.

Why then does Black decide on this capture? Is it on grounds of
economy of thought, or love of a quiet life, because he reduces the
number of possible continuations? After the stronger 20. .... P—B3;
White still need not play 21. P×P. He can defer this capture at will
while Black, in calculating the following moves, must reckon with this
pending pawn exchange which may occur at any moment.

21. R×P   P—QR4   22. P—QR3   P×P
                23. P×P

The little by-play on the QR and QKt files is not as guileless as it
may appear. Analysts at the end of the game pointed out that White
could have played for the gain of a piece by 22. Q—KKt3, (instead of
23. P—QR3). But Botvinnik refutes this claim as follows:

22. Q—Kt3, P—B3; 23. R×B, Kt×R; 24. Q×Kt, P—R4; 25. Q—
B4, P×P; 26. Kt (Q4)—Kt3, Q—Kt4; and states that the chances are
approximately equal.

But these complications lie outside the scope of our subject, and
we must not divert our attention to these, important though they
may be.

23. ....   P—B3

Safeguarding his K4.

24. QR—K1 (*No. 123*)

Pinning the Knight (Black's K Rook being insufficiently guarded);
and White will eventually succeed in attacking the Knight with one
of his own.

This position is important, because now the strategical decision has
to be made. It is apparent that, since the two white Knights are so
much more effective than the one black one, a win for White must
follow as a matter of course.

White has a choice of a number of continuations, of which the
following three are the most important:

1. Attack on K6.

2. Attack on the pinned Knight (as long as Black's K Rook is guarded only once).

3. Threat to Black's QB pawn.

None of these possibilities offers at the moment any tangible prospects, because both white Knights are half-pinned by Black's Queen, a consequence of White's 20th move (P—K4). The King therefore must use up a *tempo* in order to make the Knights mobile again, after which the threats enumerated above become actual. Thus Black has one *tempo* at his disposal, and if he makes good use of it, he will avoid considerable trouble.

It is curious to note that in this position Black has one manœuvre which minimises all three possibilities at one stroke, namely: 24. ....
B—R4, followed by 25. .... B—B2. In any event, now that the K Rook is safe and guarded his K3 is more strongly held, and the QB pawn indirectly protected as the Knight is free to move.

The point is therefore that Black can neglect his K3 for just one *tempo* because White cannot move a Knight as long as the white King is still at KKt1. Moreover, the Bishop is safer at KB2 than at KKt5, where it is exposed to attack, and the protection of Black's K3 is accordingly more secure.

24. ....   K—R1

Black did not see it.

25. K—R1

But White saw it clearly! A striking demonstration of the saying, 'When two do the same thing, it is not the same.' And now, suddenly, Black is without defence against the various threats, first and foremost 26. Kt—Q3, against both the black Knight and QB pawn.

A few possibilities after 25. K—R1:

1. 25. .... R—Q4; 26. R × B, etc.

2. 25. .... B—R4 (too late); 26. Kt (Q4)—K6, R—QKt1; 27. R × Kt, P × R; 28. Q × P, threatening mate at Kt7.

3. 25. .... B—B1; 26. Kt—R4, Q—R3 (or other Q moves); 27. Q × P, and White has won a valuable pawn.

4. 25. .... B—Q2; 26. Kt × B.

5. 25. .... R—QB1; 26. Kt—Q3, winning a pawn (26. .... Q—Kt1; 27. Kt × Kt, P × Kt; 28. R × B, P × Kt; 29. R × QP, etc.).

6. 25. .... P—R3 (relatively best); 26. P—R3, B—B1; 27. Kt—Q3, B—Kt2; 28. Kt—B3, with advantage to White.

| 25. .... | B—Q2 | 27. Q × P | Q—Q1 |
| 26. Kt × B | R × Kt | 28. Kt—B3 | |

White is a pawn ahead, though it took him a small matter of forty moves or so to win. This game demonstrates once again the value of strong squares, and in particular the power of a Knight posted on such a square.

The *assessment of this position* is more difficult than in the case of the first example, inasmuch as Black also has a strong square on which he too has posted a Knight—but, on purely arithmetical grounds, we come to the same conclusion: two strong Knights are better than one.

White's *plan* was to undermine Black's strong square at his K4, and then to exploit his own strong points by attacking and overrunning K6.

While in an end-game the King too can come into his own on a strong square, in a middle-game position the piece of real importance is the Knight, which is easy to understand. More powerful pieces, the Queen and the Rooks, are normally too valuable to fight in the front line. When a 'strong' Queen is posted at K5, she may be out of reach of the pawns—the main characteristic of the strong square—but not secure from molestation by Rooks, Knights or Bishops.

This argument does not hold good in the case of, say, a strongly posted Knight, which would have to give way only to an attack by a pawn. A threat from a Bishop or Knight may be disagreeable, but the worst that can happen is an exchange, possibly with the loss of a strong post, or else, retirement of the strong piece.

On the strength of these considerations, the Bishop too would seem to be a suitable piece to occupy a strong square, but there is a consideration which tips the scale in favour of the Knight, although Bishop can frequently carry out the same task without reference to its distance from the objective. A Bishop at QKt2 is just as effective in an attack on KKt7,

124

as when it is posted at K5. But, close to the enemy lines, a Knight is more suitable, being a short-range piece, though that is not to say that the Bishop cannot do good work from an advanced post, as is shown in the following example (*No. 124*) from the Russian Championship of 1949:

FURMAN—SMYSLOV, *Russian Championship*, 1949

Black's last move was 17. .... P—B4, which has the serious drawback of abandoning the control of his K3. But, threatened with the loss of a pawn at his QR4, Black decides on another venture, without accurately gauging its serious consequences.

18. B—Q7

White has recognised that K6 is for him a strong square, and that in this instance a Bishop is the most suitable piece for its occupation, in preference to the Knight which he could also establish there. The sequel clearly illustrates the activities of the Bishop from the strong square in question.

18. ....   Q—K4   19. B—B3

White first eliminates Black's K Bishop, whereby Black's King's field is weakened still further and correspondingly White's K6 gains in strength.

19. ....   Q×KP   20. B—K6 ch   K—R1
                      21. B×B ch   K×B

White has occupied the strong square with his Bishop, and it becomes clear why it is so difficult to drive off this piece. The black Knight is

125

miles away, and Black's Bishop is prevented from intervening (White's Bishop and Rook control his QB8), which would not be the case had the white Knight occupied K6.

22. Q—R3 (*No. 125*)

A particularly strong move, which clearly emphasises the power of the Bishop at K6. This Bishop's function is not so much to co-operate in the attack on any particular objective, as to deprive the opposing King of flight squares, so that there are direct mating threats. Incidentally, it prevents Black's Rook from occupying the QB file. Thus here also the strong piece acts in two directions, and his lines of action cannot be intercepted for the time being. The only pieces which come into consideration (the Knight at QR4 and Bishop at QKt2) are far away.

There now threatens 22. Q×P ch, K—R3; 23. Q×R ch, and as White checks with each move, Black never has the chance to play either 22. .... B×P or 22. .... Q×Kt.

22. ....   Q—KR5

Some alternative replies:

1. 22. .... K—B3; 23. Q—B3 ch, Q—K4; 24. Kt—Q4,
(*a*) 24. .... B×P; 25. P—B4, Q—K5; 26. Kt—B3 dis ch, K×B;
27. Kt—Kt5 ch, K—Q2; 28. Q—B7 ch, etc.;
(*b*) 24. .... P—B5; 25. R—K1, followed by 26. Kt—B3 dis ch.
2. 22. .... R—K1; 23. Q—Kt2 ch, K—R3; 24. R—B3, B×P; 25.

R—R3 ch, K—Kt4; 26. P—B4 ch, K—Kt5; 27. B×B, Q×B; 28. Q—B3, and wins.

23. R—B7   K—R1

If Black plays 23. .... R—K1 instead, 24. P—Q6 at once would be inferior because of 24. .... Q—K5. But after 24. P—Kt3, Q—B3; 25. Kt—B4; 26. P—Q6 is a decisive threat. The black pieces are practically stalemated, and can undertake little or nothing against the forthcoming attack.

24. R×P

This capture aggravates Black's position, in that the diagonal QR2—KKt7 cannot be left out of consideration for one moment under penalty of mate. The chief protagonist is always the strong Bishop.

24. ....   Q—B3   25. R—QB7

In order to interpose the Rook in case of a check on the first rank.

25. ....   B—R3   26. Kt—B4

The impeded position of Black's forces makes the final attack possible: the threat is 27. Kt×P ch, P×Kt (27. .... Q×Kt; 28. Q×R ch); 28. Q—R3 ch, followed by mate.

26. ....   Q—R8 ch   27. R—B1   Q—Kt2
28. R—B3

Renewing the threat 29. Kt×P ch, (29. .... Q×Kt; 30. Q×R ch, or 29. .... P×Kt; 30. R—R3 ch).

28. ....   R—Q1   29. Q—Kt2

Now that the threat from QR3 has ended the Queen transfers her activities to the long diagonal. White again threatens 30. Kt×P ch (30. .... Q×Kt; 31. R—B7 dis ch).

29. ....   Kt—B5

This loses a pawn, but is the only way of prolonging Black's resistance.

30. Kt×P ch   Q×Kt   32. Q×Q ch   K×Q
31. R×Kt dis ch   Q—Kt2   33. R—B7 ch

and White won, in the first place because of his extra pawn, but also through his strongly posted Bishop, despite the fact that it is not nearly so effective in the end-game as in support of an attack in the middle-game.

Judgment of the position in No. 125: White, although a pawn down, has the better game, as he can establish an unassailable Bishop at K6, which powerfully supports the attack on the black King.

The *plan*: attack, and again attack—above all, avoid the exchange of Queens, after which the strong Bishop would at most give White equality, being a pawn minus. Queen, Rook and Knight must support the action of the strong Bishop, which they do to the full—the black King is under constant threats of mate, with the immobile Bishop playing the chief part.

A strong square has a value in proportion to the importance of the squares which can be controlled therefrom, from which it follows that a strong square is usually more valuable on the King's side than on the opposite wing. It must be added that a strong square increases in value the closer it is to the enemy lines, which is why, in the last example, the Bishop at K6 developed such remarkable power.

In *No. 115* the strong Knight at Q4 put the opposing Bishop in the shade. In *No. 111* the strong white Queen ruled equally in all directions. Finally, there is the example *No. 117*, where the King occupies a strong square from which it dominates the field in various directions.

We have already stated that, in the end-game, the strong square can provide an exceptionally favourable location for the King. As one of the conditions governing strong squares is that they should be inaccessible to the opposing forces, the King frequently finds on them a secure and, at the same time, an active post.

This is well illustrated in the following example:

TARRASCH—TEICHMANN, *San Sebastian*, 1912

After 1. P—K4, P—K3; 2. P—Q4, P—Q4; 3. Kt—QB3, Kt—KB3; 4. B—Kt5, B—K2; 5. P—K5, KKt—Q2; 6. B×B, Q×B; 7. Q—Q2,

126

Castles; 8. P—B4, P—QB4; 9. Kt—B3, Kt—QB3; 10. P—KKt3, P—QR3; 11. B—Kt2, P—QKt4; 12. Castles KR, P× P; 13. Kt×QP, Kt×Kt; 14. Q×Kt, Q— B4; 15. Q×Q, Kt×Q (*No. 126*).

Bilguer's *Handbuch* pronounces the position to be in favour of White, with which pronouncement the reader must agree—White has a permanently strong square at Q4—though he may have some doubt as to its decisive effect. Q4 fulfils all the requirements one may expect of a strong square, but Black's position is to all appearances so sound that one may well doubt the possibility of exploiting the advantage normally derived from such a square.

Let the play speak for itself. There followed:

16. Kt—K2
On the way to Q4!

16. ....   B—Q2   17. Kt—Q4   QR—B1
Black has the only open file, and naturally endeavours to take advantage of the fact. Note that the strong Knight at Q4 guards the invaluable
pawn at QB2. It is fairly obvious that White will, at some time, advance
this pawn to QB3, but the remarkable thing is that it will be less secure
at B3 than B2, because Black can, at the right moment, play .... P—
QKt5. Moreover, White has the move P—QKt3 in reserve, which
move is more commendable with the QB pawn still on its original
square.

18. K—B2
A particularly fine move, which, with exact calculation, will relieve
the watch on Q4. The white King will occupy a temporary post at
K3, and as soon as it is safe to do so, and at the right moment, will
take over the occupation of Q4.

18. ....   R—B2   19. K—K3   R—K1
Black fears the advance P—KB5, and anticipates this manœuvre by
aiming at White's K5 with this Rook. Meanwhile, White pursues a
different plan.

20. R—B2
The object of this move is to allow the Bishop to reach Q3 *via* B1.

20. ....   Kt—Kt2   21. B—B1   Kt—R4
                          22. P—Kt3
To allow Black's .... Kt—B5 would spoil the whole of White's
scheme. The exchange by B×Kt would be practically forced, and
after .... QP×B the occupation of Q4 by the white King would
become problematical (see note to the 17th move by Black).

22. ....   P—R3
A serious positional mistake, which White refutes in striking fashion.
We have seen in Chapter V how much easier a King's side attack can
be, when the opposing King's field pawns no longer stand on their
original squares. Even when the Queens are no longer on the board
and there is practically no question of a mating attack, it can become
of great importance for the attacker to be able, in addition to his
pressure in the centre, to open a second front by clearing a file on the
K side. And the text-move provides just such an opportunity.

23. B—Q3   Kt—B3

Black eliminates the strong Knight, but an even stronger piece takes its place.

24. Kt×Kt   B×Kt   25. K—Q4 (*No. 127*)

Arrival of his Majesty. Note with what foresight White has taken the necessary measures: the Bishop at Q3 is guarding the QB pawn

now that the Knight has disappeared, and the pawn at QKt3 also has its uses: by controlling QB4 it secures the King in his commanding position against any danger of being dislodged.

25. ....   B—Q2
26. P—KKt4

On the way to opening a second front. For the time being the position of the white King is concerned only indirectly in this manœuvre, since—

127

1. Black's Q Rook is tied to the QB file, as otherwise the King would march in; and

2. Black must avoid any considerable liquidation, as the ideal position of White's King would inevitably lead to a won end-game.

26. ....   B—B1   27. P—KR4

There is now an immediate threat of 28. P—Kt5, P—KR4; 29. P—Kt6, and Black would lose his isolated KR pawn.

27. ....   P—Kt3

The typical pawn formation for defence against a pawn-storm. The idea is to keep the position closed by playing .... P—KR4 in answer to P—Kt5, or .... P—Kt4 against P—R5. In the present position this method is less effective because White has a pawn at KB4 and could answer .... P—Kt4 by an exchange at his Kt5.

28. R—R1

Against 28. P—R5, Black would play 28. .... K—Kt2. He therefore postpones this thrust.

28. ....   K—Kt2   30. R (B2)—R2 B—Q2
29. P—R5   R—R1   31. P—Kt5

Opening the KR file by force, and the win is practically an accomplished fact.

31. ....   RP×P   32. BP×P   P×P

Black has no waiting moves available: 32. .... B—K1 is answered by 33. P×P, R×R; 34. P×P, and if, instead, 32. .... R—KR2, the Rook is locked in by 33. P—R6 ch. Relatively best would be 32. .... R (B2)—B1;

| 33. R×P | R×R | 35. R—R8 ch | K—K2 |
| 34. R×R | K—B1 | 36. P—Kt6 | |

Quicker is 36. R—R8, B—B1; 37. P—R4, P×P; 38. P×P, R—B3; 39. R—R7 ch, K—K1; 40. P—R5, and Black has practically no moves.

36.	P×P;	39. B—Q3	R—B6
37. B×KKtP	P—Kt5	40. P—R3	P—R4
38. R—R7 ch	K—Q1	41. R—R8 ch	K—K2

42. R—R8. Black resigns.

A notable ending, which enables us to draw some additional conclusions:

Our *assessment* of the position must lead from the position in *No. 126* to that in *No. 127*. In the first case, the white Knight has full control of Q4, in the second the King has taken over these duties, and it is to be noted that the King here is quite safe from checks and cannot therefore be driven from his dominating post.

The *plan* is twofold.

(*a*) The occupation of Q4, free from all risks, first by a Knight, then by the King (notable moves 18. K—B2, 20. R—B2, and 22. P—QKt3).

(*b*) The opening of a second front, exploiting White's advantage in space on the K side.

To this end it is necessary to advance the pawns on that wing in order to open a file, which in turn creates the conditions in which simplification enables the strong King to take an effective part in the proceedings. (The execution of this plan was made considerably easier by 22. .... P—KR3. But for this weakening move White would have had to make preparations for its realisation by the further advance of his KB pawn.)

However, we must not take the term 'strong square' in too narrow a sense, even when the three essential conditions which were enumerated at the beginning of this chapter are satisfied, and we must in particular examine its inaccessibility to hostile pawns. There are degrees of this such as merely 'difficult of access' or 'accessible only in special and difficult circumstances.'

Here is a simple example which illustrates an oft-recurring situation:
1. P—K4, P—K4; 2. Kt—KB3, Kt—QB3; 3. B—Kt5, P—QR3; **4.**

B—R4, Kt—B3; 5. Castles, B—K2; 6. R—K1, P—QKt4; 7. B—Kt3, P—Q3; 8. P—B3, Castles; 9. P—KR3, Kt—QR4; 10. B—B2, P—B4; 11. P—Q4, Q—B2. An old acquaintance, the close defence in the Ruy Lopez.

12. P×KP   P×P
The exchange variation.

13. Q—K2   B—K3   14. B—Kt5
An inferior move, as will soon appear.

14. ....   Kt—R4   15. B×B   Kt—KB5
16. Q—K3
Not 16. Q—B1, which would lose still more material after 16. ....
B—B5.

16. ....   Q×B   17. P—QKt3 (*No. 128*)
To prevent 17. .... Kt—B5. If 17. Kt×P, the reply is 17. ....
Q—Kt4; 18. Kt—Kt4, B×Kt; 19. P×B, Q×P, with advantage to Black.

128   *129*

Let us examine the black Knight's position at KB5. The square is not a strong one in the literal sense of the word, as the Knight is exposed to attack by P—KKt3. On the other hand, this move is not immediately available because of the reply .... Kt×P ch. It will take much time and thought to make P—KKt3 possible, and we can term Black's KB5, to all intents and purposes, a strong square.

How has this come about? Originally because White played P—KR3, and then through the exchange of the black-squared Bishop (14. B—KKt5 and 15. B×B). It is important to view the position in this manner; in King's pawn openings, the normal pawn formation is pawns at K4, KB2, KKt2 and KR2 on either side. Here P—KR3 does not create a weakness at KB4, but it does imply a liability which in **certain** circumstances can lead to trouble; and here the presence at QB1 of the Q Bishop can play an important part. Let us add that the square at White's Q5 virtually represents a weakness in Black's position, which however is of little importance, since White for some time will not be able to bring his pieces to bear on that point.

We give a few more moves in this game:

    17. ....   Q—B3

Threatens, *inter alia*, 18. .... B×RP; 19. P×B, Q—Kt3 ch, etc.

    18. K—R2   QR—Q1

The reply to 18. .... Q—Kt3 is 19. Kt—R4, Q—Kt4; 20. Q—Kt3.

    19. QKt—Q2

19. Q×P can be answered by 19. .... Kt×RP; 20. Q×KP, Q—R3.

    19. ....   Q—R3

Threatens 20. .... B×RP, etc.

    20. Kt—KKt1 Q—Kt4   21. P—Kt3   Kt×RP

and Black has won a valuable pawn. (22. Kt×Kt, Q×Q; 23. R×Q, R×Kt.)

Black's KB5 has, in this example, functioned as a strong square, and has had the lion's share in the K side attack.

Now let us sum up this illustration in the usual way:

Judging the position in *No. 128:* Black has by far the better game because the Knight at KB5 cannot for the time being be driven off, and must therefore be considered a 'strong' Knight.

The *plan*: Black must as speedily as possible take advantage of the Knight's position at KB5 by a general action against White's King's field. Above all, he must not wait until White has consolidated his position by K—R2, Kt—Kt1 and P—Kt3, for then Black's KB5 is no longer a strong square.

Here is another illustration, in which the conception of a 'strong square' is on an even wider scale.

MILNER-BARRY—ZNOSKO-BOROVSKY, *Tenby*, 1928

1. P—K4, P—QB3; 2. P—Q4, P—Q4; 3. P×P, P×P; 4. B—Q3, Kt—QB3; 5. P—QB3, Kt—B3; 6. B—KB4, B—Kt5; 7. Kt—B3, P—K3; 8. Q—Kt3, Q—B1; 9. QKt—Q2, B—K2; 10. Castles KR, Castles; 11. P—KR3, B—R4; 12. QR—K1, B—Kt3; 13. B×B, RP×B; 14. Kt—K5 (*No. 129*).

The theory concludes here with the words 'White stands better.' There are indeed various factors in favour of White: chief among them is that he has the control of K5. Yet K5 is not properly speaking a strong square, since Black's KB pawn can at any time recover the control of White's K5. However, driving the Knight from his post at K5 by means of .... P—B3 implies a weakening of the pawn at K3, and the remedy could well prove the worse evil. *No. 129* illustrates the characteristics of a whole group of positions, in which a half-open file plays a dominant part. (See Chapter IX, in which the furthest square is occupied by a minor piece in order to extend the pressure on the hostile position.)

White commands the half-open K file and Black the half-open QB file. Black should, in order to take advantage of this circumstance, place a Knight on his QB5. But this square is covered by two white Knights, and furthermore, even should Black succeed in bringing a Knight to his QB5, it would not be an equivalent for White's occupation of his own K5, as this square is more central and is also in closer proximity to Black's King's field. There followed:

14. ....   Kt—Q2
Aimed at White's K5, but the drawback is that the text-move weakens Black's K side.

15. QKt—B3
Strengthening his K5.

15. ....   QKt×Kt   16. Kt×Kt
Capturing with the pawn would be against his strategical intentions.

16. ....   Kt×Kt   17. B×Kt
White has maintained his superiority. It is true, a Bishop has taken the place of the Knight, but, as the sequel shows, this in no way weakens his prospects, for here the Bishop is at least as effective as the Knight.

17. ....   Q—B3
After 17. .... P—B3; 18. B—R2, Black's K pawn is doomed to speedy destruction.

18. R—K3
A well-known recipe: the remaining white pieces must support the action of the Bishop.

18. ....   P—QKt4
An attempt at counter-action on the Q side. It comes too late, and therefore brings no relief.

19. Q—Q1

Regrouping, always with the idea of making the best use of the Bishop's strong position at K5.

19. .... P—Kt5

Consistent, but some defensive move such as 19. .... B—Q3 is preferable.

20. P—KR4 (*No. 130*)

With the clear intention of eliminating the hostile KKt pawn, after which Black's K side lies bare to the concentrated assault of the white forces.

20. .... P×P

After this ill-considered exchange, nothing will avail against White's attack. There is no doubt that at this point 20. .... P—B3 is necessary.

130

21. R×P   Q—Kt3

Now 21. .... Q—K1 is preferable.

22. P—R5   P—Kt4

Or 22. .... P—B3; 23. P×P, P×B; 24. Q—R5, and mate in a few moves.

23. P—R6

The strongest possible support for the Bishop.

23. ....   P—B3

Too late! But other moves lose as well; 23. .... P—Kt3; 24. P—R7 ch, or 23. .... P×P; 24. Q—R5, or finally 23. .... B—B3; 24. P× P, K×P; 25. Q—R5, (24. .... B×P; 25. B×B, K×B; 26. Q—R5, P—B3; 27. KR—B1,R—B2; 28. R—KR3, and wins).

24. Q—R5   B—Q1

The point of White's combination is that after 24. .... P×B; 25. Q—Kt6, B—B3 the game is decided by the invasion of the Rooks by 26. KR—B1, and there is nothing to be done against 27. R—B7.

25. Q—Kt6   Q—Kt2   26. R—B7   Resigns

Even when threatened with extinction, the white Bishop helps in giving the enemy his death-blow.

Judging the position in *No. 129:* White has the better game because of his strong square at K5 and the greater freedom of movement of his forces on the K side.

The *plan*: Support of the activities of the piece posted at K5 (Bishop or Knight) by bringing the major pieces to the K side.

The success of this operation is made considerably easier by Black's doubled KKt pawn—a complementary illustration of a weakness in the King's field such as shown in Chapter V.

We conclude with some variations from openings much in favour to-day, in which the strong square plays the most important part:

Ruy Lopez (Close Defence)
(Compare last but one example, p. 133.)

1. P—K4	P—K4	9. P—KR3	Kt—QR4
2. Kt—KB3	Kt—QB3	10. B—B2	P—B4
3. B—Kt5	P—QR3	11. P—Q4	Q—B2
4. B—R4	Kt—B3	12. QKt—Q2	Kt—B3
5. Castles	B—K2	13. P×BP	P×P
6. R—K1	P—QKt4	14. Kt—B1	B—K3
7. B—Kt3	P—Q3	15. Kt—K3	QR—Q1
8. P—B3	Castles	16. Q—K2	

Q5 is a strong square, and it must, after careful preparation, sooner or later fall into White's hands, possibly even by combinative means such as the following:

16.	Kt—KR4	18. P×B	R×P
17. Kt—Q5	B×Kt	19. B×P ch	K×B
	20. Q—K4 ch		

etc.

Sicilian Defence (Boleslavsky Variation)

1. P—K4	P—QB4	4. Kt×P	Kt—B3
2. Kt—KB3	Kt—QB3	5. Kt—QB3	P—Q3
3. P—Q4	P×P	6. B—K2	P—K4

Against accepted principles, Black weakens his pawn at Q3 as well as his square at Q4, but, on the other hand, he has free play for his pieces, which moreover frequently provides him with the opportunity of forcing .... P—Q4; thus, at one stroke, eliminating the weak pawn and the weak square, e.g.:

7. Kt—Kt3	B—K2	10. P—QR4	Kt—QKt5
8. Castles	Castles	11. K—R1	B—K3
9. P—B4	P—QR4	12. P—B5	B×Kt
	13. P×B	P—Q4	

with a satisfactory game for Black. It, however, requires careful play. For instance, if after 7. Kt—B3 (instead of 7. Kt—Kt3) Black persists in playing 7. .... B—K2, the continuation is: 8. B—KKt5, Castles; 9. Q—Q2, B—K3; 10. R—Q1, Q—R4; 11. Castles, P—QR3; 12. B×Kt, B×B; 13. Kt—Q5, B×Kt; 14. Q×Q, Kt×Q; 15. R×B, winning the Q pawn.

In this and similar variations White must make it his business to prevent Black's .... P—Q4, which forces the exchange of pawns and eliminates the existing weaknesses.

French Defence (Tarrasch Variation)

1. P—K4	P—K3	7. B×B ch	Kt×B
2. P—Q4	P—Q4	8. P×P	Kt×P
3. Kt—Q2	P—QB4	9. Kt—Kt3	Q×Q ch
4. P×QP	KP×P	10. Kt×Q	Kt×Kt
5. B—Kt5 ch	B—Q2	11. RP×Kt	B—B4
6. Q—K2 ch	Q—K2	12. B—Q2	Kt—K2
	13. B—B3		

and White has control of the strong square at Q4.

King's Indian Defence (Russian Variation)

1. P—Q4	Kt—KB3	5. Kt—KB3	Castles
2. P—QB4	P—KKt3	6. Kt—B3	QKt—Q2
3. P—KKt3	B—Kt2	7. Castles	P—K4
4. B—Kt2	P—Q3	8. P—K4	

If 8. P—Q5, P—QR4 (preventing P—QKt4); after which Black has created a strong square for himself at QB4.

8.	P×P	10. P—KR3	Kt—B4
9. Kt×P	R—K1	11. R—K1	P—QR4

The last move strengthens the black Q Knight's position. But even without 11. .... P—QR4 this Knight can be classified as 'strong,' for 12. P—QKt4 has the disadvantage for White of opening up the long black diagonal for Black's K Bishop (it is occupied by pieces only after the QKt pawn has moved).

Nimzo-Indian (Sämisch Variation)

1. P—Q4	Kt—KB3	7. B—Q3	P—K4
2. P—QB4	P—K3	8. Kt—K2	P—QKt3
3. Kt—QB3	B—Kt5	9. Kt—Kt3	Kt—B3
4. P—K3	Castles	10. B—Kt2	B—R3
5. P—QR3	B×Kt ch	11. P—K4	Q—K1
6. P×B	P—Q3	12. Q—K2	Kt—QR4

Black's Q Knight is now posted on a strong square, and although it is on an outside file, it is quite effective, for the Knight there exerts pressure on White's QB4 (the immediate threat is .... Q—R5, winning the QB pawn). In addition the Knight can at the right moment play to QKt6.

After 13. P—QR4 (preventing .... Q—R5); Black forces the advance 14. P—Q5, by 13. .... Q—K3 and obtains yet another strong square at his QB4, which the same Knight can reach either *via* QKt2 or (at the moment with the gain of a *tempo*) *via* QKt6.

CHAPTER IX

OPEN FILES

WHEN outstanding players of to-day—among them Botvinnik and Reshevsky—after 1. P—Q4, P—Q4; 2. P—QB4, P—K3 quite frequently continue with 3. P×P, P×P, one must conclude that the conception of positional play has undergone a change in the last thirty years.

One important consideration is an argument against the exchange 3. P×P. The black Q Bishop's diagonal is laid open, and the development of this Bishop, the *leit-motif* of so many variations of the orthodox Queen's Gambit, is no longer a problem. Against this, it might be argued that White exchanges his QB pawn against a centre pawn so that he obtains a pawn majority in the centre (K pawn and Q pawn against Black's lone Q pawn), but it must not be overlooked that the centre in its wider conception includes the QB and KB pawns, and we must conclude that, both before and after the exchange, the respective centres are approximately equal. If

131

then the permutations in the centre provide no compensation for White's action by helping to solve Black's main problem, the development of his Q Bishop, what is the answer to the puzzle? It lies in the QB file which has been opened by the unexpected exchange of the QB pawn.

White has the open QB file, but Black has the K file. Which of the two is the more important? We naturally assume that the QB file takes pride of place, or why should Botvinnik adopt this exchange variation? But we shall not perceive this clearly until we have seen the continuation of the play from the position in *No. 131* up to the point where the open files begin to play their part. From a profusion of available material, we have selected a game in which this feature is illustrated particularly clearly so that, after considerable simplification on either side, other characteristics lose their importance or disappear altogether.

If we ignore some few transpositions of moves, the game went as follows:

FLOHR—EUWE, *1st Match Game, Amsterdam*, 1932

1. P—Q4, P—Q4; 2. P—QB4, P—K3; 3. P×P, P×P; 4. Kt—QB3, Kt—KB3; 5. B—Kt5, B—K2; 6. P—K3, P—B3; 7. B—Q3, QKt—Q2; 8. Kt—B3, Castles; 9. Q—B2, R—K1; 10. Castles KR, Kt—B1; 11. Kt—K5, Kt—Kt5; 12. B×B, Q×B; 13. Kt×Kt, B×Kt; 14. KR—K1, QR—Q1; 15. Kt—K2, R—Q3; 16. Kt—Kt3, R—R3; 17. B—B5, Q—Kt4; 18. B×B, Q×B; 19. P—KR3, Q—Q2 (*No. 132*).

132   *133*

In the main the pawn formation here is similar to that in *No. 131*. White has the open QB file and Black the K file. To be accurate, however, as the QB file is interrupted by Black's QB pawn and the K file by White's K pawn, both these files must be described as half-open. Such half-open files carry special possibilities, which will be clearly demonstrated by the further course of the game.

20. P—Kt4

In order to follow up later on with P—Kt5, which in any event will cause a weakening of Black's right flank. This pawn-thrust is characteristically called a 'minority attack.' (Two pawns against three.)

20. ....   Kt—K3   21. QR—Kt1   Kt—B2
                  22. P—QR4   P—R3

What the opponents are playing for is quite clear. White wishes to advance P—Kt5, and Black aims at its prevention. For the present the chances are approximately equal. But such a state of equilibrium must favour the attacker, who can at will direct his forces on to some other objective, when the defender's pieces are more or less tied up.

23. Kt—B1

White transfers his Knight to the other wing, which transfer he combines with sundry threats to the valuable black Rooks.

23. ....   R—K2   24. Kt—R2
Threatening 25. Kt—Kt4—K5.

24. ....   R (R3)—K3
In order to be able to play .... P—B3 without separating the Rooks.

25. Kt—B3   P—B3   27. Kt—Kt3   R (K3)—K2
26. Kt—Q2   R—K1   28. Kt—B5   Q—B1
The white Knight has reached its destination, but cannot at present
achieve much.

29. KR—QB1   R—Q1   30. Kt—Q3   Q—Kt1
                 31. Kt—B4   Kt—K3
This means that Black gives up the fight for his QKt4. This is not
compulsory, but, taking into account that, in the mutual process of
alternation, White has improved his position, it is hardly surprising
that Black is not anxious to persevere in this course.

32. Kt×Kt   R×Kt   33. P—Kt5   RP×P
                 34. P×P (*No. 133*)
The key position in every attack on a half-open line.
Now all Black can do is to choose between (*a*) 34. .... P×P,
remaining with two weak pawns at QKt2 and Q4, or (*b*) leaving things
as they are, which burdens him with one weak pawn only at QB3.

34. ....   P×P
He decides on two weak pawns, which may conceivably bring some
compensation, but certainly not in this position. With 34. .... Q—
Q3; 35. P×P, P×P, on the whole Black has, with equal material,
fair chances of a draw.

35. R×P   P—QKt3
With 35. .... R—B3; 36. Q×R, P×Q; 37. R×Q, Black simply
throws away a pawn.

36. Q—Kt3
Everything is now forced. Both isolated pawns are under pressure
and one or the other must soon fall.

36. ....   Q—Q3
Or 36. .... Q—Kt2; 37. R (B1)—B5, R (Q1)—Q3; 38. P—K4,
K—B1; 39. P—K5, and the black Rooks must give up the protection
of one or other of the pawns.

37. R—Kt1
Black's pawn at QKt3 must fall.

This simple example clearly demonstrates the principles of half-open file strategy. After prolonged but by no means complicated manœuvring, White enforced the thrust P—QKt4—Kt5, and thereby forcibly created in the black camp such weaknesses that the loss of a pawn could not be avoided.

Perhaps the reader will ask why Black did not for his part make use of his own half-open file in a similar way, by the advance .... P—KB4—B5. The answer is that the position generally is not favourable for this manœuvre. It frequently costs a great deal of trouble to force the KB pawn forward to B4, and when it has thus advanced, it may be necessary, a consequence of the strategy of the half-open file, to play .... P—KKt4 as well, with all the ensuing hazards and with a weakening of Black's K side.

The minority attack is usually more effective on the Queen's side than on the other wing, so that even when Black's advance .... P—KB4—B5 can be carried out without much difficulty, White as well as Black must carefully consider all possibilities, such as the reader can see in the following example.

Let us first draw our conclusions from *No. 132* in the usual manner:

Assessment: White has the better chances because the half-open QB file is of greater importance than the half-open K file.

The *plan*: Advance on the Q side (P—QR4 and P—QKt4), with the white pieces posted on the QKt and QB files, for preference the Q Rook at QKt1, the K Rook at QB1, and the Queen at QB2. In addition, it is often of importance to occupy the furthest square on the QB file (here QB5) with a Knight (compare Chapter VII, *No. 119*).

This simple illustration may perhaps lead to the assumption that the half-open file is the characteristic feature *par excellence*, the key to the win in all circumstances. But the matter is not so simple, and this too can be seen in the example in question.

In the course of the game, from move 10 to move 20, we notice that White has to manœuvre with extreme accuracy to avoid the danger which threatens his King's side. These dangers occur through the advantage in space which Black is able to obtain and which makes possible such manœuvres as R (QR1)—Q1—Q3—KR3. This is further demonstrated in the following supplementary example, the Exchange Variation in the Queen's Gambit:

FLOHR—KERES, *Semmering,* 1937

(The first 13 moves as in the match game, Flohr-Euwe, p. 142.)

14. Kt—K2   Q—R5   15. Kt—Kt3 (*No. 134*)

Fine remarks here that the advance of White's Q side pawns is difficult to check. Let us examine what follows:

15. ....   QR—Q1   16. P—Kt4   R—Q3
                17. KR—K1   R—R3

The typical counter-attack.

18. Kt—B1   Kt—K3   19. P—Kt5

In view of Black's threatening position on the K side, White has not the time for quiet preparations for his own campaign.

19. ....   B—B6

A very dangerous and aggressive offer, which fails to be immediately successful only because of White's subtle defence.

20. P×B   Kt—Kt4
21. B—B5

To defend his KB3 would be ineffective either by 21. B—K2, because of 21. .... Kt—R6 ch, or by 21. Q—K2, because of 21. .... Q—R6, along with 22. .... Kt× P ch. The text-move, by guarding the square KR3, is intended to parry the mating threat 21. .... Kt×P ch; 22. K—Kt2, Q—R6 ch; 23. K—R1, Q×P mate.

134

21. ....   Kt×P ch   22. K—Kt2   Q—R4

After 22 .... Kt×RP; 23. Kt×Kt, Q×Kt ch; 24. K—B1, Black's attack has run its course. After the text-move Black threatens 23. .... Kt—R5 ch, winning back the piece, or else, more straightforwardly, 23. .... Q×B.

23. Kt—Kt3   Kt×R ch   24. R×Kt   Q×P ch
                25. K—B3

Black's attack is repulsed; the material on either side is approximately equal (Rook and two pawns for two minor pieces). Although this game ended in a draw, the course of the game shows clearly that Black's attack is not to be taken lightly, and, upon examination of *No. 134*, we arrive at the following conclusion: White has the better chances on the Q side, Black on the K side.

Assessment: It is, in the nature of things, impossible to decide which side has the pull. Let it suffice to say that White's action is more lasting and Black's more fierce.

White's plan: Attack on the Q side by means of the well-known advance P—QKt4—Kt5, together with a firm defensive hold on his right wing, and counteract Black's numerical superiority there by keeping his minor pieces close at hand.

Black's plan: Attack at all hazards on the K side. The defence of the Q side is just possible by bringing back the black pieces from the K side if the attack there has to be abandoned. Once White has played P—QKt5, Black must on no account capture the pawn. It is easier for Black to defend his QB3 from the flank than to defend his QKt2 or Q4.

Now another example. Here Black also takes advantage of his half-open file:

BOUWMEESTER—EUWE, *Amsterdam*, 1950

1. P—Q4, Kt—KB3; 2. P—QB4, P—K3; 3. Kt—QB3, P—Q4; 4. B—Kt5, QKt—Q2; 5. P×P, P×P; 6. P—K3, P—B3; 7. B—Q3, B—K2; 8. Q—B2, Kt—R4; 9. B×B, Q×B; 10. KKt—K2, P—KKt3; 11. Castles KR (*No. 135*).

135136

The situation here differs from that in preceding examples, because of the pawn at Black's KKt3, which makes a K side attack by Black still possible, but very much harder to carry out. Black sets out on another tack.

11. ....   P—KB4

The minority attack on the King's side.

12. QR—Kt1

White prepares for the usual action on the Q side. Note that 12. P—QR3 loses a *tempo* (in the game the pawn goes to QR4 in one move—see move 14). Furthermore, White has left out the thematic QR—QB1. As mentioned before, the right place for the Q Rook in this variation is QKt1.

12. ....   Castles   13. P—QKt4   P—QR3

Not with any idea of frustrating White's advance, nor yet to retard it, but rather to involve the Rook's pawns in the conflict and to make sure, by means of exchanges, that Black is not left with a weak QR pawn.

14. P—QR4   P—B5
The counter-stroke.

15. Kt×BP   Kt×Kt   16. P×Kt   R×P
               17. Kt—K2   R—B3
Black's action has achieved the following: (*1*) the KB file is open, and above all, (*2*) White's Q pawn is weak.

18. P—Kt5   RP×P   19. P×P   Kt—B1
According to the principle that one weak pawn is less damaging than two.

20. P×P   P×P
In this position the chances are fairly equal; White's Q pawn is at least as weak as Black's QB pawn, and the example demonstrates anew the conflict between the minority attacks on the QB file and the K file respectively. However, as we said before, the minority attack on the K file is by nature less effective than that on the QB file, because White's KB pawn does not become isolated as does the black QKt pawn which, after .... BP×P, remains thoroughly weak.

We have more than once established the fact that defence pure and simple is not only more difficult but also less effective than active defence. Whenever Black commits himself without reservation to the defence in the Queen's Gambit, he is from the first restricted to one line of action. Although it is possible theoretically to revert to an active defence, in practice this must fail through the piling up of difficulties.

Here are two recent examples which illustrate this point:

VAN DEN BERG—KRAMER, 1950

1. P—Q4, Kt—KB3; 2. P—QB4, P—K3; 3. Kt—QB3, P—Q4; 4. B—Kt5, B—K2; 5. Kt—B3, Castles; 6. Q—B2, QKt—Q2; 7. P×P, P×P; 8. P—K3, P—B3; 9. B—Q3, R—K1; 10. Castles KR, Kt—B1; 11. QR—Kt1.

This appears to be stronger than 11. Kt—K5, as played in two previous examples, which merely leads to simplification.

11. ....   P—KKt3 (*No. 136*)
Blocking the KKt file.

Black has no counter-chance: in this position, White's minority attack is driven home with the utmost smoothness.

12. P—QKt4	P—QR3	15. P—Kt5	RP×P
13. P—QR4	Kt—K3	16. P×P	B—KB4
14. B—R4	Kt—Kt2	17. P×P	P×P
	18. Kt—K5		

Black's weak QB pawn is set upon without delay.

18.	QR—B1	20. Q×B	R—B2
19. R—Kt7	B×B	21. R×R	Q×R
	22. R—B1		

Threatening to win a pawn by 23. B×Kt, B×B; 24. Kt×QP.

22.	Q—Kt2	23. Q—Kt1	

In order to win the QB pawn after the exchange of Queens.

23.	Q—R3	24. Kt—R2	R—R1

And now White can win quickly by 25. Kt×QBP.

KOTOV—PACHMAN, Venice, 1950

1. P—Q4, P—Q4; 2. P—QB4, P—K3; 3. Kt—QB3, Kt—KB3; 4. B—Kt5, B—K2; 5. P—K3, Castles; 6. Kt—B3, QKt—Q2; 7. R—B1, P—QR3; 8. P×P, P×P; 9. B—Q3, R—K1; 10. Castles, P—B3; 11. Q—B2, Kt—B1; 12. P—QR3, P—KKt3; 13. P—QKt4, Kt—K3 (*No. 137*).

This position bears the same character as the preceding one—Black has no counter-chances.

14. B×Kt

A noteworthy exchange frequently seen in this kind of position, and for the following reasons:

1. A Knight is more apt to impede White's strategy than the black K Bishop.

2. By forcing the Bishop away from its present diagonal, White is able immediately to carry out his plan of attack without let or hindrance.

14.	B×B	17. P×P	B—B4
15. P—QR4	Kt—Kt2	18. B×B	Kt×B
16. P—Kt5	RP×P	19. P×P	P×P

The situation is now clear: Black has a weak QB pawn without any compensation. White won after various and protracted manœuvres, some on the Q side, others on the K side—the usual tactics whenever the weak pawn cannot be captured by direct means (see Chapter VII).

Are, then, in the Exchange Variation of the Queen's Gambit, no defensive measures available against the minority attack, and is Black reduced to counter tactics such as were shown in the first examples? The situation is not as black as all that, but the correct counter-measures

137	*138*

must be taken in time. If Black succeeds in posting a Knight at Q3, he can answer P—QKt4 with .... P—QKt4 without losing QB3, and then the minority attack is no longer dangerous, because Black can seal up the QB file by .... Kt—QB5.

Here is an example:

1. P—Q4, P—Q4; 2. P—QB4, P—K3; 3. Kt—QB3, Kt—KB3; 4. B—Kt5, B—K2; 5. P—K3, Castles; 6. R—B1, QKt—Q2; 7. P×P, P×P; 8. Kt—B3, P—B3; 9. B—Q3, Kt—K1; 10. B×B, Q×B; 11. Castles, QKt—B3; 12. P—QR3, Kt—Q3 (*No. 138*).

Here Black's position is more favourable than in any of the previous examples because he can, in reply to 13. P—QKt4, play 13. .... P—QKt4; 14. Kt—K2, Kt—B5, or 14. Kt—K5, B—Q2; 15. P—B3, Kt—B5, and he has nothing more to fear. As a rule, however, Black cannot be sure of reaching this improved position. If White delays playing R—QB1, or changes over to the development Q—B2, with B—Q3, Black will not find it easy to effect the desired formation. Be that as it may, we have discovered an important weapon for the defence: a Knight at Q3, and this can in all circumstances be a guiding line for the correct defence.

Up to now our treatment of half-open files has been closely connected with the minority attack, and as far as we have been dealing with the Exchange Variation of the Queen's Gambit, the attacker had hardly an alternative. But the characteristic half-open file can also occur in a different form.

A simple illustration is given in (*No. 139*).
White, with the move, wins a pawn:

    1. Kt—Q5

An outpost on the advanced square on the half-open file (see Chapter VIII). Black's QB pawn is threatened and cannot be guarded (1. . . . . QR—B1 loses the exchange by 2. Kt—K7 ch). There is nothing else but:

    1. . . . .   P—QB3

with a weakening of the Q pawn, which in this case is immediately fatal.

139   *140*

    2. Kt—B3   QR—Q1   3. KR—Q1
and the Q pawn falls. (2. Kt—K7 ch, also wins.)

Two tactical points govern this simple example: (*a*) the check at K7, and (*b*) the position of White's Q Rook at Q2, which enables White to double Rooks without any loss of time.

Without these more or less accidental factors, the gain of a pawn does not arise from the possession of a half-open line, but a direct consequence is the pressure that is exerted against the hostile position. Thus, in the English Opening, after 1. P—QB4, P—K4; 2. Kt—QB3, Kt—KB3; 3. Kt—B3, Kt—B3; 4. P—Q4, P—K5, the position is said to be bad for Black, because of 5. Kt—Q2, Kt×P; 6. Kt (Q2)×P, Kt—K3; 7. P—KKt3, Kt×Kt; 8. Kt×Kt, B—Kt5 ch; 9. B—Q2, B×B ch; 10. Q×B. White ultimately obtains command of his Q5, and Black cannot play . . . . P—QB3 without weakening his Q pawn.

An altogether different example of a half-open file is shown in *No. 140*.
White played:

    1. P—B5

A minority attack, undertaken, not with the object of creating pawn weaknesses, but in order to eliminate the obstructing Q pawn, so that the half-open Q file becomes an open file.

1. ....   P×P

Black has no option. If 1. .... R—Q1; 2. P×P, R×P; 3. R×R, P×R; 4. K—B4, the Q pawn is lost, and after 2. .... P×P; 3. K—B4, K—Kt1; 4. K—Q5, K—B2; 5. R—B2, R—Q2; 6. R—B8, Black also faces a hopeless task.

2. P×P

Note that White has allowed his own pawns to become isolated. On the other hand, he now has control of the open Q file along which his Rook can penetrate the enemy lines.

2. ....   K—Kt1   3. R—Q7   R—QB1
4. K—B4

and it will be very hard for Black to hold out.

The transition effected here in a few moves has brought us to a new subject: the *fully open file* and the *seventh rank*.

Here is, to begin with, a standard example, which will illustrate this conception in a more precise form.

VAN VLIET—ZNOSKO-BOROVSKY, Ostend, 1907

1. P—Q4, P—Q4; 2. P—K3, P—QB4; 3. P—QB3, P—K3; 4. B—Q3, Kt—QB3; 5. P—KB4, Kt—B3; 6. Kt—Q2, Q—B2; 7. KKt—B3, P×P; 8. BP×P (*No. 141*).

In this position is to be found a note-worthy opportunity for Black to obtain an advantage along the open QB file with the help of a few tactical turns.

8. ....   Kt—QKt5
9. B—Kt1

To all appearances entirely satisfactory. The Knight will be driven away by P—QR3 without losing a *tempo*, though also without a gain in time, for not only would the black Knight have to retire, but the

141

white Bishop could not remain at QKt1 where it seriously hinders the Q Rook.

9. ....   B—Q2   10. P—QR3   R—B1

The first spoke in the wheel. If 11. P×Kt, Q×B; 12. R×P, Q×P; 13. Castles, Q×KtP, Black has won a pawn.

11. Castles   B—Kt4

This is the second spoke. 11. .... Kt—B7 is also playable, but less effective.

12. R—K1   Kt—B7   13. B×Kt   Q×B
14. Q×Q   R×Q (*No. 142*)

The result of Black's strategy is now apparent: Black's Q Rook obstructs White's development and can, in conjunction with other pieces, initiate all kinds of activities. The success of such manœuvres stands or falls by the lodgment of the Rook at QB7, leaving the other Rook to play its part afterwards, so that the importance of the seventh rank rather increases than otherwise. In addition, the minor pieces (Bishop at QKt4 and Knight at KB3) also participate, both in order to maintain or even increase the pressure on White's position and also, when opportunity arises, to take advantage of favourable circumstances.

142

143

15. P—R3

In order to prevent .... Kt—Kt5, but at this point 15. Kt—Kt1 at once is preferable.

15. ....   B—Q3   16. Kt—Kt1

The characteristic regrouping of forces. The Knight makes for QB3 in order to cut off the Rook. Although there can be no question of its capture, this manœuvre would at least eliminate the QB file as a base for further operations.

16. ....   Kt—K5

Preventing 17. Kt—B3.

17. KKt—Q2

With the idea of carrying out after the exchange of Knights the manœuvre indicated above.

17. ....   B—Q6   18. Kt×Kt   B×Kt

With a threat against the KKt pawn, so that White has to give up his plan.

19. Kt—Q2   K—Q2   20. Kt×B   P×Kt (*No. 143*)

The situation is clarified: the black Rook at QB7 is stronger than ever. With the support of the second Rook at hand, it has become a practical impossibility to drive off the advanced Rook. The most White can hope for is to obtain a measure of relief by exchanging one of the Rooks.

So much for the first part of Black's programme: occupation of the seventh on an open file. The second part, exploiting the advantages realised, is less easily managed, and the minor pieces, after helping the attainment of the first part of the programme, have to be delivered to the Moloch of exchanges. Black must then evolve a fresh plan in order to exploit his advantage, and its basis—as usual in such cases—is the greater mobility of the King on the attacking side, the defending King being mostly confined to the first rank.

21. R—Kt1

In order to play 22. P—QKt4 and 23. B—Kt2. White has hardly anything else, for if, e.g. 21. K—B1, intending to play 22. R—K2, Black replies with 21. .... KR—QB1, and the white Rooks cannot leave the first rank.

21. ....   KR—QB1   22. P—QKt4   KR—B6
                  23. K—B1

To play 23. B—Kt2, at once, would cost a pawn: 23. .... R—Kt6; 24. B—R1, R×RP.

23. ....   K—B3

The King marches on, and nothing can stop him.

24. B—Kt2   R—Kt6   25. R—K2   R×R
                  26. K×R   K—Kt4

The relieving exchange of Rooks has come too late: the black King's entry is conclusive.

27. K—Q2   K—R5   28. K—K2

White can only wait.

28. ....   P—QR4

New lines of attack which settle Black's positional superiority. White can no longer hold out.

This particularly fine example of open file and seventh rank is taken from Nimzowitsch's *My System*. This outstanding chess master, a thinker of the very first rank, was, alas, prematurely taken from us in 1935 at the age of forty-eight. His work on the whole has not had the full recognition it deserves. Perhaps the bulk of the chess public of twenty-five years ago, when Nimzowitsch wrote his works on the strategy of chess, was not yet ripe for studies in this field. It is another proof of Nimzowitsch's greatness that theories evolved at the time should be valued even more highly in the light of present-day experience. Nimzowitsch lays particular stress on a number of main principles such as the blockading of a passed pawn, and he pays much attention to open lines, so that it is significant that we should to-day recognise and adopt many of his views.

Let us now recapitulate our findings on the positions in *Nos. 141* and *142*.

Assessment of No. 141: Black has the better chances on the QB file, and relies not so much on the position of his Queen at QB2 as on the respective development of the black and white Knights. Once the QB file is open, the Knight is more effective at QB3 than at Q2, so much so that where the Knight stands on the wrong square (Q2) it is quite usual to give up two *tempi* to bring the Knight to the correct square (QB3) *via* Kt1. Further analysis establishes the fact that we have here one of the minor advantages of the central formation in which a pawn at QB4 is opposed to a pawn at QB3. Here the black Knight, unlike his opposite number in the white camp, is able to reach QB3.

Once the white Knight has got on the wrong track (Q2), the QB file will be opened. In principle, recapture with the K pawn in such cases is preferable, but here 8. KP×P should lose a pawn. However, it is on the whole reasonable, and tactically entirely justified, to give up a pawn, with all the risks attending gambit play (8. .... Q×P; 9. Kt—B4, Q—B2; 10. Kt (B4)—K5), rather than voluntarily to submit to a definite positional disadvantage. On psychological grounds, too, you force the opponent into a variation which he never intended, and which is entirely different from the straightforward path which he had mapped out for himself.

The *plan*: Take advantage of the open file, sometimes quickly—as in the game, with .... Kt—B5; .... B—Q2; .... R—B1—B7,—sometimes step by step by steady development and later concentration of forces—doubling on the QB file, manœuvres such as .... Kt—QB3—R4—B5, in order to establish an outpost, advance of the Q side pawns, etc. By the second method the gain of two *tempi* is turned into pressure. The real object of these operations is the occupation of the seventh rank.

Assessment of No. 142: A considerable preponderance for Black on account of the absolute command of the QB file and the occupation of the seventh rank.

The *plan*: (*a*) Preservation of the advantages already acquired by the activity of the minor pieces (B at QKt4 and Kt at KB3) and the mobilisation of the second Rook. (*b*) A combined attack by the Rook at QB7 and the minor pieces—so that, as in the game—the Rooks and the King finally work together.

Nimzowitsch makes a number of weighty remarks on the subject of open files, for instance, he quotes the conception of the *restricted advance*, which is of great importance and which is illustrated in the following examples, together with other factors of moment in the treatment of open files:

NIMZOWITSCH—PRITZEL, Copenhagen, 1922

1. P—Q4, P—KKt3; 2. P—K4, B—Kt2; 3. Kt—QB3, P—Q3; 4. B—K3, Kt—KB3; 5. B—K2, Castles; 6. Q—Q2, P—K4; 7. P×P (the open file which White clearly feels is more favourable to himself than

to Black); 7. .... P×P; 8. Castles, Q× Q ch; 9. R×Q, P—B3 (holding White's Q5, but relinquishing the hold on his own Q3) (*No. 144*).

It is obvious that White has an advantage on the open Q file, but it is not so clear how he is to turn this advantage to account. Of course, there can be no question of an immediate penetration along the open file.

10. P—QR4

144

Attack on the flank frequently goes well with operations on the open file. The main object is to create weak points which may then be occupied by minor pieces which co-operate with the Rook on the open file.

10. .... Kt—Kt5 11. B×Kt B×B
    12. Kt—K2 Kt—Q2

Nimzowitsch observes that the correct defensive formation is: the Knight at QR3, the K Rook at K1, and the K Bishop at KB1, the last piece guarding his Q3.

13. KR—Q1 Kt—Kt3 14. P—QKt3 B—B3

It is clear that Black wishes to contest the Q file by .... QR—Q1, and so nullify White's advantage.

15. P—B3   B—K3   16. P—R5

Frustrating Black's plan, and justifying White's flank attack in another sense than above.

16. ....   Kt—B1   17. Kt—R4

In order to occupy QB5, and thereby to add force to the operation on the Q file. Without the advance of the QR pawn White's efforts would have been in vain; in this connection we realise that the note to Black's 12th move is now clear: the Knight at QR3 would have blocked the path of White's QR pawn, and moreover would have guarded Black's QB4.

17. ....   P—Kt3

An excellent parry, based on a tactical chance: 18. P×P, P×P; 19. Kt×P, Kt×Kt; 20. B×Kt, and now Black wins the exchange by 20. .... B—Kt4.

18. R—Q3 (*No. 145*)

Here we see the restricted advance along the open file: the Rook will be placed on a selected square on the open file, in front of its own pawns, aiming horizontally at hostile squares or pawns. In this way the neighbouring files also become, as it were, open files, and the attacker has the advantage of being able to choose between various alternatives or even to try these out one after the other. Throughout the sequel we can see that in this position the restricted advance is by no means confined to the QB file.

18. ....   P×P

Black should play 18. .... R—Kt1; 19. R—B3, P—B4, and although White then registers a success in that his Q5 becomes free, Black's defensive prospects would be better. The consequences of the text-move are much more serious.

19. R—B3   Kt—K2   20. R—B5

Again the restricted advance, this time to the QR file *via* QB5.

20.	KR—Kt1	22. R×RP	K—Kt2
21. KKt—B3	P—QR3	23. Kt—Kt6	R—R2
	24. Kt (B3)—R4	R (R2)—Kt2	

Black cannot avoid losing a pawn, one threat being 25. Kt—B5 (if 25. .... R×Kt; 26. Kt×B ch, etc.).

25. R×RP   Resigns

An impressive triumph of the open file—*via* a flank attack and restricted advance.

The Rook's file takes a special place in open file strategy. It is true that squares away from the centre are of lesser importance, but on the other hand, they fall perhaps more easily into the grasp of a would-be conqueror. Q2, for instance, is much easier to defend than QR7. The manœuvres which are required in order to open the QR or KR file

145

146

are described elsewhere (Chapters III and VI), but the following example (*No. 146*), which combines both operations, demonstrates the strategy of the seventh rank, starting from QR7, which falls first.

CAPABLANCA—TREYBAL, *Carlsbad*, 1929

A war on two fronts in the true meaning of the word, and on both fronts White is the attacker, although the attack on the right flank seems to be marking time. Here White preserves the option to exchange pawns or to advance the KR pawn. The threat of an exchange at KKt6 ties up some important hostile units, but White can hardly effect this exchange before he can decide with certainty what the outcome will be, and this is not the case as yet. Neither can he consider playing P—R6 ch until he has obtained, and can maintain, a decisive advantage on the other wing. The decision rests entirely with White's judgment at what stage P×P must bring about a considerable deterioration of Black's position so that his KR pawn will be in need of support. The transfer of the white Queen to the KR file will then force Black to play .... P—KR3, and the opening of that file will follow with all its fatal consequences.

First of all White secures fresh opportunities on the Q side:

1. P—Kt5

This puts Black in a quandary: should he capture, allow White to capture, or to advance the pawn? Let us first examine the continuation 1. .... P—R4. White wins a pawn quite simply by 2. P—Kt6, Q—Q1;

3. Q—B3, Q—R1; 4. Kt—Q2, followed by 5. Kt—Kt3, etc. Allowing
White to capture implies the protection of the QR pawn by .... B—
B1, as 1. .... Q—B1 is insufficient because of 2. P×RP, P×QRP;
3. R—QKt1, with R—Kt6, preceded perhaps by the decisive P—R6
ch, depriving Black of all counter-play on the K side. Incidentally,
the same system is also effective against the stronger 1. .... B—B1,
thus: 2. P×RP, P×QRP; 3. P—R6 ch, K—B1; 4. R—QKt1, B—Kt2;
5. R—Kt6, Q—B1; 6. K—Kt3, followed by 7. R—QKt2, and Black
is completely tangled up.

From the above, it is clear that Black has no option but to capture
with the R pawn. After 1. .... BP×P; 2. P—R6 ch, K—B1; 3. P—
B6 dis ch, the result is clear, as Black loses a piece.

| 1. .... | RP×P | 2. P—R6 ch |

White chooses this line for the reasons already given: (*a*) he has
provided for decisive developments on the Q side, and (*b*) Black is
thereby bereft of any counter-chance.

| 2. .... | K—B1 | 4. P—Kt6 | Q—Kt1 |
| 3. P×P | K—K2 | 5. R—R1 | |

The picture has changed in material aspects: an open file over which
White has complete mastery, for 5. .... Q—R1 is refuted by 6. Q—
Kt2, while Black, on account of the unfortunate disposition of his
forces, cannot possibly bring a Rook to QR1. This perhaps is saying
too much, as it can be done, though it is very much like a box puzzle,
and would cost an enormous amount of time: Q—K1, K—Q1, Q—K2,
R—K1, Q—B1, K—K2, and if Black wants to use both Rooks, R—Q1,
KR—K1, K—B1, K—Kt1, KR—B1, QR—K1, Q—Q1, Q—K2,
R—Kt1, R (B1)—B1, Q—B1.

| 5. .... | R—QB1 |

Black has to put up with the unfavourable distribution of Queen—
Rook—Rook.

| 6. Q—Kt4 | KR—Q1 | 7. R—R7 |

The seventh rank, the conquest of which has not caused White
much trouble.

7.	K—B1	9. KR—R1	K—Kt1
8. R—KR1	B—K1	10. R (R1)—R4	K—B1
	11. Q—R3	K—Kt1 (*No. 147*)	

Black can but wait, while White in the meantime has completed
the disposition of his forces, with the major pieces trebled on the QR
file, and in readiness to strike along the seventh rank. But how? This

is less complicated than one might think. White plays his Knight to
QR5, and if then Black guards his QKt pawn with .... R—Q2, there
is the surprising combination Kt×KtP, R×Kt; R—R8, and the Queen
is caught. Black can thwart this plan only by moving his Knight to
Q1. But this he can do only by making room for the Knight with

.... R—Q2, when R—R8 is immediately
decisive. Thus the black Rooks can
operate only horizontally: .... B—Q2;
.... R—K1, when, it may be added, ...
Kt—Q1 is hardly feasible, although the
white Knight at QR5 is disconnecting the
Rooks on the QR file, so that R—R8 is
no longer threatened. This plan of defence fails because of B—R6, as the
further course of the game will show.

147

The only really effective disposition of
Black's forces would be: K—B1, Kt—R1,
B—B2—Kt1, Kt—B2, R—K1, and Black
can now answer Kt—B5 with .... Kt—Q1, as, resulting from the
better position of his Bishop, the 'killer,' B—R6 is no longer possible.
This ingenious 'box puzzle' fails of course on account of the time
element.

12. K—Kt3

White does not wish to play 12. Kt—Q2 at once, because of the
reply 12. .... Kt×KtP, and if 13. P×Kt, Q—R7 ch. Therefore the
preparatory 12. K—Kt2 is essential. The text-move achieves nothing,
for after 13. Kt—Q2 Black still plays 13. .... Kt×KtP.

| 12. .... | B—Q2 | 14. Q—R1 | K—Kt1 |
| 13. K—R4 | K—R1 | 15. K—Kt3 | |

Could Black have imagined that White was going to waste so much
time, the manœuvre shown above might after all have been considered.

| 15. .... | K—B1 | 16. K—Kt2 | |

At last the King finds the right square, and now matters are getting
serious.

| 16. .... | B—K1 | 17. Kt—Q2 | B—Q2 |
| | 18. Kt—Kt3 | R—K1 | |

Here we may mention again that 18. .... B—K1; 19. Kt—R5, R—
Q2 fails against 20. Kt×KtP, R×Kt; 21. R—R8.

| 19. Kt—R5 | Kt—Q1 | 20. B—R6 | P×B |
| | 21. R×B | | |

The strategy of the seventh rank has triumphed. The threat besides 22. R×RP is 22. Kt—Kt3, followed by 23. R×QRP, and the doubling of the Rooks on the seventh rank.

    21. ....   R—K2
Hastens the end.

    22. R×Kt ch   R×R   23. Kt×P   Resigns
There is no stopping the united passed pawns.

This example demonstrates clearly how important it is to have freedom of movement within your own lines. White is able to reap the advantage of the open file and the seventh rank, while Black is reduced to clumsy manœuvres, which, compared to his opponent, leaves him at a great disadvantage in time.

One last example in which the great pioneer of open-file strategy, Nimzowitsch, emphasises that the seventh rank can compensate for a considerable deficiency in material (*No. 148*).

SÄMISCH—NIMZOWITSCH, *Copenhagen*, 1923

148   *149*

It is Black's move. His Knight is threatened as well as his Q pawn, while White can also play P—K5, and there follows a surprising offer of a piece.

    1. ....   BP×P   2. Q×Kt   R×P
Nimzowitsch himself commented as follows: 'Two pawns, the seventh rank and an inextricable Q side, all that for merely a piece!'

    3. Q—Kt5   QR—KB1   4. K—R1
Not 4. Q—K3, because of 4. .... R (B1)—B6.

    4. ....   R (B1)—B4   5. Q—K3   B—Q6
Threatens to win the Queen by 6. .... R—K7.

6. QR—K1   P—R3 (*No. 149*)

White is in *Zugzwang*. He cannot move without losing a piece (apart from P—R3, P—Kt3, and P—KR4—but these moves will soon be exhausted). For observe the following:

7. B—QB1, B×Kt; or 7. R—QB1, R—K7; or 7. KR—B1, B×R; or 7. B—KB1, B×B; or 7. K—R2, R (B4)—B6; or 7. P—Kt4, R (B4)—B6; 8. B×R, R—R7 mate.

Apart from all this, Black could have exchanged two Rooks for Queen and Bishop, but the waiting move is stronger and brings more substantial gain. The immortal *Zugzwang*, a monument worthy of Nimzowitsch the thinker.

Three principles have provided the subject matter of this chapter: half-open files, open files and the seventh rank. They differ individually, but have so much in common that an exhaustive study of each one separately is scarcely possible.

Besides the vertical and horizontal lines, along which the major pieces operate, the chessboard also contains diagonal lines, the hunting ground of the Bishops and, at times, of the Queen. The character of these diagonals is of a different kind, if only because the trebling of pieces is here materially impossible, and further, because hostile pawns bear a different relation to diagonals as compared with files and ranks. A file, once open, remains open—except for possible exchange transactions—but the diagonal, e.g. KKt2—QKt7, can be blocked by pawns at QB6, Q5, K4 and KB3. A discussion of the diagonal does not therefore fit into the framework of this chapter. But, in conclusion, we shall say this concerning the nature of a diagonal: Once we have placed a Bishop in an attacking position against the opposite hostile flank (B—Kt2 or B3 or B—Q3), it is generally desirable to advance the pawns on the threatened flank, in order to assist the work of the Bishop (thus in this case P—QKt4–5 against QB6 or P—KR4–5 against KKt6). In this way the diagonal is used to its greatest effect. The reader will find an example of this type of pawn advance in Game III, Chapter X.

CHAPTER X

ILLUSTRATIVE GAMES

THE gulf which, in all spheres of human endeavour, separates theory from practice can be seen also in chess. The player who, armed with the knowledge acquired from the study of the foregoing chapters, settles down to practical play with eager anticipation may well experience disappointment. He does not succeed in obtaining a pawn majority on the Q side or in occupying a strong square, or when he does, he finds himself in a mating net on the opposite flank. The teachings of theory seem to take on a different aspect in practical play and, besides, there are many more in addition to those for which we were able to find room in these pages.

The examples shown hitherto were carefully chosen as illustrating each characteristic by itself and alone on the scene from which the correct line of play could in every case be worked out with precision, while the correlation between judging and planning stands out clearly. In Chapter II we have said that a position containing several of the features we have discussed is more difficult to handle unless the player has a thorough grasp of each and every one of these characteristics individually.

It is, however, unavoidable that at times we should meet with some feature with which we are unfamiliar, however comprehensive we attempted to make this book. It would be quite senseless to speak of *all* characteristic ones. Every peculiarity of the chessboard, be it to all appearances ever so insignificant, may become the basis of an assessment and a plan.

In order to facilitate as far as possible the transition from theory to practical play, we shall in this the last chapter discuss five modern games chosen at random from master practice. In these games the characteristics which we have been discussing will appear in more or less straightforward form, but in addition other elements will play their part and will present an outline of the various aspects which we were obliged to leave outside the scope of our investigations. We shall in the case of each game recapitulate its course and enquire into the question of judging and planning at various critical stages of the play.

GAME No. I

DR. M. EUWE—S. RESHEVSKY
World Championship Tournament, Moscow, 1948
Nimzo-Indian Defence (Milner-Barry Variation)

1. P—Q4	Kt—KB3	3. Kt—QB3	B—Kt5
2. P—QB4	P—K3	4. Q—B2	Kt—B3
	5. Kt—B3	P—Q3	

In the preceding chapters no special attention was paid to the opening. Investigations began when one or the other feature had materialised. That feature then determined both the assessment of the position and the plan evolved from it. But little attention was given to the manner in which the situation arose.

The openings cover a very large field. We shall make some remarks concerning the initial phase, though only, of course, on broad lines. The opening presents on the whole a struggle for the command of the centre: he who holds sway in the centre can procure for his pieces the greater mobility and at the same time gain an advantage in space. Each player strives to achieve some particular pawn formation in the centre, which formation frequently governs the further course of the game. It follows that at the beginning of the game, the forces as far as possible are directed towards the centre—centralisation.

So far, all the moves played illustrate similar ideas, even 3. ....
B—Kt5, although in this case indirectly so, by pinning the Knight and thus interrupting its effect on the centre. Black aims at the central formation Q3—K4, against which White can react in a number of different ways, as we shall see.

6. B—Q2

In preparation for 7. P—QR3, so that, after an exchange at QB3, he can recapture with the Bishop, bringing an additional piece to bear on K5.

6.	Castles	7. P—QR3	B×Kt
8. B×B	P—QR4		

Right on the target is 8. .... Q—K2 or 8. .... R—K1, preparing for .... P—K4, but White then plays 9. P—QKt4, soon to be followed by P—Kt5, dislodging the Knight from a centralising position. The text-move prevents White's P—QKt4, and so, however unlikely it may appear, it still conforms to the principle of centralisation.

9. P—K3

After this Black realises his intention, which he could not do had White played 9. P—K4, for then 9. .... P—K4 at once costs a pawn, while after the preparatory 9. .... Q—K2, White himself can continue with 10. P—K5.

        9. ....   Q—K2   10. B—Q3

This move is open to the objection that White, before long, will be exposed to the threat of a fork by .... P—K5.

        10. ....   P—K4 (*No. 150*)

Black has reached his strategic target, and White must now decide which stand he will take against Black's formation in the centre. In general, there is a choice of three ways in which to proceed against this fairly frequently recurring configuration: capture by P×P, advance by

                     150   151

P—Q5, or letting things remain as they are. This last method cannot be seriously considered; it would mean loss of time, as White must then provide against .... P—K5, which threatens to win a piece. Therefore, either advance or capture, leading to entirely divergent types of position. The advance P—Q5 leads to a closed game presenting extremely difficult problems, which of course does not mean that White must avoid this line of play. He prefers, however, the alternative method (the exchange of pawns in preference to the pawn advance), and that for a very special reason: the possession of two Bishops. Experience teaches that two Bishops are stronger than either two Knights or Knight and Bishop. This advantage increases where the position has an open character, and in consequence White has no interest in a pawn advance and the consequent closing of the position.

        11. P×P   P×P   12. Castles KR

White does not as yet fear 12. .... P—K5, because of the reply 13. B×Kt (13. .... P×KB; 14. B×Q, P×Q; 15. B×R).

        12. ....   R—K1

But now 13. .... P—K5 is an actual threat.

13. B—B5

White cannot preserve the 'two Bishops.' After 13. Kt—Kt5, there follows: 13. .... P—K5 (after all), as the sequel 14. B×Kt, P×KB; 15. B×Q, P×Q; 16. B—B5, R—K4 wins for Black, while 13. Kt—Q2, P—K5; leads to troublesome consequences. Furthermore, 13. B—K2 can be answered by 13. .... B—Kt5, followed by 14. .... P—K5. Finally, 13. P—K4 is out of the question. White buries his K Bishop and abandons the control of his Q4.

13. ....   B×B   14. Q×B (*No. 151*).

14. ....   Q—K3

Forcing the exchange of Queens, as White's K4 is under fire and 15. Q—Q3 fails against 15. .... P—K5. The significance of this forced exchange lies chiefly in the fact that Black takes command of his K5.

15. Q×Q   R×Q

Now only has the game taken on a definite character, which is characterised by the open Q file, and thus comes within the scope of Chapter IX on open files: occupation of the open file and invasion of the seventh rank. The reader will see this happen also in this game, but not at once. There will be preparatory skirmishes relating to minor features, which however, for the time being, overshadow the chief feature, the open file. Mainly concerned are, first, the weakness of White's QB4 (should Black be able to play .... P—QR5), and furthermore, the insecure position of White's Bishop at QB3 (if Black plays .... Kt—K5).

16. P—QKt4

The drawback of this move is that White will soon be forced to play P—Kt5, when his QB pawn will become hopelessly weak. But neither would 16. P—QKt3 solve White's problem: 16. .... Kt—K5; 17. B—Kt2, Kt—B4, and White is in sore straits. (18. P—QKt4, Kt—R5.)

On the whole, the best continuation is 16. KR—Q1, after which Black carries out his positional threat 16. .... P—R5, and so deprives White's QB4 of the possible protection by P—QKt3. But White then need not fear .... Kt—K5, as he can play B—K1, and eventually drive back the black Knight by Kt—Q2.

In the sequel it turns out to be a great handicap for White that it appears to be impossible to drive off the black Knight after .... Kt—K5.

Finally, another alternative can be considered: 16. Kt—Kt5, R—Q3;

17. P—B3. The awkward .... Kt—K5; is eliminated, but White must expect to remain at a disadvantage on the open Q file.

    16. ....   Kt—K5   17. B—Kt2   P—B3

Clearly not 17. .... P×P; 18. P×P, R×R; 19. R×R, Kt×KtP, because of 20. R—R8 ch, with mate to follow. But after the text-move White is threatened with the loss of a pawn, which forces him to weaken his position still further.

    18. P—Kt5   Kt—K2   19. KR—Q1   R—Q3

At last the struggle for the open file, but with a wholly divergent point. For instance, White cannot exchange on Q6, for after 20. R×R, P×R the QB file is opened, and White's QB pawn is doomed to fall, e.g.: 21. R—QB1, R—QB1; 22. K—B1, R—B4; 23. K—K2, Kt—B1; 24. Kt—Q2, Kt×Kt; 25. K×Kt, Kt—Kt3; 26. K—Q3, P—Q4; 27. P×P, R×P ch, followed by 28. .... R×P.

This serious limitation of White's free choice of moves ensures for Black from this point the command of the open Q file.

    20. K—B1   Kt—B1

The Knight is making for QKt3, in order to strike at the weak QB pawn.

    21. KR—B1

White must relinquish the Q file now or on the next move. 21. K—K2 is answered by 21. .... Kt—Kt3 (22. QR—B1, R×R loses a pawn). The text-move at least prevents 21. .... Kt—Kt3.

    21. ....   P—QB4 (*No. 152*)

A particularly effective continuation, which turns his QKt3 into a strong square, which means that the square will be beyond the reach of hostile pieces and pawns, a splendid starting-point for the Knight.

    22. B—B3

Here 22. P×P e.p., R×P leaves the weak QB pawn defenceless. Nor is 22. K—K2, Kt—Kt3; 23. R—B2, QR—Q1 any more attractive.

    22. ....   Kt×B

This Bishop could play an important part in guarding White's Q2, and is therefore eliminated.

    23. R×Kt   P—K5

Black takes his chance of driving the Knight to an unfavourable square.

24. Kt—Kt1 Kt—Kt3

Before invading Q7 Black must first make sure of the assistance of his second Rook: after 24. .... R—Q7; 25. K—K1, R—Kt7; 26. R—Q1, Kt—Kt3; 27. R—Q2, R—Kt8 ch; 28. R—Q1, his satisfaction would have been short-lived.

152

153

25. Kt—K2 P—B4

Or 25. .... R—Q7; 26. Kt—Kt3, R—K1; 27. K—K1, etc.

26. K—K1 QR—Q1 27. R—B2 (*No. 153*)

A temporary equilibrium has been established. White has only just managed to prevent Black from breaking in at Q1 or Q2. But that is all he has to show while in other respects all the trumps are in Black's hand. He has command of the strong square at his QKt3, from where White's QB pawn is kept under fire, and this permanent threat makes it impossible for White to use his Rooks actively on the Q file. There is nothing that White can undertake, and Black can strengthen his position at leisure before embarking on decisive operations. The sequel requires little comment, but is typical of this type of situation.

27.	K—B2	29. Kt—B1	R—Q6
28. Kt—Kt3	K—K3	30. Kt—Kt3	P—Kt4
	31. Kt—K2	Kt—R5	

In order to strengthen his position by .... Kt—B6 or Kt7, according to circumstances.

| 32. Kt—Kt3 | K—K4 | 33. Kt—B1 | P—R4 |

All is smooth and unhurried.

34. P—B3

White still tries to put up a fight, but for Black this is the signal for the final attack.

34. ....   R—Kt6 (*No. 154*)

In order to bring his Knight to Q6 by way of QKt7. As Black could not obtain mastery over his Q8 and Q7, he uses Q6 as a thoroughfare in order to put the finishing touches to the disposition of his forces.

154

35. P×P

The opening of the KB file can benefit Black only, but White's position has long been untenable.

35.	P×P
36. R—B2	Kt—Kt7
37. R—B2	Kt—Q6 ch
38. K—K2	R—KB1

Black has control of his KB7 (the seventh rank) and penetrates White's position *via* this square with decisive vigour.

39. Kt—Q2	R—B7 ch	41. R×R	Kt×R ch
40. K—Q1	R—Kt7	42. K—B1	R×P

White resigns. In a hopeless situation he loses at least two pawns.

Judging and planning at various stages of the game:

(*1*) After 5. .... P—Q3.

Assessment: White appears to have a slight lead in the centre (the result of having the move).

Plan (for White): To oppose Black's formation in the centre (Q3 and K4). The counter-measures can be: direct or delayed action or preparation of an attack against the hostile centre formation. The execution of this plan could be, for instance: 6. P—QR3, B×Kt ch; 7. Q×B. Now Black's .... P—K4 is prevented. But this seems to be only temporary, as Black can play 7. .... Q—K2 and immediately realise .... P—K4. However, there follows 8. P—QKt4, directed against Black's centre, and if then 8. .... P—K4; 9. P×P, P×P; 10. P—Kt5, winning the K pawn.

A different method is adopted in the game: 6. B—Q2, in order to proceed, after 6. .... P—K4, with 7. P—QR3, B×Kt (7. .... P×P; 8. P×B, P×Kt; 9. B×P, plays into White's hands); 8. B×B. Here again the attack against the formation in the centre. Black now gets into difficulties after 8. .... Q—K2; 9. P×P, P×P; 10. P—QKt4 (10. .... P—K5; 11. P—Kt5, P×Kt; 12. P×Kt, and White's two Bishops hold sway over the open field).

In the execution of his plan, White has faltered by omitting to play

9. P—K4, by which Black's formation Q3 and K4 could definitely have been prevented. For his part, Black has, with 8. .... P—QR4, frustrated an indirect attack on his centre by White's P—QKt4.

(*2*) After 14. Q×B (*No. 151*).

Assessment: The open Q file is the battle ground along which the decision will be fought. The mastery of this file will depend on Black's pieces being tied or otherwise to other points. White must here take into account the helplessness of his QB4 (even after P—QKt3, because of the possibility .... P—QR5), and Black on the other hand, the vulnerability of his K4.

Plan (for Black): Exchange Queens in order to free his K4, whereby not only will .... P—KB3; relieve the King of his guard duties, but also make an attack possible on White's Bishop at QB3, which would break up White's entrenchments.

Plan (for White): To safeguard QB4 and prevent .... Kt—K5, and if this proves impossible, provide a suitable retreat for the Bishop (e.g. at K1 after the K Rook has vacated KB1).

We have seen in the game that Black succeeded in carrying out his plan, while White failed to do so.

(*3*) After 21. .... P—QB4 (*No. 152*).

Assessment: Black has a strong square for his Knight at his QKt3, and since White's K Rook is tied to the protection of his QB4, Black has free play along the Q file.

Plan (for Black): Play the Knight to QKt3, double Rooks, deal with any obstacles preventing the Rooks from breaking in (e.g. 22. .... Kt×B).

(*4*) After 27. R—B2.

Assessment: As before.

Plan (for Black): Circumvent by pressure on the QB pawn or by other means any attempt by White to free his game. As soon as it becomes clear that the opponent has no further counter-play, do everything possible to help the coming liquidation, as for instance, advance on the extreme King's wing, bringing the pawns nearer the queening squares.

GAME No. II

N. KOPYLOV—M. TAIMANOV

U.S.S.R. Championship, Moscow, 1949

Slav Defence

| 1. P—QB4 | Kt—KB3 | 3. P—Q4 | P—Q4 |
| 2. Kt—KB3 | P—B3 | 4. P—K3 | B—B4 |

The formation of the centre on either side is provisionally completed: White, Q4 and QB4; Black, Q4 and QB3. There is a certain tension which could be relieved by White with P×P or P—B5, by Black with .... P×P. In principle, any of these moves has some small drawback, so that the tension in the centre frequently endures right into the middle-game.

5. Q—Kt3   Q—Kt3

Black is not afraid of a doubled pawn, as after 6. Q×Q, P×Q; he obtains an open file.

6. P—B5

White fears the doubled pawn even less, and had Black now been forced to exchange Queens, the text-move would be very effective. But Black does not have to exchange; he retires the Queen, and White then has to contend with the awkward consequences of the changes in the centre brought about by the text-move.

6. ....   Q—B2   7. Kt—B3   QKt—Q2
        8. B—Q2   P—K4 (No. 155)

This advance clearly demonstrates the objection to White's sixth move, P—B5. Black has now formed a centre Q4—K4, which White cannot invalidate because of the vulnerability of his own QB4 (9. P×P, Kt×BP; 10. Q—Q1, KKt—Q2).

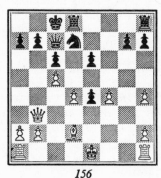

155   156

9. Kt—KR4

White aims at a forcible solution of his problems in the centre. He finds himself in an unhappy position, in which he cannot undertake anything there, but must constantly reckon with Black's possible advance .... P—K5, followed eventually by an attack on the K side. Owing to the line of play adopted by White, there is no solution, at most a change in the nature of his difficulties.

The correct plan would have been quietly to continue his development (B—K2, Castles KR, and if necessary P—KR3), together with, or better, perhaps, *preceded* by, some action on the Q side (Q—R3, P—QKt4, with possibly P—Kt5). However, White's handicap in this manœuvre is that Black's Q Bishop cuts across his position and prevents the white Q Rook from occupying the QKt file by R—Kt1. For this reason White had better proceed by stages in the sense that, after P—QKt4, Black's centre is under fire. As soon as White's QB5 is twice guarded (by QKt4 as well as Q4), he can consider exchange by P×P. If Black forestalls this eventuality by playing .... P—K5, his Q Bishop's diagonal towards QKt8 is intercepted. See assessment and plan at the end of the game.

9. ....   B—K3 10. P—B4

A consequence of the preceding move, which forced White to declare himself, but this flank attack is by no means unfavourable for Black.

10. ....   P×QP 11. P×P Kt—K5

The refutation of White's strategy. The threat is 12. .... Kt×B, followed by 13. K×Kt, Q×P ch; while after 12. B—K3, Black can reinforce his K5 by 12. .... B—K2; 13. Kt—B3, QKt—B3. Black's K5 becomes a strong square within the meaning of Chapter VIII, and operations against White's position can be intensified.

12. Kt×Kt P×Kt 13. B—B4 B—K2

A venomous intermediary move which further increases Black's advantage. The white Knight has no flight square.

14. B×B B×Kt ch 15. P—Kt3 P×B
16. P×B

Of course 16. Q×P ch, B—K2 loses a piece.

16. ....   Castles QR (*No. 156*)

Let us investigate the damage. Both players have weak pawns, but White's are on black squares and his Q Bishop has become a bad, a very bad, Bishop.

17. KR—Kt1

Not 17. Q×P, because of 17. .... KR—K1; 18. Q—R3, P—K6, with a decisive preponderance for Black.

17. ....   Kt—B3

Black estimates the respective chances very accurately, and offers a pawn in order to obtain a favourable ending. Inferior is 17. .... P—KKt3; 18. P—R5, and White gets rid of at least one of his weak pawns.

18. Q×KP ch   Q—Q2   19. Q×Q ch   R×Q
20. B—K3   Kt—Q4

White has a bad Bishop, and Black has a Knight on a strong square. Together this represents ample compensation for the latter's minority of one (weak) pawn.

21. K—K2 (*No. 157*)

21. ....   R—B1

Attacking one of the weak pawns, but, be it noted, without being compelled to capture. Liquidation would mean the exchange of a strong Knight for a bad Bishop, a decision which Black would hardly consider when he holds a decisive advantage. But after 22. R—Kt5, Kt×P ch; 23. B×Kt, R×B; 24. K—K3, R×P; 25. R—Kt2, R—KB2; Black is a good pawn ahead.

157

158

22. QR—KB1   R—B4   23. R—Kt5   QR—KB2
24. R×R

Here White misses an opportunity to get into comparatively smooth waters: 24. R (B1)—KKt1, P—KKt3 (24. .... Kt×P ch; 25. B×Kt, R×B; 26. R×P would lead to an easy draw); 25. P—R5, with some counter-chances. Taimanov quotes the following: 25. .... R×R; 26. R×R, R—B4; 27. P×P, R×R; 28. P×R, P×P, and an ending has resulted in which Black, in spite of being one pawn short, has excellent winning chances. The black King marches straight to his KB4, and White has practically no resource. The consequences of the text-move are more serious still.

24. ....   R×R   25. R—KKt1   P—KKt3
26. R—Kt4

White employs his pieces in a purely defensive manner, a procedure seldom to be recommended.

26. ....   K—Q2   27. B—Q2   K—K3
28. P—QR3   Kt—K2 (*No. 158*)

Regrouping of the black forces: the King at Q4, the Rook at KR4, the Knight at KB4 (likewise a strong square). Once this new formation is achieved, White's Q4 can no longer be held, and the passed K pawn can come into its own.

29. R—Kt3

White discovers his last counter-chance: attack on Black's Q side pawns, indeed, the only vulnerable spot in Black's position.

29.	R—R4	30. R—Kt3	R×RP

The treatment of the ending presents no particular difficulties for Black. It is not a question of capturing pawns, but rather of carefully analysing White's random attempts at counter-action, which attempts might otherwise become dangerous.

31. R×P	R×P ch	32. K—Q1

Not 32. K—K3, Kt—B4 ch, winning the Bishop.

32.	Kt—B4	33. R×QRP	R—R8 ch

Waiting to see whether White will fall into the trap (34. K—B2, Kt×P ch; 35. K—B3, Kt—Kt4 ch).

34. K—K2	R—R7 ch	36. R—Q7 ch	K—B5
35. K—Q1	K—Q4	37. P—Q5	R—R8 ch

Not 37. .... P×P, because of 38. P—B6, R—R8 ch; 39. B—K1. After the text-move 38. B—K1 fails against 38. .... Kt—K6 ch and 39. .... Kt×P.

38. K—K2	P×P	40. K—B2	Kt×P
39. P—B6	Kt—Q5 ch	41. P—Kt3 ch	K—B4

Black is well advised in holding on to his Q pawn.

42. P—Kt4 ch	K—B5	43. R—QB7	K—Q6

Black now wins comfortably with his united passed pawns.

44. R×Kt	R—R7 ch	48. P—Kt5	R—Kt5
45. K—Kt3	R×B	49. R—K5	P—Q5
46. P—R4	P—K6	50. P—R5	K—Q7
47. R—K6	R—Kt7	51. P—R6	R—R5

White resigns.

Judging and planning at various stages in the game:

(*1*) After 6. P—B5.

Assessment: Black has now the better game, because White's QB pawn requires the support of his Q pawn, which pawn is working at barely half strength. This is always the case when a unit is overloaded by having to perform some other task.

Plan (for Black): In order to exploit this advantage, Black without delay prepares for .... P—K4.

(2) After 8. .... P—K4 (*No. 155*).

Assessment: By reason of the greater elasticity of his centre, Black has a certain advantage.

Plan (for White): To force Black to declare his intentions in the centre. This is feasible, as he has further cover for his QB5, namely Q—R3, as well as P—QKt4. In between he will add B—K2, to keep the King in readiness for castling, and P—KR3, vacating KR2 for the K Knight. If Black later on continues with .... P—K5, the Knight gets back into the game *via* R2—B1—Kt3, when it is a point in White's favour that Black's Q Bishop no longer controls White's QKt1.

If Black, however, takes the Q pawn, White's Knight can return to KB3 under excellent conditions. If Black allows the tension to continue, White can at the right moment play P×P, and Kt—Q4, conquering the strong square Q4. When all this has come to pass according to plan, there follows, as an offshoot of White's strategy, the advance P—QKt5, together with operations on the open file. (We have seen that White, in this game, decided on an entirely different and less commendable line of play.

(3) After 21. K—K2 (*No. 157*).

Assessment: Black has posted his Knight on a strong square, while White has a bad Bishop. White's pawn majority on the K side (three pawns in ragged formation KR2, KR4 and KB4, against Black's KR2 and KKt2) is an insufficient compensation.

Plan (for Black): Attack on White's KB4, simplification by exchanges, the King playing an important part in these operations. Because of White's Bishop being 'bad,' Black's King has a free run along advanced white squares, and these increase in importance as the Rooks disappear from the board.

GAME No. III

J. R. CAPABLANCA—A. LILIENTHAL, *Moscow*, 1936

Réti's Opening

1. Kt—KB3	P—Q4	5. P—Kt3	Kt—B3
2. P—B4	P—QB3	6. B—Kt2	QKt—Q2
3. P—QKt3	B—B4	7. Castles	P—KR3
4. B—Kt2	P—K3	8. P—Q3	B—K2

White has selected a formation rather off the beaten track, but one which thirty years ago would have been called modern. Its chief characteristic is a prolonged delay in the final disposition of the centre. The pieces, certainly, are directed towards the centre, but the pawns are held back. In this game the K pawn does not move forward until the 50th move. It is claimed that this idea of holding back the centre has this advantage, that it can be timed according to the opponent's mode of procedure: an advantage which, however, in principle is now held, in master practice, to be little more than theoretical. That, however, such a modern build-up can contain no little venom can be seen here, should Black play 8. .... B—Q3 instead of the text-move. In that case there follows 9. P—K4, and now, after 9. .... P×KP; 10. P×P, Kt×P; 11. B×P, Black can no longer castle on the K side, while after 9. .... B—KKt5; 10. R—K1, White also obtains a big advantage.

> 9. QKt—Q2   Castles   10. R—B1 (*No. 159*)

White could advance in the centre by either P—K4 or P—Q4. The most usual method is to try for P—K4 (perhaps after the preparatory

move Q—B2), although the drawback of this manœuvre is that his Q3 could become weak (exchange by Black at his K5, followed by .... Kt—B4—Q6). On the other hand a premature P—Q4 is unfavourable, because it gives Black's Q Bishop a splendid diagonal. In the game under review, White does neither one nor the other, but waits to see whether there might be an opportunity to employ either of these tactical methods in the centre in more favourable circumstances.

159

> 10. ....   P—QR4   11. P—QR3

The object of this move is to enable White to play P—QKt4, in reply to .... P—R5, preventing Black from opening the QR file to his advantage. In such positions the capture on Black's QR5 hardly ever deserves consideration, because a white pawn at his QR4 usually becomes untenable, so that White is left with a weak pawn at QR3.

> 11. ....   R—K1   12. R—B2

To let the Queen go through (see the following move).

> 12. ....   B—R2

A preventive manœuvre, in case White should sooner or later be able to play P—K4.

13. Q—R1

This doubling on the long diagonal is characteristic of the modern principle which requires pieces to be directed against the centre in preference to the occupation of the centre by pawns. With the text-move White exercises pressure on K5.

13. ....   B—B1

Logical is 13. .... B—Q3; threatening .... P—K4—K5, which would force White to give up his waiting policy. Black decides on this course seven moves later; the intervening moves are of little importance, and might well have been omitted as far as the reader is concerned.

14. R—K1

The raid 14. Kt—K5, Kt×Kt; 15. B×Kt would rather favour Black, who could then play .... Kt—Q2, to be followed by .... P—B3 and .... P—K4.

14. ....   Q—Kt3   16. R—KB1   B—B1
15. B—R3   B—QB4   17. R (B2)—B1

Taking the Rook away from the black Bishop's diagonal, enabling him to play P—Q4, if necessary.

17. ....   QR—Q1   18. KR—K1   B—QB4
                  19. R—B1

White intends to play P—Q4, after all.

19. ....   B—B1   20. B—Kt2   B—Q3

At last this move, which opens a new phase in the game.

21. Kt—K5

White must on no account allow .... P—K4. Note that the text-move has here a different significance than on move 14 (see note thereto), in that Black now would have to exchange the Bishop as well as the Knight if he wishes to play .... Kt—Q2.

21. ....   B×Kt   22. B×B   Kt×B
                  23. Q×Kt   Kt—Q2

Not so good is 23. .... P—Q5, because of 24. P—B5, when the white Knight can get to Q6 *via* QB4.

24. Q—Kt2   Kt—B3

Black also plays a waiting game, tactically perhaps not a bad idea. In the book of the tournament, Capablanca gives 24. .... P—QB4,

followed by the Knight manœuvre Kt—Kt1—B3. White then achieves
nothing by capturing at Q5, as then the K file is opened and White's
K2 is exposed to attack (25. P×P, P×P; 26. B×P, R×P).

25. P—QKt4 (*No. 160*)

We have here an example of the half-open diagonal (KKt2 to QR8)
blocked by hostile pawns at QKt7, QB6 and Q5. It is to be noted
that such a half-open line generates as a rule greater power than a fully
open one, particularly when the blockade

160

is by two (instead of three) pawns, as will
later be the case in this game (see next
diagram) after Black has unjustifiably
exchanged his Q pawn.

Tactically, the line to adopt consists
in attack by pawns and pieces on the
blockading pawns; then, by means of exchanges or pawn advances, the creation
of weaknesses which will be under fire on
the long diagonal by the Bishop at KKt2.
The execution of these manœuvres begins
with the text-move. White is ready either
to operate on open QR and QKt files or to advance the QKt pawn
still further.

Note that Black's Q Bishop cannot compare in effectiveness with
White's K Bishop, especially as White's Q pawn which blocks the
diagonal is quite unassailable.

25. ....   RP×P   26. Q×P

White seizes the opportunity to exchange Queens. This is of importance in the forthcoming positional onslaught, the effect of which
would be impaired by the presence of too many major pieces.

26. ....   Q×Q

Practically forced: after 26. .... Q—B2; 27. R—Kt1, R—K2; 28.
R—Kt3, Black's QKt2 becomes dangerously weak.

27. P×Q   R—R1   28. R—R1

All according to plan.

28. ....   Kt—Q2

To the rescue of the threatened wing.

29. Kt—Kt3   K—B1   30. R—R5

An important move. He prepares for the doubling of his Rooks, while an exchange at QR5 would bring the Knight to a strong post. Playable too is 30. R×R, R×R; 31. Kt—R5, but the move chosen allows more varied possibilities.

    30. ....   P×P

Positionally a mistake, through which an entirely new position arises. Correct is 30. .... R×R; 31. Kt×R, R—Kt1, or alternatively the continuation recommended by Capablanca: 30. .... K—K2; 31. KR—R1, R×R; 32. R×R, K—Q3; 33. R—R7, K—B2; 34. Kt—R5, R—QKt1, when Black has not much to fear.

    31. P×P   Kt—Kt3   32. R×R   R×R
                33. Kt—R5 (*No. 161*)

The attack on the half-open diagonal in its most characteristic form. A white Knight threatens both the blockading pawns, which pawns

161   162

cannot be moved, for if either moves the other one falls; furthermore, the deadly P—Kt5 is in reserve. Black has the option of playing .... R—Kt1 or .... R—R2. White wins by an attack, in the first case, by pawns, and in the second by pieces, as follows:

1. 33. .... R—Kt1; 34. P—Kt5 (White could first make some further preparations without impairing the effect), 34. .... P×P; 35. P×P, Kt—Q4 (there is nothing else); 36. B×Kt, P×B; 37. R—Q1, R—Q1 (37. .... B—K5; 38. P—B3); 38. Kt×P, R—Kt1; 39. Kt—Q6, K—K2; 40. R×P, and now neither 40. .... R—Q1; 41. Kt—B5 ch, nor 40. .... K—K3; 41. R—Q2, allows Black any counter-chance.
2. 33. .... R—R2 as in the game.

    33. ....   R—R2   34. R—Q1

With the powerful threat 35. B×P, P×B; 36. R—Q8 ch, K—K2; 37. Kt×P ch, K—B3; 38. Kt×R.

After 34. .... K—K2 this threat becomes even more emphatic (35.

B×P, R×Kt; 36. P×R, and the Knight is attacked), and 34. ....
P—B3 loses a vital pawn after 35. R—Q8 ch, K—K2; 36. R—QKt8.

    34. ....   K—K1
The best move, but also insufficient.

    35. Kt×KtP (*No. 162*)
An elegant triumph of the attack on the half-open diagonal.

| 35. .... | R×Kt | 37. P—B5 | K—K2 |
| 36. B×P ch | R—Q2 | 38. B×R | Kt×B |

The combination has yielded ample material advantage, Rook and
two united passed pawns for Knight and Bishop.

| 39. P—B6 | Kt—Kt3 | 40. P—B7 |

All goes smoothly. Black cannot avoid the loss of a piece.

    40. ....   B—B4
To reach the queening square just in time by .... P—K4.

    41. R—Q8
Simpler is 41. P—K4, and now:

1. 41. .... B×P; 42. R—Q8, B—Kt2; 43. R—QKt8, or
2. 41. .... B—Kt5; 42. P—B3, B×P; 43. R—Q8.

| 41. .... | P—K4 | 43. P—Kt5 | K—Q3 |
| 42. R—QKt8 | Kt—B1 | 44. P—Kt6 | Kt—K2 |

Or 44. .... K—B3; 45. P—Kt7, K×P; 46. P×Kt (Q) ch, B×Q;
47. R—R8, and the advantage of the exchange is conclusive.

    45. R—KB8
Once again White leaves out of consideration a quicker way to win:
45. P—B8 (Q).

1. 45. .... B×Q; 46. P—Kt7, B—K3; 47. R—Q8 ch.
2. 45. .... Kt×Q; 46. P—Kt7, again winning a piece.

However, the text-move also wins.

45.	B—B1	50. P—K4	Kt—K2
46. R×P	Kt—Q4	51. P—B3	K—Q2
47. R×P	Kt×KtP	52. P—R4	K—K1
48. R—R7	Kt—Q4	53. R—KB6	Kt—Kt1
49. R×P ch	K×P	54. R—B6	Resigns

Judging and planning:

(*1*) After 20. B—Kt2.

Assessment: There is in the centre an extensive no-man's-land, which affords White in particular considerable freedom of movement.

Plan (for Black): To put an end to this situation by enforcing .... P—K4, and so attain in the centre a clear and definite preponderance (20. .... B—Q3).

Plan (for White): To frustrate Black's intentions (21. Kt—K5).

(*2*) After 24. .... Kt—B3.

Assessment: White's K Bishop operates along the half-open diagonal on which are placed three hostile and vulnerable pawns.

Plan (for White): Attack on the Q side with pieces (28. R—R1 and 29. Kt—Kt3) and pawns (25. P—QKt4).

(*3*) After 31. P×P.

Assessment: As before, except that the blockading pawns at Black's QKt2 and QB3 have become considerably more vulnerable because of Black's heedless exchange of his Q pawn (30. .... P×P).

Plan (for White): Attack on QKt7 by pieces (33. Kt—R5) and pawns (see the variation given in the note to White's 33rd move).

GAME No. IV

D. BRONSTEIN—M. BOTVINNIK

22nd Game, World Championship Match, Moscow, 1951
Dutch Defence

1. P—Q4	P—K3	4. B—Kt2	B—K2
2. P—QB4	P—KB4	5. Kt—QB3	Castles
3. P—KKt3	Kt—KB3	6. P—K3	P—Q4

Already the provisional formation in the centre is established, Q4 and K3 on either side. But whereas White's QB4 exercises pressure on the centre, Black has provided counter-pressure on White's K4 by bringing his own pawn to his KB4. The consequence of all this is that White can at will modify the situation in the centre, either by P—B5 (as a rule not to be recommended, see Game No. II), or by the exchange P×QP (see Chapter IX on the half-open file).

Black's .... P—KB4, on the other hand, has slightly weakened his K3 and his K4 is made accessible, though on the other hand his own Knight can occupy his K5. In addition, moving the KB pawn opens for Black's Queen the way to the enemy K side (.... Q—K1— R4), which sally could easily become very dangerous.

7. KKt—K2

Directed principally against the manœuvre indicated above, ...
Q—K1—R4, but this development of the Knight at K2 has the further
advantage to enable White to drive off the advanced black Knight by
P—KB3. White could achieve this also by immediately playing his
Knight to K5 (Kt—B3—K5), but then Black could exchange this Knight
after .... QKt—Q2, and the white pawn at K5 could become a weakness which Black would seal off.

7. .... P—B3   8. P—Kt3 Kt—K5

The black Knight's jump to K5 works out differently than does the
corresponding move by White. An exchange of Knights opens the KB
file for Black after .... BP×Kt. On the other hand, it must not be
overlooked that White can drive away the Knight by P—B3. Note
also that 8. .... QKt—Q2 has its draw-
back because of 9. Kt—B4 (weakness at
Black's K3).

9. Castles Kt—Q2
10. B—Kt2 QKt—B3 (*No. 163*)

163

Both sides have completed their deployment, and now comes the most difficult
phase of the game. What is to be done?
The white formation on the left wing
points to operations on the Q side, but
Black seems set for an attack on the K
side.

11. Q—Q3

One more waiting move, which has, however, a slight drawback, in
that the Queen stands in the way of manœuvres such as Kt—B4—
Q3—K5.

11. .... P—KKt4

Black is first in making a decision: action on the K side. What
continuation has he in mind? Presumably .... Q—K1—R4, with
.... Kt—Kt5 and .... B—Q2—K1—Kt3, also eventually, should a
favourable opportunity arise, ... P—B5. But, for the time being,
no concrete results are to be expected from this attack.

12. P×P

White's rejoinder: this exchange initiates an attack on the Q side.

12. .... KP×P

After 12. .... BP×P, White starts an attack along the open QB
file. Now his operations will be based on the half-open QB file (the
minority attack).

13. P—B3

Before continuing with P—QR3 (to which Black would probably have replied 13. .... P—QR4), White drives away the troublesome Knight.

13. ....   Kt×Kt

Against 13. .... Kt—Q3 White could have replied 14. P—K4. A general exchange, 14. .... QP×P; 15. P×P, P×P; 16. Kt×P, Kt×Kt; 17. B×Kt, Kt×B; 18. Q×Kt, looks quite favourable for White if various holes in Black's King's field are taken into account.

14. B×Kt

After 14. Kt×Kt, P—B5 is very embarrassing. As matters stand, the text-move fits in best with White's plan (P—QKt4).

14. ....   P—Kt5

A doubtful move. It is true that 15. P—K4, up to a point, carries a threat (compare note to Black's 13th move), but it could be satisfactorily parried by 14. .... B—K3 (15. P—K4, QP×P; 16. P×P, P×P; 17. B×P, Kt×B; 18. Q×Kt, B—Q4).

15. P×P   Kt×P   16. B—R3   Kt—R3

Black can hardly allow 17. B×Kt, P×B, as he would get into difficulties (as set out above). It is unfortunate for Black that he cannot retire the Knight to KB3. He will later on lose two *tempi* and bring this Knight from his outlying post to his K5.

17. Kt—B4   B—Q3   18. P—QKt4

The well-known minority attack.

18. ....   P—R3   19. P—R4   Q—K2
20. QR—Kt1

All on normal lines. Playable too is the immediate advance 20. P—Kt5, but the opportunity of doing so later will not melt away.

20. ....   P—Kt4 (*No. 164*)

A positional misconception. While it stops White's intended action, it brings trouble to Black: the weakening of his QB3 and the opening at a chosen moment of the QR file by White. Correct is 20. .... B—Q2, with a probably tenable game. The text-move would have been barely sufficient had the Knight been able quickly to reach Black's K5, but that awkward beast is far away.

21. B—KKt2

An immediate threat of 22. Kt×P, perhaps preceded by an exchange at Kt5. Possibly, however, 21. R—Kt2 and 22. R—R1 may be stronger.

21. ....   Kt—Kt5

Gaining a *tempo* (attack on K6).

22. B—Q2   Kt—B3   23. R—Kt2

In order to let the K Rook through.

23. ....   B—Q2

The bulletin mentions 23. .... Kt—K5, so that after 24. B—K1, P×P, the white K Rook should be cut off. But White has something better in 24. R—R1, Kt×B; 25. Q×Kt, followed by 26. Kt—Q3.

24. R—R1   Kt—K5
25. B—K1   KR—K1
26. Q—Kt3

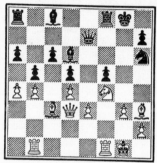

164

Guarding QKt4, so that the Rook at Kt2 can move to R2, doubling Rooks on the QR file.

26. ....   K—R1
27. R(Kt2)—R2

A gradual development of the attack; White now threatens to win a pawn by 28. P×P.

27. ....   Q—B1

Guarding the Q Rook, which parries the threat. This attempt to make a stand on the QR file should be preceded by 27. .... B×Kt; because now the white Knight will play an important part in the proceedings. Meanwhile we can establish the fact of the superiority of White's attacking formation QR4 and QKt4 to Black's QR3 and QKt4. White has doubled Rooks on the QR file, and this Black cannot emulate (27. .... R—R2; 28. P×P). Along the QR file Black is condemned to passivity, with his important pieces inactive.

28. Kt—Q3

To bring the Knight to the central square K5, where it can intervene decisively, for Black cannot then eliminate the Knight without conjuring up serious dangers along the long black diagonal. Note also that White need not fear the combination 28. .... P×P; 29. R×P, P—B4, because of the simple continuation 30. KtP×P, B×R; 31. R×B, after which White wins the Q pawn as well, and wins easily with two united passed pawns.

28. ....   QR—Kt1

Black abandons the QR file. He has no suitable waiting moves, and White can in any event play 29. Kt—K5.

29. P×P   RP×P   30. R—R7 (*No. 165*)

The seventh rank.

30. ....   R—K2

After 30. .... R—R1; 31. Kt—K5 is likewise very strong.

165

31. Kt—K5   B—K1

Hastens the end; but after 31. .... B ×Kt; 32. P×B, B—K3; 33. Q—B2, Black would have suffered a more leisurely extinction.

32. P—Kt4

The decisive break-through, bringing the Q Bishop to life. The threat is B—R4, when Black must allow his opponent the command of the seventh rank, with fatal consequences.

32. ....   P×P

In time trouble, Black misses the continuation 32. .... Q—Kt2, when he could have held his second rank at the cost of a pawn. (33. R×R, Q×R; 34. P×P, B×Kt; 35. P×B, Q×KP; 36. R—R7, etc.).

33. B×Kt   P×B   34. B—R4

Part of White's strategy, of which successive phases have been: contesting the QR file, conquest of that file, and contesting the seventh rank, which now is completely overrun.

34. ....   R×Kt

A despairing sacrifice. After 34. .... R×R; 35. R×R, the threat 36. Kt—B7 ch can hardly be met by 35. .... B×Kt, because of 36. P×B, followed by 37. B—B6, again with serious loss in material for Black.

35. P×R   B×KP   36. R—KB1   Q—Kt1

Alternative lines have much the same result:

1. 36. .... Q—Q3; 37. B—Kt3, B×B; 38. Q—B3 ch, etc.
2. 36. .... Q—R3; 37. B—Kt3, B×B; 38. Q—B3 ch, etc.

37. B—Kt3

An elegant finish. Black cannot accept the Queen sacrifice because of mate in two (38. R—B8 ch and 39. B×B).

37. ....   B—Kt2   38. Q×Q ch   Resigns

Judging and Planning:

(*1*) After 10. .... QKt—B3.

Assessment: White has greater freedom on the Q side, Black on the K side.

  Plan (for White): Attack on the Q side (P×P and P—QKt4–5).

  Plan (for Black): Attack on the K side (.... P—KKt4, followed by .... Q—K1—R4).

(*2*) After 20. .... P—Kt4.

Assessment: White has a clear advantage in his pawn formation on the Q side (R4 and Kt4 against R3 and Kt4), which enables him to open the QR file at a favourable moment.

  Plan (for White): Doubling Rooks along the QR file, to which end White's QKt4 must be adequately protected. The ultimate object of this manœuvre is the occupation of the seventh rank.

(*3*) After 30. R—R7.

Assessment: White has a Rook on the seventh.

  Plan (for White): The complete supremacy over the seventh rank by Kt—K5, P—KKt4, and B—KR4. These moves give White an undoubted advantage because various black units are tied to the defence of the seventh rank, and also because the double exchange at K5 opens a diagonal for White's QB with decisive results.

GAME No. V

DR. S. TARTAKOWER—DR. M. EUWE, *Venice*, 1948

Giuoco Piano

1. P—K4	P—K4
2. Kt—KB3	Kt—QB3
3. B—B4	B—B4
4. P—B3	B—Kt3
5. P—Q4	Q—K2
6. Castles	P—Q3
7. P—KR3	Kt—B3
8. R—K1	Castles (*No. 166*)

166

A well-known type of battle array: K4 and Q4 on the attacking side against the defensive K4 and Q3. White has therefore the option of altering the formation in the centre either by P×P or P—Q5. As in either case Black's K Bishop gets into action, neither continuation can at present be entertained by White. His chance lies rather in forcing Black to effect **the** exchange, which brings for him a most favourable change in position. For then White's K pawn recovers his mobility, which carries with it all manner of attacking chances.

9. Kt—R3

In combination with the next move an original way to strive for the target we have described. White has in view Kt—B2—K3—Q5.

9. ....   Kt—Q1

Better is 9. .... K—R1, in which case White can hardly play 10. B—B1, on account of 10. .... P×P; 11. P×P, Kt×KP. The object of the text-move is to anticipate Kt—B2—K3—Q5 by .... P—B3.

10. B—B1

Now 10. .... P×P; 11. P×P, Kt×P is bad because of 12. Kt—KKt5, followed by 13. P—B3 (this line of play for White would fail if the black Knight were still at QB3, making .... P×P possible).

10. ....   Kt—K1

Better is 10. .... Kt—Q2, as will be seen before long. The object of the text-move is to give the K pawn effective support by .... P—KB3.

11. Kt—B4   P—KB3

Black has secured his K pawn, and White's plan, of which his last three moves formed a part, apparently has achieved nothing.

12. P—QR4

A characteristic manœuvre, which takes advantage of the immobility of Black's Bishop at his QKt3. The threat P—R5 forces Black to

167

move either his QR pawn or QB pawn, both of which guard the Bishop, and thus Black will finally lose a pawn. Had Black played his K Knight to Q2 instead of K1, Black would have escaped material loss, although his formation (Knight at Q2, Knight at Q1, and Bishop at QB1) would not have been particularly easy to disentangle.

12.	P—B3
13. Kt×B	P×Kt
14. Q—Kt3 ch	Kt—K3
15. Q×P	P—Kt4 (*No. 167*)

A well-known recipe: he attacks White's K side, weakened by the advance of the KR pawn, by the advance of his own KKt pawn. Black decides the more readily on this course, as after the setback in the last few moves he has little to lose.

16. B—QB4

White takes Black's action too lightly. He should have left this Bishop at KB1 to take part in the defence and continued with 16. P—KKt3, preventing Black's .... Kt—B5 more effectively than is the case after the text-move.

16. ....   P—R3

So as to recapture with the KB pawn should White play 17. P×P.

17. P—R4   K—R2

Now 17. .... P—Kt5 has no object. The primary object of Black's strategy is to open the KKt file.

18. P×KtP

This is in conflict with the ideas of the defence. White opens the KR file for his opponent.

18. ....   RP×P   19. P×P   QP×P

This is what White has been playing for; the KB file has remained closed, and White has the run of the black diagonal QR3—KB8, but it is clear that the time element will be against him, e.g.: 20. P—QKt3, R—R1; 21. B—R3, Q—KB2; and already 22. .... Q—R4 is threatened.

20. B—K3   R—R1   21. P—KKt3

He again, and voluntarily, weakens his K side. Best was the King's immediate flight *via* B1 and K2.

21. ....   K—Kt3
22. K—Kt2

In order to reply to 22. .... Q—R2 with 23. R—R1, but Black has more strings to his bow.

22. ....   Kt—B5 ch (*No. 168*)

A fairly obvious offer of a Knight, in accordance with the principles laid down in Chapters V and VI; White's guarding pawn at Kt3 is eliminated and, at the same time, Black's Q Bishop will be given the opportunity to intervene with the gain of a *tempo*.

168

23. P×Kt   B—R6 ch   24. K—Kt3

After 24. K—Kt1, KtP×P, White's position is beyond hope, as Black's Queen threatens to take part in the struggle on the KKt file with 25. .... Q—Kt2.

24. ....   KP×P ch   25. B×P   Q—Q2

The mating threat at White's KKt4 leads to a further collapse of the white forces. The white Knight must move to R2, where it is out of action and itself becomes a target.

26. Kt—R2   P×B ch   27. K×P   R—R5 ch

Black must proceed with the utmost energy, as his own King is not safe and is threatened with a check by R—KKt1.

28. K—K3

Other possibilities are:

1. 28. K—B3, B—Kt7 ch; 29. K×B, Q—R6 ch; 30. K—Kt1, Q×Kt ch; 31. K—B1, Q—R8 ch; 32. K—K2, Q×P ch; 33. K—Q2, Q×B, etc.

2. 28. K—Kt3, R—Kt5 ch, and now:

(*a*) 29. K—B3, B—Kt7 ch; 30. K—K3 R×P mate;

(*b*) 29. K×B, R—Kt4 dis ch; 30. K—R4, Q—R2 mate.

28. ....   B—Kt7   29. Kt—B3   R×P ch (*No. 169*)

White has built up a new line of defence, which, however, the text-move renders useless. The white King, bereft of all help and with the additional handicap of his Queen's vulnerable position, is exposed to attack by three black pieces.

30. K×R   Kt—Q3 ch   31. K—Q3

If 31. K—B4, Q—B4 ch, etc. Fatal also is 31. K—K3, Kt×B ch; and 31. K—Q4, Kt—B1 dis ch.

31. ....   Q—B4 ch   32. K—Q4   Q—B5 ch
                     33. K—Q3

If 33. K—B5, Q×B ch; 34. K×Kt, Q—Q4 ch, then—

1. 35. K—B7, Q—Q1 ch; 36. K×P, Q—B1 mate.

2. 35. K—K7, Q—B2 ch; 36. K—Q6, Q—B1 ch;

(*a*) 37. K—Q7 or K6, B—R6 ch, etc.;

(*b*) 37. R—K7, R—Q1 ch; 38. K—K6, B—R6 mate.

33. ....   Q×B ch   34. K—B2   B×Kt

Black's attack, for the time being, has come to an end, but on balance the situation is far from unfavourable for him, namely Knight and Bishop against Rook and pawn, with a very promising position. White's counter-action, 35. R—Kt1 ch, K—B2; 36. Q—B7 ch, K—K3; 37. QR—K1 ch, leads to nothing because 37. .... B—K5 ch; 38. K—B1, R×P, etc.

35. P—Kt3

Here 35. Q—Q4 leads to a lost ending after the exchange of Queens.

| 35. .... | B—K5 ch | 37. R—Kt1 ch K—B2 |
| 36. K—Kt2 | Q—Q6 | 38. QR—QB1 |

This gives Black the opportunity for an elegant final combination. Insufficient, however, was:

1. 38. QR—Q1, Q—B7 ch;
  (*a*) 39. K—R1, R×P ch; 40. P×R, Q×RP ch; 41. K—Kt2, Kt—B5 ch; 42. K—B1, Q—B7 mate;
  (*b*) 39. K—R3, Kt—B5 ch; 40. P×Kt, R×P mate.
2. 38. Q—B7 ch, K—K3; 39. QR—QB1, Q—Q7 ch;
  (*a*) 40. K—R3, Kt—Kt4 ch, etc.;
  (*b*) 40. K—R1, Kt—B5, and wins.

169

170

However, White could still hold out with 38. Q—B5, as 38. .... Q—B7 ch; 39. K—R3, Kt—Kt4 ch; 40. K—Kt4, achieves nothing. The best for Black is then to play for the end-game by 38. .... Q—Q7 ch; 39. K—R3, Q—Q4.

38. ....   Q—Q7 ch   39. K—R3

If, instead, 39. K—R1, there follows 39. .... Kt—B5; 40. Q×P ch, K—K3, and now:

1. 41. P×Kt, R×P mate.
2. 41. R—Kt1, Q×P ch; 42. K—R2, R×P ch; 43. P×R, Q—R6 mate.

39. ....   Kt—B5 ch (*No. 170*)

With this offer and that on the next move the white King's last defences on the Q side are destroyed.

40. P×Kt   R×P ch   41. K×R   Q—R7 ch
42. K—Kt4   Q—Kt7 ch

White resigns, for after 43. K—R5, Black mates with 43. .... Q—R6.
After 43. K—B5, White loses the Queen (43. ..... Q×P ch; 44. K—Kt4,
Q×Q ch; 45. K—R3, B—B7; etc.).

Judging and Planning:

(*1*) After 8. ..... Castles.
   Assessment: White's position in the centre is more aggressive, but
he can hardly benefit from this fact, because Black can force him to
give up his strong pivot at K5.
   Plan (for White): To play his Knight to QB4, laying stress, if occasion arises, on a tactical point due to the immobility of Black's Bishop
at his QKt3; but he must be prepared to switch over to another course
by bringing his Knight to Q5 either *via* QB2 and K3 or QB4 and K3.

(*2*) After 15. Q×P.
   Assessment: White has an extra pawn, but his King's field is weakened
by the advance of his KR pawn to R3.
   Plan (for Black): To assault White's K side by .... P—KKt4–5;
strengthened possibly by Kt—KB5.

(*3*) After 22. K—Kt2.
   Assessment: White's King's side is seriously weakened, and, at the
moment, Black has a preponderance in available forces, but must not
wait until White strengthens his defence, say by 23. R—R1.
   Plan (for Black): Destruction of White's battlements by the sacrifice
of a Knight at Black's KB5, in order to force an immediate break-
through by the attacking forces.

(*4*) After 29. Kt—B3.
   Assessment: White's King is poorly protected and his pieces stand
unguarded, while the Queen can easily become the victim of a double
attack on the King and herself.
   Plan (for Black): To eliminate White's defending K pawn by a
sacrifice and afterwards to throw all his forces into the battle.